Macmillan
Work Out
Series

Work Out

26. JAN. 1989 This book is to be returned on or before
the last date stamped below.

conomic History

16. MAR 1989   2/6/94

GCSE

The titles
in this
series

MACMILLAN
WORK OUT
SERIES

Work Out

Social and Economic History

GCSE

S. Mason

Editorial Consultant
Jon Nichol

MACMILLAN
EDUCATION

First published 1988

Published by
MACMILLAN EDUCATION LTD
Houndmills, Basingstoke, Hampshire RG21 2XS
and London
Companies and representatives
throughout the world

Printed in Great Britain by
The Bath Press Ltd, Avon

British Library Cataloguing in Publication Data
Mason, Simon
Work out social and economic history GCSE.
—(Macmillan work out series).
1. Great Britain. Social conditions,
1700–1980
I. Title
941.07
ISBN 0–333–46767–1

To all pupils, past and present, at
Bishop Fox's School, Taunton

Contents

Preface

This book has been written specifically for pupils taking examinations in GCSE Social and Economic History. It provides candidates with a complete course guide to the examination, together with tips on how to answer questions and how to carry out a thorough revision programme.

Work Out Social and Economic History is based on an analysis of all the syllabuses and papers set by the GCSE examination boards. The aims and objectives of examiners have changed radically over the past few years. Candidates are expected to 'know, understand and do' more than simply regurgitate facts learned during the course. They are expected to have acquired knowledge relating to historical understanding, concepts, empathy and skills. This has made GCSE examinations much more demanding for pupils and their teachers, but it has also made the process of learning History much more interesting.

The book has been structured to meet the demands of all the GCSE Social and Economic History syllabuses. Each chapter contains a fact file, a guide to questions, model answers and a 'test yourself' section, and is linked to a specific GCSE assessment objective. The specimen questions are similar to those set on GCSE papers. These questions and their answers are my sole responsibility.

If any candidate would like further advice or clarification of any issues raised by the book, I can be contacted via the publishers.

Bridgwater, Somerset, 1988   Simon Mason

Acknowledgements

The author and publishers wish to thank the following who have kindly given permission for the use of copyright material:

Cambridge University Press for material from *Abstract of British Historical Statistics*, by B. R. Mitchell and P. Deane, 1962.

Illustrated London News	Mary Evans Picture Library
British Museum Newspaper Library	Camera Press
Manchester City Art Gallery	BBC Hulton Picture Library
Manchester City Libraries	Keystone Collection
The Science Museum	Raissa Page
The Mansell Collection	J. Allen Cash Ltd

Every effort has been made to trace all the copyright holders, but if any have been inadvertently overlooked the publishers will be pleased to make the necessary arrangement at the first opportunity.

The author would like to thank Margaret Jelfs for her help in preparing and typing the manuscript.

The cover picture is *Work*, by Ford Madox Brown (courtesy of Manchester City Art Gallery).

Organisations Responsible for GCSE Examinations

In the United Kingdom, examinations are administered by the following organisations. Syllabuses and examination papers can be ordered from the addresses given here:

Northern Examining Association (NEA)

Joint Matriculation Board (JMB)	**North Regional Examinations Board**
Publications available from:	Wheatfield Road
John Sherratt & Sons Ltd	Westerhope
78 Park Road	Newcastle upon Tyne NE5 5JZ
Altrincham	
Cheshire WA14 5QQ	

Yorkshire and Humberside Regional Examinations Board (YREB)
Scarsdale House
136 Derbyside Lane
Sheffield S8 8SE

North West Regional Examinations Board (NWREB)
Orbit House
Albert Street
Eccles
Manchester M30 0WL

Midland Examining Group (MEG)

University of Cambridge Local Examinations Syndicate (UCLES)
Syndicate Buildings
Hills Road
Cambridge CB1 2EU

Southern Universities' Joint Board (SUJB)
Cotham Road
Bristol BS6 6DD

West Midlands Examinations Board (WMEB)
Norfolk House
Smallbrook
Queensway
Birmingham B5 4NJ

London and East Anglian Group (LEAG)

University of London School Examinations Board (L)
University of London Publications Office
52 Gordon Square
London WC1E 6EE

East Anglian Examinations Board (EAEB)
The Lindens
Lexden Road
Colchester
Essex CO3 3RL

Associated Lancashire Schools Examining Board
12 Harter Street
Manchester M1 6HL

Oxford and Cambridge Schools Examination Board (O & C)
10 Trumpington Street
Cambridge CB2 1QB

East Midland Regional Examinations Board (EMREB)
Robins Wood House
Robins Wood Road
Aspley
Nottingham NG8 3NR

London Regional Examining Board (LREB)
Lyon House
104 Wandsworth High Street
London SW18 4LF

Southern Examining Group (SEG)

The Associated Examining Board (AEB)
Stag Hill House
Guildford
Surrey GU2 5XJ

University of Oxford Delegacy of Local Examinations (OLE)
Ewert Place
Banbury Road
Summertown
Oxford OX2 7BZ

Southern Regional Examinations Board (SREB)
Avondale House
33 Carlton Crescent
Southampton
Hants SO9 4YL

South-East Regional Examinations Board (SEREB)
Beloe House
2–10 Mount Ephraim Road
Royal Tunbridge Wells
Kent TN1 1EU

South-Western Examinations Board (SWExB)
23–29 Marsh Street
Bristol BS1 4BP

Scottish Examination Board (SEB)

Publications available from:
Robert Gibson and Sons (Glasgow) Ltd
17 Fitzroy Place
Glasgow G3 7SF

Welsh Joint Education Committee (WJEC)

245 Western Avenue
Cardiff CF5 2YX

Northern Ireland Schools Examinations Council (NISEC)

Examinations Office
Beechill House
Beechill Road
Belfast BT8 4RS

Introduction

How to Use This Book

This book gives you the core information which you need to take any examination in Social and Economic History. I have planned the book for study at home or in class, or for just before the examination. While you are working through the book, I hope you learn a great deal about the changes which have taken place in the world you live in. My aims are to teach you to enjoy the study of History and to be successful in passing History examinations.

I have tried to write the chapters in a logical sequence, although you can work through them in whichever order you think best.

Chapter 1 tells you how to organise your revision programme and gives you the information you need to make the best possible use of your time. The second part of Chapter 1 explains how to tackle GCSE questions. Many of these questions are based on historical *evidence*. Answering them is like solving clues in a crossword puzzle — you have to work out what the question means before you can answer it. Once you get the knack, they are easy to understand.

Chapters 2–11 deal with one topic each. The chapters are linked to one specific assessment objective (see below). Each chapter is in sections which have a common pattern:

1. An 'information file' containing the facts that you need to know so as to be able to understand the topic.
2. A guide to examination questions and hints on how to answer those questions.
3. Source material, if needed.
4. Model answers, if needed.
5. A 'Work Out' of short-answer questions to allow you to test your knowledge of the information file and the source material.

Sections 3 and 4 will look at how to approach the different kinds of questions which the GCSE boards will ask you. You can apply the lessons you learn from these sections to questions asked about the topics covered in other chapters.

The GCSE examiners will expect you to be able:

1. To recall, evaluate and select knowledge relevant to the context and to deploy it in a clear and coherent form.
2. To make use of and understand the concepts of cause and consequence, continuity and change, similarity and difference.
3. To show an ability to look at events and issues from the perspective of people in the past.
4. To show the skills necessary to study a wide variety of historical evidence, which should include both primary and secondary written sources, statistical and visual material, artefacts, textbooks and orally transmitted information.

(i) By comprehending and extracting information from it.

(ii) By interpreting and evaluating it — distinguishing between fact, opinion and judgement; pointing to deficiencies in the material as evidence, such as gaps and inconsistencies; detecting bias.

(iii) By comparing various types of historical evidence and reaching conclusions based on this comparison.

(*GCSE National Criteria for History* — Assessment Objectives)

These assessment objectives can be summarised as follows:

1. Knowledge and understanding.
2. Concepts.
3. Empathy.
4. Skills.

Revision

'What's the best way to revise?' I get asked this question at least once a day during the weeks and months leading up to the History examination. There's no easy answer to the question. However, learning should be *fun*. Your revision should be enjoyable and rewarding. It's all too easy to write off examinations and revision as 'boring'. The more you learn about History, the more interesting it becomes. A few years ago a girl I was teaching in Devon told me: 'I didn't get much out of the lessons but once I started revising, everything became much clearer. It all fell into place.'

If you are finding your revision boring, ask yourself *why*? Do you find the subject matter uninteresting or is it the revision technique you are using which is at fault? In nine cases out of ten, improving your revision technique can make examination work much more interesting. Chapters 1 and 12 give you advice on how to plan your revision course and how to use the revision methods which suit *you* best. Read these chapters carefully and work through the exercises in each section.

The Examination

You are likely to be slightly nervous on the day of the examination. Try to relax! The GCSE examination is supposed to let you show what you 'know, understand and can do'. If you have planned your revision carefully, you may find yourself enjoying the examination!

There are *two* main types of question in the History examination.

(a) Short-answer Questions

Short-answer questions mainly test *recall* (memory). These can be of three types:

(i) *Open-response Questions*

Here you are asked to write a word or short sentence in answer to a question — for example:

Which part of Britain produced the most coal in 1700?

You can find further examples of this type of question at the end of each chapter.

(ii) *Multiple-choice Questions*

These give you a number of options. Only one of the options is correct. You choose your answer from the list of possible options — for example:

Which development in communications do you associate with the name of Guglielmo Marconi?

A Road-building
B Semaphore
C Wireless telegraphy
D Television

(iii) *Source-based Questions*

You will find many source-based questions on GCSE papers. You will be given a map, a photograph, a graph, a document or a set of statistics and you will be asked questions which are based on these sources — for example:

December 26, 1835
The Railway is now in progress. I am the engineer to the finest work in England — a handsome salary — £2000 a year.
Clifton Bridge — my first child, my darling, is actually going on — Glorious!

Name the engineer who wrote this entry in his diary on Boxing Night 1835.

(b) Extended-answer Questions

Extended-answer or essay-type questions will appear on most GCSE examination papers. Sometimes they will be divided up into several parts. For further guidance on essay-writing, refer to Chapter 3.
  A typical GCSE essay question may look like this:

  (i) How did the development of steam power affect the iron and textiles industries in the eighteenth and nineteenth centuries?
  (ii) In the nineteenth century new sources of power, such as electricity, oil and petroleum, were introduced. What effect did these new sources of power have on transport, communications and the economy?

1 Course Planning

Your GCSE History examination will award a large number of marks for source- or evidence-based questions and coursework. What do we mean by a historical source? Historical sources are the raw material which a historian uses to write History. A historian's sources are of two main kinds. *Primary sources* are the evidence which the past has left behind. *Secondary sources* are what historians have already written about the topic. This book is a secondary source for the study of Social and Economic History. You can read more about primary and secondary sources in Chapter 6.

Before we begin work on how to handle sources, we have to take a few basic steps linked to your own GCSE paper. The first step is to find out how much of the course is linked directly to source-based work.

Activity 1

(a) Look at your History syllabus. Work out the proportion (the percentage) of the marks which are tied directly to the use of sources.
(b) Split your work on sources into two parts:
    (i) Source-based work linked to the examination(s).
    (ii) Source-based work linked to coursework (see Chapter 12).

Activity 2

Take a copy of last year's examination papers or your examination syllabus. Read through the source-based questions on the papers.

(a) List the different types of sources which have been used (e.g. maps, diagrams, pictures, graphs).
(b) What sort of questions have been based on the sources (e.g. short-answer, extended, multiple-choice)?
(c) Are questions directly linked to the sources or is *additional* information required?

Activity 3

Look at Figure 1.1. It shows the opening of the Liverpool and Manchester Railway in 1830. What other kinds of sources could you look at to find out about this event? Draw up your ideas in the form of a spider diagram with a *sources* box at the centre. Draw arrows and boxes for the different kinds of sources. We have put visual material (pictures) in for you as an example.

Figure 1.1

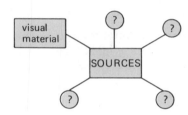

At the end of this section you will find a list of some of the sources you could have included on your spider diagram.

Primary and secondary sources are of little use unless you ask questions about them. You ask questions to get your sources to tell you things. Questions can be very varied and fall under a number of headings.

On your GCSE papers you will find a wide range of questions. They fall into a number of different kinds. This chapter looks at different types of question. Chapters 2–11 guide you through examples of each kind.

What types of question will you have to answer? We have sorted them into the categories listed in Table 1.2. The table should help you to answer source-based questions.

Activity 4

Take last year's papers or your syllabus. Tick the source-based questions which are linked directly to the sources and which do not require extra information. As you work through this chapter, see which headings in the table your ticked questions come under. Then copy out the table, making a note of them.

Answering Source-based Questions

When you are looking at a source-based question, how can you recognise what kind it is? Questions are like puzzles. Their meaning is wrapped up in the way they are written. Fortunately, the question will contain clues in the form of *keywords* or phrases. There is a list of these in Table 1.1.

Table 1.1 Index of keywords and phrases

Keyword/phrase	Question type
Explain	Recall
Name	Recall
Select an example of	Recall
What is meant	Recall
What clue/evidence	Source/external knowledge
Support	Source/external knowledge
Explain	Source/external knowledge
Why	Source/external knowledge
Whether or not	Source/external knowledge
How trustworthy	Source/external knowledge
Arguments/conflicts	Source/external knowledge
Agree/disagree	Source/external knowledge
How far	Source/external knowledge
Using information/sources	Own historical account
Bias/prejudice	Value of sources
Which sources/evidence	Value of sources
Primary/secondary	Value of sources
Bias/propaganda	Value of sources
Reliability/trust	Value of sources
Other sources/information	Value of sources
Which sources/evidence	Value of sources

Sorting out the meaning of a source-based question requires a great deal of patience. The first step isn't too obvious — you have to see whether the questions are actually linked to the sources or not. Boards sometimes ask questions linked to a source without any reference to it at all! The two CSE questions below were linked to a picture of Robert Owen's school for his factory employees in New Lanark:

(1) Outline the part played by the government in education up to 1869.

(9 marks)

(2) In 1870 the government took over the provision of elementary education in England and Wales. Why did the government feel this action to be necessary?

(15 marks)

These are essay-type questions. You can find out how to answer them in Chapter 7. We can now move on to look at the headings in Table 1.2: Types of Source-based Questions.

(a) Recall

The meaning of words, phrases, dates and facts in the source. These questions can be asked without any reference to the document. The questioner just wants you to write what you know about the word, phrase, fact or date.

Table 1.2 Types of source-based questions

Question type	Y Pa S/W Qn	Y Pa S/W Qn
(a) Recall		
(b) Information linked to *external* knowledge		
(i) Explanation		
(ii) Test against		
(iii) Identify person, place, thing, concept		
(iv) Identify idea inside another source		
(v) Explain contradiction or agreement between sources		
(c) Use of sources to write own historical account		
(d) Value of sources to the historian		
(i) Detection of bias		
(ii) Reliability of the sources		
(iii) Other sources about the subject		
(iv) Dating of source, placing it in context		
(v) Identification of sources		

Example: 1988 S 2 5a

Y	1988
Pa	Paper number, 2
S (or W)	Summer (or winter)
Qn	Question number, 5a

Examples

  (i) What is meant by the following words and phrases used in the sources?

     laissez-faire; free trade; mercantilism; the 'slave triangle'

  (ii) Source A refers to 'some eminent engineers' responsible for improving Britain's roads. Name *two* well-known engineers who improved the country's road network between 1800 and 1830.

 (iii) Name the 'lady with the lamp' portrayed on the right of the picture.

(b) Information in Source Linked to External Knowledge

This will ask you to link information inside the source or sources to what you already know about the topic. This type of question has five main varieties.

(i) To explain why something happened, what the source is about, what light it throws on the topic.

1. With explicit reference to sources A and B, explain why the six Dorset labourers were transported to Australia in 1834.
2. Explain the cartoon.
3. Why has the cartoonist drawn Lloyd George as a giant and referred to a well-known children's story in source E?

(ii) To test the source against an existing historical opinion.

1. Explain, whether or not, in your opinion, the sources support the following statement: The term 'workshop of the world' could justifiably be applied to Britain between 1850 and 1875 since she had the world's biggest industrial output.
2. The Industrial Revolution destroyed the domestic system and there is no evidence that in doing so it made life better for the people. (E. J. Hobsbawm). Is this view supported or contradicted by sources B, C and D? Explain your answer.
3. The engineering skill of George Stephenson was essential for the development of railways. Using the sources, explain how far you agree with this opinion.

(iii) Evidence inside the source which enables you to identify a person, place, thing, concept or idea.

1. What evidence is there in source B which helps you to identify A the speaker B the place?
2. What evidence can be drawn from sources C and D to show the difficulties that the duplication of railway lines would create for the railway companies?
3. Using all the sources, explain the various methods employed by the Liberals to set up a 'welfare state' in the period 1906–1914.

(iv) Evidence inside the source which enables you to identify a person,
place, thing, concept or idea *inside another source*.

1. How can you use maps B and C to explain the movements of
   population in Britain between 1800 and 1900?
2. In what ways does the evidence in sources A and B support the
   views advanced in sources C and D?
3. Which of the schools listed in source B might the child in source A
   have attended?

(v) The explanation of contradictions or agreement between sources.

1. Is the writer of source F's argument undermined by the evidence
   produced in sources D and E?
2. How far did the terms of the 1819 Factory Act (source B) go
   towards satisfying the demands of Robert Owen (source E)?
3. Source C shows women and children working underground in
   appalling conditions. This proves that Lord Londonderry's statements in source A are lies. Do you agree with this conclusion?

(c) The Use of the Sources to Write Your Own Historical Account

1. Using information which you have extracted from sources A–H, write
   your own account of the reasons for the population increase in Britain,
   1750–1850.
2. Use all the sources to explain why some people were against the idea of
   enclosing fields in the late eighteenth century.

(d) The Value of the Sources to the Historian

There are a range of questions which ask you to look at the sources as if you were
a historian. Such questions apply a number of tests to the sources. Below are the
main types of such questions.

(i) *The Detection of Bias in the Source*

1. What three words and phrases used by the writer of source E show bias?
2. How effective is source F as a piece of propaganda?

(ii) *The Reliability of the Source*

1. What questions would you ask about the reliability of the evidence which the writer of source E uses to support his opinions?
2. How trustworthy is the view given by the cartoon?
3. What questions would you ask about the reliability of the evidence which the writer of source D uses to support his opinions?
4. The authors of sources C and D wrote about the same event, yet their accounts differ considerably. Does this mean that one of them was lying? Explain your answer fully.

Keywords/Phrases
reliability; trust; trustworthy; truth

(iii) *Other Sources about the Subject*

1. What other sources of information are likely to be available to a historian writing about Peterloo?
2. Where else could you look for sources of information about the Chartists?

Keywords/Phrases
other sources; other information; evidence

(iv) *Dating of Sources/Placing Them in Context*

1. What evidence is there in source D which helps you to identify

   A the speaker   B the place   C the occasion on which the speech was made?

2. What evidence is there that source D was written in 1820 rather than 1850?
3. Write down when you think picture C was engraved. Give your reasons in as much detail as possible.

(v) *Identification of Sources*

1. B, C and D describe how the domestic system worked in different parts of the country. Which of the sources do you think describes the domestic system in the West Riding of Yorkshire? Give reasons for your choice.
2. Which of the sources A–D is most likely to have been written by Feargus O'Connor? Give reasons for your choice.

Keywords/Phrases
which sources/evidence are more likely to be; which sources are

(vi) *The Difference between Primary and Secondary Evidence*

1. From the sources, give *one* piece of primary evidence and *one* piece of secondary evidence which tells us about people's attitudes to the Corn Laws in 1846. Explain why the examples you have chosen are regarded as being primary or secondary.
2. Would you say that source D is primary or secondary? Give reasons for your choice.

> *Keywords/Phrases*
> primary; secondary; evidence; sources

When you feel confident that you can sort out the different kinds of source-based question, you can begin to work through the exercises in Chapters 2–11. Each chapter focuses on one aspect of the course you will need to answer for your GCSE examination. Table 1.1 on p. 6 summarises the most important keywords and phrases.

(e) Consortia Guide

To make sense of Table 1.3 look at the *left-hand column* for the topic covered. Then go across to your *board heading*. Find the entry for your board:

Table 1.3   Consortia guide

Topics	London	Midland	Northern	Southern
Agriculture	DOC/SA/MC/E/P 70% re/co/ev/em	DOC/SA/P 40% re/co	DOC/SA/E 30% re/co/em/ev	DOC/SA/E 50% re/co/ev
Industry	DOC/SA/MC/E/P 70% re/co/ev/em	DOC/SA/P 40%	DOC/SA/E 30% re/co/em/ev	DOC/SA/E 50% re/co/ev
Growth of towns	DOC/SA/MC/E 70% re/co/ev/em		DOC/SA/E 30% re/co/em/ev	
Communications	DOC/SA/MC/E 70% re/co/ev/em	DOC/SA/ PA/ 40% re/co	DOC/SA/E 30% re/co/em/ev	DOC/SA/E 50% re/co/ev
Trade	DOC/SA/MC/E/P 70% re/co/ev/em		DOC/SA/E 30% re/co/em/ev	
Population	DOC/SA/MC/E/P 70% re/co/ev/em	DOC/SA/P 40% re/co	DOC/SA/E 30% re/co/em/ev	

Table 1.3 Consortia guide (cont'd)

Topics	London	Midland	Northern	Southern
Poor law	DOC/SA/MC/E/P 70% re/co/ev/em	DOC/SA/P 30% re/co/ev	DOC/SA/E 40% re/co/em/ev	P/E 30% re/co/em
Corn law				P/E 30% re/co/em
Social reform	DOC/SA/MC/E/P 70% re/co/ev/em	DOC/SA/P 30% re/co/ev		
Chartism			DOC/SA/E 40% re/co/em/ev	P/E 30% re/co/em
The economy	DOC/SA/MC/E 70% re/co/ev/em			
Trade unions	DOC/SA/MC/E/P 70% re/co/ev/em	DOC/SA/P 30% re/co/ev	DOC/SA/E 40% re/co/em/ev	P/E 30% re/co/em
Medicine	DOC/SA/MC/E/P 70% re/co/ev/em	DOC/SA/P 30% re/co/ev		
Welfare state			DOC/SA/E 40% re/co/em/ev	P/E 30% re/co/em
Education	DOC/SA/MC/E/P 70% re/co/ev/em	DOC/SA/P 30% re/co/ev	DOC/SA/E 40% re/co/em/ev	
Role of women	DOC/SA/MC/P 70% re/co/ev/em			
	Ten topics (45%) Examination $1\frac{3}{4}$ hours Ten topics (25%) Examination $1\frac{1}{2}$ hours Coursework 30%	Four themes (40%) Examination $1\frac{3}{4}$ hours Two topics (30%) Examination $1\frac{1}{2}$ hours Coursework 30%	Two themes (30%) Examination $1\frac{1}{2}$ hours Four themes (40%) Examination 2 hours Coursework 30%	Three themes (50%) Examination 2 hours Two topics (30%) Examination 1 hour Coursework 30%

1. The first letters, in BLOCK CAPITALS, will tell you the kind of answer you will have to give (see Table 1.4).
2. The entry below that in figures will tell you the percentage of the total marks.
3. The entry below that will tell you the *skills* being tested.

For example, the entry for the *Agriculture* topic for the London Board translates as in Table 1.4.

Table 1.4

1		DOC	document questions
		SA	short answers
		MC	multiple-choice
		E	essays
		P	paragraph
2		70%	the marks are worth up to 70% of the total
3		re	recall
		co	concepts
		ev	evidence
		em	empathy

Answer to Activity 3 (Spider Diagram)

On the diagram you could have included:

visual material
newspaper reports
maps
biographies
eyewitness accounts
history books
letters
magazines
cartoons
paintings
TV programmes/videos
railway museums
safety regulations
accident statistics

2 Population

Examination Guide

'There are three kinds of lies:
lies, damned lies, and statistics.'

(Mark Twain, *Autobiography*)

In your GCSE exam you are almost certain to get questions based on statistics. GCSE assessment objective (4) states that a candidate should be able to 'show the skills necessary to study a wide variety of historical sources such as . . . statistical and visual material'. What form will these statistics take?

You may be asked to answer questions on (a) line graphs, (b) bar graphs, (c) statistical maps, (d) pie graphs or (e) tabulated information. Look at the examples given in Figures 2.1–2.4 and Table 2.1. Match up these statistics with (a) to (e) above.

Statistics can be used to 'bend the truth'. Look at the two examples in Figure 2.5. Would you vote for the progressive retardists or not? Give reasons for your answer.

Government officials are very good at using statistics to suit their own ends. On 8 March 1987 a leader article in the *Observer* newspaper stated:

'There have been no fewer than 18 changes in the way official unemployment statistics have been compiled . . ... The independent Unemployment Unit calculates that the monthly total would be 400 000 higher if it was based on the methods of calculation used by the Whitehall statisticians in 1979.'

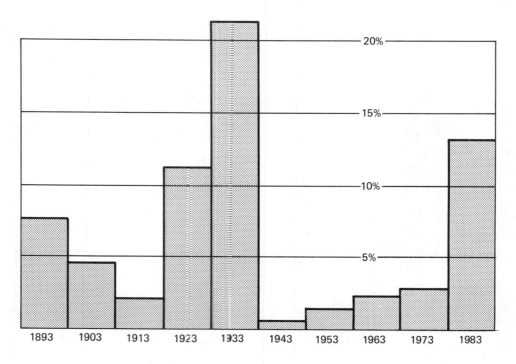

Figure 2.1   Percentage of the workforce unemployed

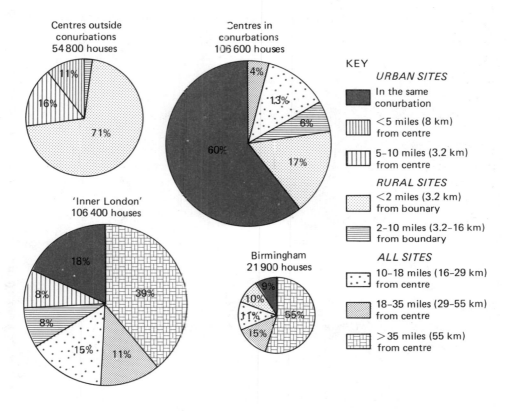

Figure 2.2

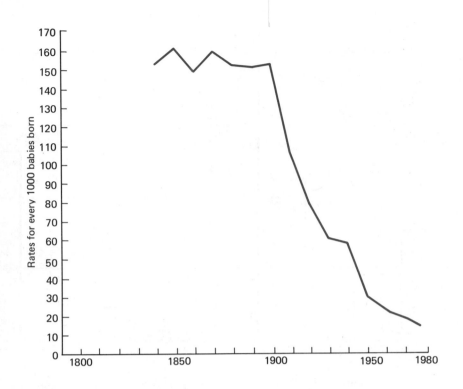

Figure 2.3 England and Wales infant death-rate (under 1 year old), 1840–1980

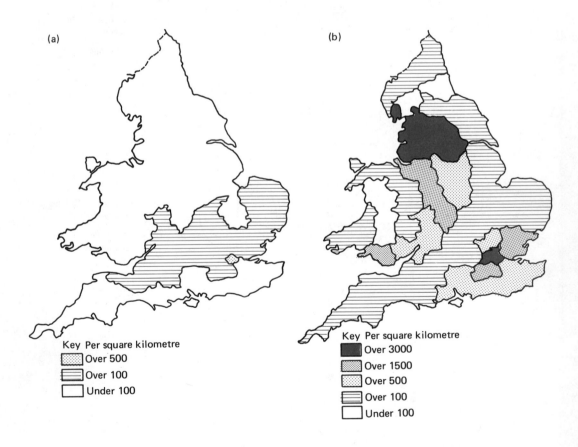

Figure 2.4 (a) Population in 1740; (b) population in 1900

Table 2.1 Population, 1801–1977

| Date | Population (millions) | | | Rate of growth (England and Wales, annual average percentage increase) |
	England and Wales	Scotland	Ireland	
1801	8.9	1.6	5.2	1.1
1811	10.2	1.8	6.0	1.43
1821	12.0	2.1	6.8	1.81
1831	13.9	2.4	7.8	1.58
1841	15.9	2.6	8.2	1.43
1851	17.9	2.9	6.5	1.27
1861	20.1	3.1	5.8	1.19
1871	22.7	3.4	5.4	1.32
1881	26.0	3.7	5.2	1.44
1891	29.0	4.0	4.7	1.17
1901	32.5	4.5	4.5	1.22
1911	36.1	4.8	4.4	1.09
1921	37.9	4.9	4.3 (1926)	0.49
1931	40.0	4.8	4.3 (1936)	0.55
1951	43.8	5.1	4.3	0.48
1961	46.1	5.2	4.3	0.52
1971	48.7	5.2	4.5	0.26
1977	49.1	5.2	n.a.	0.01

Source: B. R. Mitchell and P. Deane, *Abstract of British Historical Statistics*, Cambridge University Press, 1962, pp. 6–7; *Britain 1979*, London, HMSO, 1979, p. 7.

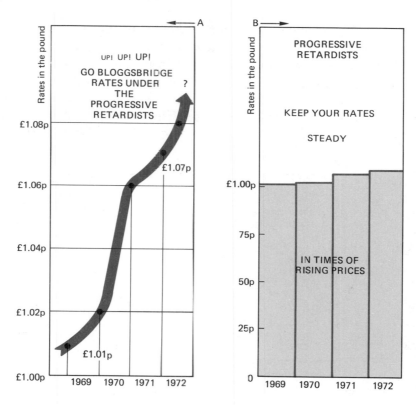

Figure 2.5 Two different ways of showing the same information may produce two quite different impressions

2.1 Introduction

Table 2.2 shows one of the most important trends in English history. From 1100 to 1700 there had been only a slight increase in the population of England and Wales. There had been a rough balance between the *birth-rate* (the number of births per thousand population per year) and the *death-rate* (the number of deaths per thousand per year). In the eighteenth century two important changes took place. There was

- a sudden increase in the population;
- a movement of population from the countryside to the growing towns and cities.

Table 2.2 Population of England and Wales, 1700–1790 (thousands)

1700	5475	1750	6467
1710	5240	1760	6736
1720	5565	1770	7428
1730	5796	1780	7953
1740	6064	1790	8675

John Rickman's survey — from *Abstract of British Historical Statistics*, B. R. Mitchell and P. Deane.

2.2 Reasons for Population Increase

Historians have been discussing this question for many years. No one knows the correct answer, but demographers (people who study population figures) have been able to make a number of intelligent suggestions.

A great deal of debate (discussion) has centred around the death-rate and the birth-rate (see Section 2.1). If the birth-rate was increasing and the death-rate decreasing, the population would increase. Figure 2.6 shows the birth-rate and death-rate for 1700–1840. You can see that the birth-rate reached its peak in 1790 and then started to decline. The death-rate started to fall after 1730 and continued to decline, apart from the periods 1760–1780 and 1820–1830. This

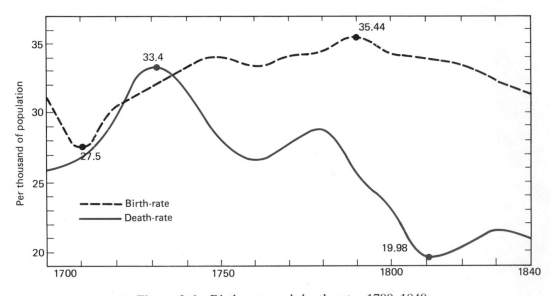

Figure 2.6 Birth-rate and death-rate, 1700–1840

helps to explain why population figures increased after 1730. The next questions we need to ask are *why* did the birth-rate go up and *why* did the death-rate go down? Again, no one can be certain of the answers to these questions. Below are listed eleven factors which may help to explain changes in the birth-rate and death-rate.

(a) Reasons for the Rise in the Birth-rate

1. Under the old system of apprenticeship, young craftsmen were not supposed to marry. By the 1770s boys were no longer forced to become apprentices or farm labourers when they were very young. So young people were free to get married and have families at an earlier age.

Table 2.3 Average age of marriage and childbirth in 1700 and 1800

	1700	1800
Marriage	27	20
Childbirth	33	31

2. The growth of the textile, iron and coal industries by 1800 led to higher wages. With more money in their pockets, people could afford to get married earlier.
3. By the 1770s some children were working in cotton spinning mills. Some historians have argued that couples had bigger families because they realised that their children could become wage-earners at an earlier age.
4. Improvements in housing, food and sanitation may have led to a higher birth-rate.

(b) Reasons for the Decline in the Death-rate

1. *Food and diet* In the eighteenth century people had more money to spend on food and the *quality* of their food improved. Great changes were taking place in agriculture. There was more meat and milk on sale and both could be bought in winter as well as summer. More people were eating potatoes and vegetables. There was a series of good harvests and there were few famines. Improvements in transport (canals and roads) made it easier to send food from farms to towns. An increase in trade with other countries meant that more food was imported from abroad.
2. *Infant mortality* The infant mortality rate (death-rate among babies) went down. Mothers enjoyed a better diet (see above), the rate of miscarriage (babies being born dead) fell, babies were born stronger and mothers were able to feed their children more adequately. There were also improvements in hygiene and midwifery.
3. *The environment* By the 1840s attempts were being made to pave the streets, get rid of sewage and provide people with pure water. Housing gradually improved. Coal became cheaper and heating people's homes became easier.
4. *Medicine* Medical knowledge increased in the eighteenth and nineteenth centuries, but most historians now believe that medical advances did little to bring down the death-rate much between 1780 and 1820. Hospitals were built only in the larger towns and they affected the

health of only small numbers of people. Most advances in medicine were expensive and only rich people could afford them.

5. *Alcohol* Gin was a killer. It was so cheap that people drank it in large quantities. In 1751 Parliament placed a tax on gin. Distillers were no longer allowed to sell direct to the public. By 1800 more people were drinking tea.

6. *Hygiene* After 1790, factory-made soap became cheaper and people washed more often! With higher wages people could afford better-quality clothes. Many of the clothes on sale were made of factory-made cotton cloth, which is an easier fabric to wash than wool. More people wore underclothes and nightshirts. With greater cleanliness, the fleas, lice and ticks which had spread diseases began to disappear.

7. *Population checks* Britain lost few men in major wars and there were fewer famines or outbreaks of epidemic diseases.

2.3 Thomas Malthus (1766–1834)

By the 1790s reporters, authors and pamphleteers were looking at the question of the rise in population. In 1798 the Reverend Thomas Malthus published a book called *An Essay on the Principles of Population*. He argued that it was a natural thing for population to grow *slowly*. Wars, famines and diseases which killed large numbers of people were nature's way of preventing the population increasing too quickly. If these *checks* on population did not happen, the population would increase more rapidly than food production and there would not be enough food to go round. Malthus suggested that, to prevent a population explosion, people should not marry at too early an age and that they should be aware of the dangers of having large families.

Many influential people read Malthus' book. His ideas made them think that Britain would soon be facing a famine. To make matters worse, Britain was fighting a war against France between 1793 and 1802 and this led to serious food shortages. John Rickman, a government official, had the idea of carrying out a census (population count) to see how big the population was. Rickman's census showed that the population of England and Wales was over nine million. The government decided to hold a census every ten years. A census is still taken today.

Fortunately Malthus' ideas have been proved wrong. The growth of population meant that there were more people to feed than ever before, but mass hunger and poverty did not take place in Britain on a wide scale. The increase in population encouraged farmers to put more money into agriculture and to produce greater quantities of food. The growth of population was a factor in the number of industrial goods we were producing and by the 1850s Britain had become 'the workshop of the world'. This increase in industrial production made it possible for British merchants to sell goods to other countries and eventually led to an improvement in the standard of living for most people in Britain.

2.4 Changes in Population Distribution

During the eighteenth century many people left their home areas and moved to other parts of the country to find work. The decline in the old wool-producing areas of East Anglia, Somerset, Devon and the Cotswolds provided people with fewer jobs, while the iron, coal and cotton areas of the North Country and the West Midlands became important 'growth areas'.

The main growth area was around London. London was famous for its agricultural markets and the cloth, building and brewing trades. It was the biggest port in England. It was also the centre of banking, the law and central government. Table 2.4 shows the growth of Greater London between 1801 and 1911. The second-biggest growth area was in Lancashire. Two important towns, Liverpool and Manchester, became centres of the cotton industry. Many workers came over from Ireland to find jobs in the cotton mills. Between 1751 and 1801 the population of the county more than doubled. A similar movement of people took place in the West Midlands. Thousands of people went to live in Birmingham and Coventry, the centres of the metal trades. Craftsmen set up small industries in backyard workshops, making goods such as locks, bolts, pins,

Table 2.4 Population of Greater London, 1801–1911 (thousands)

1801	1117	1861	3227
1811	1327	1871	3890
1821	1600	1881	4770
1831	1907	1891	5638
1841	2239	1901	6586
1851	2685	1911	7256

buttons and nails. Goods such as these were later sent to many different parts of the world. The coal and wool industries of the West Riding of Yorkshire attracted many thousands of workers to the North. The West Riding had fast-flowing streams for water power and plentiful supplies of coal. Cloth was made in large industrial villages which were scattered across the country. In Staffordshire and Shropshire, the centres of the coal and iron industries, industrial sites were similarly spread out. It was not until the nineteenth century that large industrial towns became common in these areas.

By 1800 the population distribution of Britain was developing in four ways. The population was increasing very rapidly, towns were growing at the expense of country areas (see Table 2.5) and the coalfield areas of Lancashire, Staffordshire and Warwickshire were expanding. Large numbers of people continued to move northwards. This movement of people carried on throughout the nineteenth century. A further feature of nineteenth-century population change was a huge increase in the number of people who moved into or out of Britain. Between 1840 and 1914 about 19 million people left the United Kingdom for countries outside Europe. Greater numbers of people than ever before left *Ireland* after a disastrous potato famine in 1846. Six hundred thousand Irish left

Table 2.5 Net gain (+) or loss (−) by migration in England, 1841–1911 (thousands)

Period	London	Other towns	Coal-mining districts	County areas
1841–1851	+274	+386	+82	−443
1851–1861	+244	+272	+103	−743
1861–1871	+262	+271	+91	−683
1871–1881	+307	+297	+84	−837
1881–1891	+169	−31	+90	−845
1891–1901	+226	+294	+85	−660
1901–1911	−232	−89	+114	−295

Source: *Home and Foreign Investment 1870–1913*, A. K. Cairncross.

their home country to settle in Lancashire or Clydeside. Thousands more travelled to North America. You can read more about population movements in Section 6.10.

As overseas trade expanded in the nineteenth century, the population of ports and coal-mining areas near the coast grew rapidly. By 1901, 49 out of 66 towns with a population of over 50 000 lay in a broad band stretching from Dover to Liverpool.

Other towns got bigger as a result of specific industries. Swindon, for example, grew in size as a result of the railway industry, while Blackpool's expansion was due to a huge increase in the holiday trade.

Since the First World War (1914–1918), two factors have brought about important changes in where British people work and live:

- The 'old' industries (coal, iron, steel, textiles) never recovered from the depression of the 1930s. Thousands of workers left the coal-mining areas of Wales, the North and the North-west to look for jobs elsewhere.
- The development of *electrical power* meant that British industries no longer had to be based on or near coalfields. Electrical power can be transmitted over great distances quickly and cheaply. One result of this was the rapid expansion of population and industry in London and the Home Counties. This process is still going on today. Unemployed workers from the North, Wales and the West Midlands are moving southwards to look for jobs in the new technological and service industries of the prosperous South-east.

2.5 The Effects of Population Growth

The growth of population between 1700 and 1900 may have helped the growth of Britain's economy. There were more people to work in factories and on farms and there were more people with money to spend on *consumer goods* (e.g. food and clothing). The notes below show how population growth may have affected the economy.

(a) Farming

There were more people to feed. More money was invested in farming so that farmers could grow more wheat and vegetables and rear more cattle. Without extra food there could not have been extra people! The increased demand for food encouraged farmers to develop new agricultural methods.

(b) Industry

The growth in population meant a growing demand for goods such as coal, textiles and ironmongery. These industries expanded and flourished to meet this demand. However, in some industries an increase in the number of workers available may have slowed down the rate of technological change. There is little point in introducing labour-saving machines in factories if labour is cheap. Some historians have argued that industrial changes were a *cause* of population increase and not the *result* of it.

(c) The Poor

There were more poor people to feed and clothe than ever before. Towards the end of the eighteenth century, the *poor-rate* (money collected for the poor) increased sharply. The old system of poor relief began to break down. Government officials began to consider other ways of looking after the poor. In 1834 the government introduced a new system of poor relief under the terms of the Poor Law Amendment Act (see Section 8.5).

(d) Emigration

More people emigrated to countries such as Australia, Canada and the U.S.A. in the nineteenth century as the statistics in Table 2.6 suggest.

Table 2.6 Outward and inward movements of population, 1876–1885 (excess inward, +; outward, −) (thousands)

| Date | Total | To or from | | |
		U.S.A.	Canada	Australia
1876	−38	+1	−3	−30
1877	−31	−1	−2	−26
1878	−58	−21	−4	−32
1879	−126	−72	−14	−36
1880	−181	−140	−16	−18
1881	−190	−146	−18	−17
1882	−225	−153	−34	−30
1883	−246	−145	−37	−64
1884	−151	−94	−22	−36
1885	−122	−80	−11	−31

(e) Exports and Imports

With factories producing more goods, Britain was able to export a greater number of industrial products abroad than ever before. Selling these products abroad made money for the country and later led to an improvement in our standard of living. Britain came to rely on imported food and raw materials. By the twentieth century, about four-fifths of all the food eaten by British people came from abroad. This led to many problems during wartime, when imported food supplies were threatened by enemy ships, submarines and aircraft.

SPECIMEN QUESTIONS AND EXAMINATION GUIDANCE: POPULATION

GCSE examiners may set you questions like the ones below. Some questions, such as 1(a), simply require you to read off information from the table. Others are more difficult and require a higher level of reasoning.

Before answering any questions on any form of statistics do bear the following points in mind:

- You need to read the information on the vertical and horizontal axes of a graph very carefully.
- Look at the title or heading at the top of the table. What does this tell you about the information displayed below?
- Do make sure that the *units* along both axes are clear in your mind. (Do they mention 'hundreds', 'thousands' or 'millions'?)

- Do the statistics show an overall decline or increase in prices, wages, population figures, etc.?
- Why has the examiner set you this particular exercise? Is he trying to catch you out in any way?

Try to answer the specimen questions based on the statistics below.

The working population: age groups showing the percentage of men and women available for work (1975)		
Percentage of total population		
Date	A (under 16 years)	B (men 16–65; women 16–60)	C (men over 65; women over 60)
1921	27.16	64.5	7.9
1931	23.8	66.6	9.6
1951	22.2	64.0	13.8
1955	22.6	63.1	14.3
1960	23.3	62.1	14.6
1965	24.1	60.8	15.1
1975	26.0	58.2	15.8

1. (a) What percentage of the population was below the age of 16 in 1955?
   (b) What was the percentage increase in numbers of senior citizens between 1951 and 1965?
   (c) In 1960 the country's population was 51.5 million. Calculate the number of people in group B in 1960.
   (d) Add together the two non-working groups and draw a bar-graph to show the relative sizes of the working and non-working populations in 1921, 1951 and 1975.
   (e) Why have the ages 16, 60 and 65 been used in the statistics?
2. Show the three sets of figures in a *three-line* graph.
3. (a) Of what value are these statistics to demographers and historians?
   (b) What factors not shown on the graph might have made the size of group C increase between 1921 and 1975?
   (c) Why do you think there was a percentage increase in group A after 1951?
   (d) What sort of long-term trends do these statistics show?

GCSE essay-type questions on population growth may ask you to *explain the reasons* for population growth. You also need to know about population distribution (see Section 2.4) and the effects of population growth (see Section 2.5). Use sketch maps and statistics in your answers, if you can.

Forget the idea that statistics are boring! They form an important part of our lives. They form the basis of government planning, consumer research and economic development. They can be as interesting and entertaining as a good book or film! It can be fascinating to work out why prices rise or fall, why population figures increase or decrease, why certain industries produce different quantities of goods at different times. You *will* need a certain amount of mathematical ability to enjoy statistics, but a high level of maths is not necessary for GCSE History examinations.

Look again at the statistics in Figures 2.1–2.4, at the beginning of the chapter. Write down any ideas which occur to you about the way in which the information has been presented.

Example	What type of statistical evidence is it?	How is it displayed?	What information can be obtained from the statistics?
Figure 2.1			
Figure 2.2			
Figure 2.3			
Figure 2.4(a)			
Figure 2.4(b)			

WORK OUT SHORT-ANSWER QUESTIONS: POPULATION

1. What was the population of England and Wales in 1700?
2. Define birth-rate and death-rate.
3. What is a demographer?
4. What is the infant mortality rate?
5. Which alcoholic drink led directly to the deaths of thousands of people in the eighteenth century?
6. What was the title of Thomas Malthus' book about population?
7. Write down *two* of the checks on population mentioned by Thomas Malthus in his book.
8. Why was it difficult to import food into Britain between 1793 and 1815?
9. Who was John Rickman?
10. According to Rickman's census, what was the population of England and Wales in 1800?
11. How often is a census taken in Britain?
12. Name three wool-producing areas which were in decline by the early eighteenth century.
13. Which county in the North-west of England had become a major 'growth area' by 1750?
14. Which two towns in the North-west had become centres of the cotton industry by 1801?
15. Upon which industry was Swindon's prosperity based?
16. What was the poor-rate?
17. Which Act of Parliament changed the system of poor relief in 1834?
18. In which country was there a disastrous potato famine in 1846?
19. What percentage of Britain's food was being imported by 1914?
20. Name *four* of Britain's 'old' industries which were in decline by the 1930s.

3 Agriculture

Examination Guide

Agriculture is a popular topic with all examination boards. Work out from the past papers all the questions asked on agriculture. Note which are the most popular areas examined — and base your revision upon them. You should also note the trend towards setting questions on more recent social and economic history. It would be dangerous to assume that no questions will be set on the twentieth century.

If you cannot get old papers, you should be well prepared for questions on the eighteenth and nineteenth centuries. Most questions set on the eighteenth century are either descriptive, empathetic or based on a short extract, a picture or a set of statistics. You should have a detailed knowledge of the *enclosure movement* — why, how, when and where enclosures took place and their results.

Nineteenth-century agriculture is a slightly less popular topic. You may be asked to answer a question on the *Corn Laws* or to explain why the 'Golden Age of Agriculture' occurred. A popular question involves asking candidates to write about the main developments in farming through the eyes of an old farm worker or his boss. You may also be asked to write about agriculture as part of a question combining two or more topics — for example:

- The Tolpuddle Martyrs (trade unions and agriculture).
- The Speenhamland System (the Poor Laws and agriculture).
- The Game Laws (law and order and agriculture).
- Railways (transport and agriculture).
- Growth of cities (population and agriculture).

Topic Guide

Use the following topic headings to help you in your revision. Tick each box as soon as you have completed each topic in your revision.

Agriculture in the 18th century
(open fields, strips, balks, fallows, etc.)

*Enclosures**
(what? when? why? where? results? etc.)

Improvers
(Tull, Coke, Bakewell, Townshend, Young)

French wars (include effects of wars on farming)
*Corn laws** (include Anti-Corn Law League and repeal)
*'Golden Age' (1846–1870)** (improvements in machines, fertilisers, etc.)
*Great depression (1870–1914)** (causes, effects, government intervention)
First World War (U-boats, government measures, Corn Act)
1918–1939 (depression, technical advances, Marketing Act)
Second World War (Government control, rationing, W.L.A.)
Since 1945 (Agriculture Act, intensive farming, E.E.C.)

*Important topics.

3.1 Introduction

Today so many people live in towns and work in factories that we tend to forget that agriculture is still one of our most important industries. As many as 648 000 people (2.6 per cent of the working population) have jobs in agriculture. Farmers grow crops and rear livestock on 19 million out of the 24 million hectares of farmland in Britain. In 1978 exports of cattle and sheep, agricultural products, machinery and chemicals were worth £3743 million. Yet fewer farm workers are needed than ever before. New crops, improved breeds of animals and high technology are three factors which have made this possible. This chapter looks at the way in which agriculture, the oldest industry in the world, has changed over the past 300 years.

3.2 Agriculture in 1700

In 1700 the economy of Britain was mainly based on farming. More people worked in agriculture than in any other part of the economy. British farmers grew enough food to feed the whole population. The land also provided the raw materials needed for Britain's main industry, woollen cloth, as well as for making other goods such as beer, shoes, furniture, carts, ships and houses.

(a) The Open-field System

Half the farmland in Britain was still farmed by the *open-field system* — Figure 3.1. In such areas the arable (farm) land around each village was divided up into

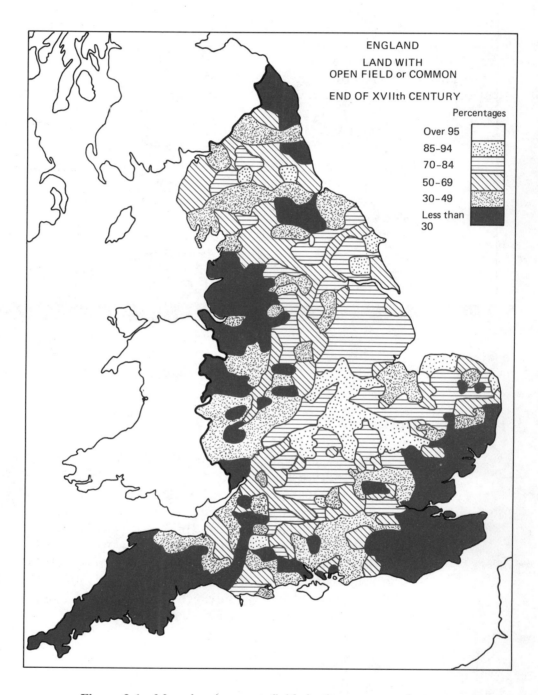

Figure 3.1   Map showing open fields in the seventeenth century

between two and five large, unfenced fields. The large fields were split up into many 200-metre-long strips. Each strip was about one acre in area. An acre was roughly the amount of land a farmer could plough in a day. Stones, posts or ridges of unploughed land, called *balks*, separated the strips from each other.

The crops grown in the open fields were usually winter wheat, spring oats and barley. One field was usually left fallow (empty) so that the soil could regain its goodness. The crops were sown in rotation, as Table 3.1 shows.

Table 3.1

Year	West field	South field	Mill field
1702	Spring barley	Winter wheat	**Fallow**
1703	**Fallow**	Spring barley	Winter wheat
1704	Winter wheat	**Fallow**	Spring barley
1705	**Three-year crop rotation starts again**		

(b) The Farming Community in 1700

In open-field villages there were five main social groups.

(i) *Big Landowners who Owned 300–2000 Acres*

Often the chief landowner was the *squire*, who owned most of the land in and around the village. He was usually a Justice of the Peace (a local magistrate) and would take an active part in running local affairs and choosing the county's Members of Parliament.

(ii) *The Rector or Vicar*

He was sometimes the younger son of the squire or another important landowner. He farmed or rented out the *glebe*, land which belonged to the church.

(iii) *Freeholders and Copyholders*

These were wealthy farmers who owned the land they farmed. The copyholders owned their land because their right to the land was mentioned on village documents which survived from the Middle Ages.

(iv) *Smallholders*

These were farmers who rented about 20 acres of land from the squire, the rector or freeholders. Often they ran small farms.

(v) *Squatters*

These were poor farmers who lived in shacks on the common land, part of which they cleared to grow crops on. They had no legal rights to the land they farmed.

Only groups (i), (ii) and (iii) had legal proof (documents) that they owned the land they farmed.

(c) Advantages and Disadvantages of Open-field Farming

(i) *Advantages*

- In 1700 open fields provided nearly everyone in Britain with enough food to eat.
- Even the poorest farmers had some land upon which to grow food.
- The villagers farmed the land on a co-operative basis — the villagers planned the year's farming together, and shared oxen, ploughs and farm tools. At harvest time everyone helped to gather in the crops.
- Villagers had the right to graze animals on the common land, fallow fields and pasture. They could collect firewood, nuts and berries from the woodland and graze pigs there.

(ii) *Disadvantages*

- One-third of the land used for growing crops (arable land) grew nothing, as it was *fallow*. Within the open fields, land was also wasted on balks and cart-tracks.
- Labour was wasted because the fallow land was ploughed to keep down the weeds.
- Time was wasted in walking from one strip to another. In 1763 Richard Derby of Hanslope, Buckinghamshire, owned 26.5 acres of open field land spread over three fields in 24 strips.
- It was hard to raise healthy animals on the open fields and common land. Diseases such as foot and mouth disease and sheep liver rot spread easily. *Selective breeding* (mating your best animals to produce strong, healthy stock) was impossible.
- In winter there was rarely enough hay to keep all the farm animals alive. Cattle had to be killed off in the autumn and their meat salted down.
- It was hard to raise healthy animals on the open fields and common land. Diseases such as foot and mouth disease and sheep liver rot spread easily. *Selective breeding* was impossible.
- New farm machines could not be used easily on strips.
- Open fields were difficult to drain.

3.3 The 'Agricultural Revolution'

Leading historians, such as J. H. Clapham in *An Economic History of Modern Britain*, used to think that between 1750 and 1850 medieval methods of farming disappeared in favour of modern methods. Clapham called this sudden and dramatic change the 'Agricultural Revolution'. Central to his view of the 'Agricultural Revolution' was the enclosure movement (see Section 3.4) and the work of four great farming improvers — Jethro Tull, Turnip Townshend, Thomas Coke and Robert Bakewell (see Section 3.5).

Historical evidence for this sudden change came from writers such as Arthur Young, Nathaniel Kent and William Cobbett, who wrote between 1768 and 1830. However, we now think that these contemporary writers were exaggerating the changes which had taken place. They wanted to persuade farmers and estate owners to take up the new ideas and farming methods.

Since the 1950s and 1960s historians such as J. D. Chambers and G. E. Mingay have shown that the idea of a sudden change in agriculture may be wrong. The process of change which affected British agriculture widely from 1750 began in the sixteenth century and is still going on today. Many key changes, such as crop rotation, selective breeding and model estate management, began before 1700.

The pace of change varied greatly from area to area. The history of farming is made up from lots of local histories. Farms and farming techniques differ according to soil, climate and landscape; who owned the land; and the distance from centres of change, such as London. Few changes were introduced everywhere at the same time. There was a long time between the invention of a new machine or the introduction of a new crop and their general use in farming. Ideas spread at a speed of about one mile a year from the point at which the change was introduced. For these reasons the term 'Agricultural Revolution' has to be treated with some caution, although it is still useful as a term of reference.

(a) Causes of the Agricultural Revolution

Often you are asked a question which requires you to explain the causes of the Agricultural Revolution. Below are six causes of change which historians have identified:

1. The population of Britain grew quickly between 1700 and 1900, and rose from about $5\frac{1}{2}$ million to 32 million. This created a demand for more food. Farmers could make large profits, and the price of land went up.
2. New farming methods which were becoming popular before the end of the seventeenth century were not suited to open-field farming.
3. There were a number of large landowners, owning over 500 acres, who were keen to try out new ways of running their estates and farms.
4. During the early eighteenth century, landowners were able to set up large, compact farms as a result of 'voluntary enclosure' (see Section 3.4). This meant that they exchanged scattered strips of land to get their land together in one place.
5. The scientific discoveries of the seventeenth century were gradually being applied to farming.
6. Frequent wars and poor harvests meant that the price of wheat was often high. High prices could mean high profits, and give farmers the incentive to produce more food.

3.4 Enclosure

We use the term 'enclosure' to describe open grassland which has been fenced off to turn it into fields. In the North and West of Britain many fields had already been enclosed by 1700. These enclosures were needed for cattle farming and sheep farming. Most of the land which had not been enclosed lay in a wide stretch running from Yorkshire through the Midlands to Bristol and Dorset (see Figure 3.2).

Before 1760 most 'Voluntary' enclosures resulted from villagers swapping parcels of land so that their holdings were in one place. After 1760 *parliamentary enclosure* became more common. The process of parliamentary enclosure was as follows.

- The squire and the landowners called a meeting to discuss plans for enclosure.

31

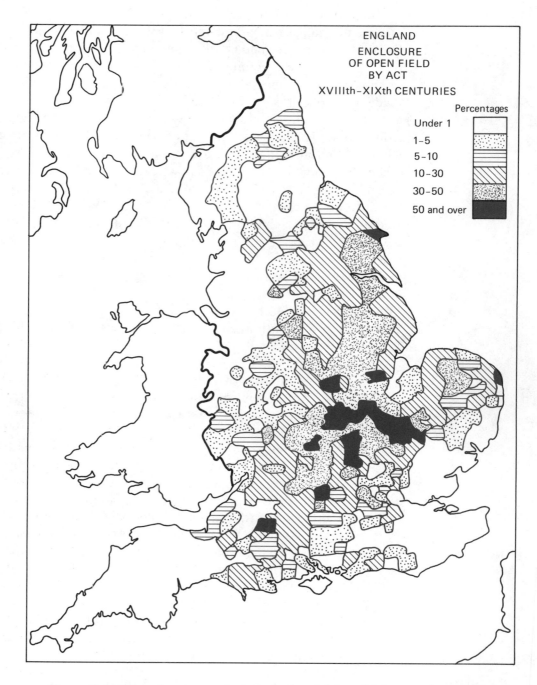

Figure 3.2 Map showing enclosures in the eighteenth/nineteenth centuries

- A notice stating that an enclosure was planned had to be fixed to the door of the parish church for three Sundays in August or September.
- A petition was sent to Parliament. The petition had to be supported by *the owners of four-fifths of the land*. The squire and three or four of the chief landowners usually owned four-fifths of the land.
- Parliament discussed the petition and usually passed an *Enclosure Act*.
- Between three and seven *commissioners* visited the village to survey the area and to try to decide who the land belonged to. They drew up a map showing the new enclosed fields, roads and paths and who owned them.

In 1801 Parliament passed a *General Enclosure Act*. This made it cheaper and simpler to enclose a village. However, each parish still needed its own Act. After 1836 an Act was unnecessary if two-thirds of the villagers agreed to enclose. But by this time the main period of enclosure was nearly over.

Table 3.2 Parliamentary enclosure acts

1750–1759	137	1800–1809	847
1760–1769	385	1810–1819	853
1770–1779	660	1820–1829	205
1780–1789	246	1830–1839	142
1790–1799	468	1840–1849	46

Today there is only one village in England which is not completely enclosed — Laxton, in Nottinghamshire. In certain parts of Laxton, strip farming still carries on.

(a) The Effects of Enclosure

Contemporary writers and poets, such as William Cobbett and Oliver Goldsmith, thought that enclosure caused suffering and distress among the poor. They talked to farmers who had lost their land, their cattle and their self-respect, and came to the conclusion that enclosure worked to the advantage of the rich and powerful. This view is often quoted in school history textbooks:

Wealthy landowners and large farmers definitely benefited by the enclosures . . . but to thousands of small farmers and cottagers, and to the squatters on the commons, the enclosures brought great suffering.
(D. P. Titley, *Machines, Money and Men*, 1977)

We now know that the hardship experienced by the poor in the late eighteenth and early nineteenth centuries was the result of high prices and taxes, high unemployment and low wages. Recent research has shown that enclosure *increased* the number of farming jobs in most areas. As soon as the fences had been put up and ditches had been dug, there were new farmhouses and roads to be built and maintained. The new machines which were used on the enclosed fields were not labour-saving; new farming methods required more men per acre than were needed under the strip system, and after enclosure many more acres were being cultivated. People did *not* leave the land in large numbers as a result of enclosure. In 1811 there were 697 353 families employed in farming; 20 years later there were 761 348.

Most historians would agree that the six main effects of enclosure were:

1. Farmers had the chance to alter their methods of farming without worrying about what their neighbours were doing. They could try out new machines, crops and fertilisers.
2. There was a greater area of arable land in England, because common land, wastes, paths and meadows had been ploughed up.
3. Huge estates were formed containing large farms. Many landowners were able to rent them out to new tenant farmers, who would use improved methods.
4. *Some* of the copyholders, smallholders and squatters who could not prove ownership of the land they had farmed or who could not afford the high cost of enclosure had to give up their land. Some became 'landless labourers'.

5. Many farmers became rich. They could invest more money in their farms and employ more farm workers.
6. The appearance of the countryside changed. Strips, balks, commons and areas of woodland disappeared. New farms, roads, hedges and fences appeared in their place.

SPECIMEN QUESTIONS, EXAMINATION GUIDANCE AND MODEL ANSWER: ENCLOSURE

(a) Essay

Why and with what results were fields in the Midlands and South enclosed between 1750 and 1850?

This 'traditional' essay question is really asking two questions: *Why* were fields enclosed? What were the *results* of enclosures? Therefore, you can assume that half the marks will be awarded to *why* and half the marks to the *results*. Your essay plan could look something like this:

PARAGRAPH 1
Introduction (include reference to population).
PARAGRAPH 2
Profits gained from enclosure.
PARAGRAPH 3
Machinery and enclosure.
PARAGRAPH 4
Results (1).
PARAGRAPH 5
Results (2).
PARAGRAPH 6
Conclusions (sum up the available evidence).

Model Answer

The increase in the population of England and Wales from 6.5 million in 1750 to 17.9 million in 1850 was probably the most important single development to affect farming in the eighteenth and nineteenth centuries. The growth of towns from 1750 onwards and the outbreak of the wars with France in 1793 were further factors in the enclosure movement, as was the enthusiasm of many farmers and landowners for the new farming methods popularised by Bakewell, Townshend and Coke.

The increased demand for food and the likelihood of making large profits probably encouraged farmers to make maximum use of their land and to increase the amount of grain and meat produced on their farms. Enclosure had an important part to play in both developments. Machinery such as Tull's seed-drill or horse-drawn hoe was not suited to strip farming, which still existed in the Midlands and South of England in 1750. The 'open-field' system made a profit in some areas, but in others it was clear to farmers that strip farming wasted time and labour. One-third of the arable land lay fallow. After an enclosure award had taken place, the commons, fallows and marshes were drained and cultivated.

More crops could be grown on a scale large enough to make heavy investment in the land worth while.

The effects of enclosure were many. Historians and agriculturalists still argue over whether the poor suffered as a result of enclosure. There has also been a long-running debate over whether the small farmer benefited or suffered as a result of having his land enclosed. Recent detailed study has shown that the number of small farmers declined during the early eighteenth century but rose during the main period of enclosure. Where farmers could afford the cost of enclosure, and where soils were good, the small farmer flourished.

A further result of enclosures was that the amount of land under cultivation increased by between 100 and 150 per cent. Farmers who were able to enclose on a large scale became very wealthy as the demand for food increased and the price of grain went up. Enclosure undoubtedly provided jobs for the rural poor in the form of hedging, ditching, digging drains and making new roads. Once the fields were enclosed, the new methods required more men and women per acre — not fewer. A greater area of arable land under cultivation and an increased rate of agricultural production provided thousands of new jobs.

The old idea that the rural poor were driven off their patches of land by greedy and unprincipled farmers, M.P.s and commissioners has been discredited. It is now known that the agricultural population increased from 697 353 families in 1811 to 761 348 families in 1831. Nor is there much evidence to suggest that poverty increased substantially as a direct result of enclosure. Areas such as Sussex and Kent, which experienced few enclosures between 1750 and 1850, had as high a proportion of paupers as did Dorset and Leicestershire, where the number of enclosures was high. Even so, contemporary writers such as Arthur Young and William Cobbett believed that enclosure had a very bad effect on the poor. Modern economic historians such as J. D. Chambers and G. E. Mingay do not deny that there was a great deal of suffering among the poor during this period — merely that enclosure was the cause of it. Modern historians suggest that poverty increased as a result of population growth, an inadequate system of poor relief, low wages and high unemployment after the Napoleonic Wars. In the words of Chambers and Mingay: 'There was in fact no general exodus of unemployed rural labour, pauperised by enclosure, to seek work in the towns'.

(b) Documentary Question

Notice is hereby given that an application is intended to be made to Parliament in the forthcoming session for leave to bring in a Bill for dividing, allotting and enclosing the Open and Common fields, common meadows, Common Pastures, and other Common lands within this Parish of Weston Turville in the County of Buckingham.

All those who have objections to the same must record them . . ..

(A notice placed on the church door on 10 September 1797)

1. Why was this petition being sent to Parliament?
2. What were the 'common meadows'?
3. What sort of people might have raised objections to the application?
4. Why might these people have had difficulty in making their objections felt?
5. If the bill had been passed, how might the appearance of Weston Turville have changed?
6. For what reasons was land enclosed in the eighteenth century?

A documentary question like this is fairly easy to score marks on. You will normally find the number of marks awarded for each question in brackets after the question. How many marks do you think each question (1)–(6) is worth?

The mark scheme gives you a guide to how much you are expected to write in each answer. If you see that a question is worth 6–10 marks, your answer should consist of a short paragraph. If a question is worth only 1 mark, you need only write down one fact to earn that mark.

These questions are often quite interesting to answer and they can be fun. You can put yourself in the place of a historical researcher asking questions about the past through the use of documentary evidence. They also contain a number of pitfalls for weaker candidates. Do *not* assume that all the information you need to answer a documentary question can necessarily be found in the passage. To obtain a good mark on a documentary question, you need to use:

- Your knowledge of History.
- Your powers of comprehension.
- Your vocabulary.

3.5 Agricultural Improvers

When revising this topic, you should remember that the following 'great names' in agriculture were not necessarily the first men to use the ideas and inventions historians before 1960 gave them credit for. The improvers were often merely building on the work many previous generations of farmers and landlords had carried out. In any case, it was many years before the majority of farmers accepted ideas and 'inventions'.

Many of the improvers were great lords, such as the Marquis of Rockingham or Lord Braybrook. Others were local gentry or rich tenant farmers with long leases. As these farmers travelled up and down the country on business, they noted down the improvements they saw being introduced on other farms. Also, they could pick up ideas at agricultural shows. They tried these out on their own farms when they got home. We should think of these farmers as being the first of many thousands of 'improving landlords'. It was the work of these landlords which allows us to talk of an 'Agricultural Revolution'. The well-known improvers were as follows.

(a) Jethro Tull (1674–1741)

Tull started off in life as a lawyer but took up farming because he suffered from poor health. He worked on his father's farm at Mount Prosperous, in Berkshire. By about 1701 Tull had developed a seed-drill designed to sow seed in rows, evenly spaced out and at a regular depth. This was an improvement on the traditional system of *broadcasting* (throwing seed down onto the ground in handfuls). In 1714 Tull produced a horse-drawn hoe which was used for clearing weeds growing between the rows of crops. Tull's inventions were described in his book, published in 1733, *The New Horse Hoeing Husbandry*. Many of his ideas were rather far-fetched (he was, for example, against the use of manure on arable land), and he found himself mocked by other eighteenth-century writers.

(b) Charles 'Turnip' Townshend (1674–1738)

A famous diplomat, Townshend gave up politics in 1730 and retired to his great estates at Raynham, in Norfolk, to concentrate on farming. He became well known for his interest in the *Norfolk four-course rotation* (a rotation which alternated turnips and clover with wheat and barley). He also improved the quality of the soil on his land by draining it and adding *marl* (a mixture of clay and lime), which turned sandy swamps into rich, arable land.

(c) Thomas Coke (1750–1842)

Coke (pronounced 'Cook') followed Townshend's example in using marl (clay and lime), to improve the quality of the soil on his estates at Holkham, in Norfolk. He fed his cows on cattle-cake and grew a new root crop, swedes. He gave his tenant farmers long leases on condition that they used the new methods of farming. He also organised annual sheep-shearing festivals known as 'Coke's Clippings', which thousands of people attended between 1778 and 1821.

(d) Robert Bakewell (1725–1795)

Bakewell was a stock-breeder from Dishley, Leicestershire. He selected the finest and fittest types of cattle, sheep and horses, and tried breeding from them. He created new breeds of sheep ('New Leicesters'), longhorn cattle and shire horses. Visitors from all over Europe visited his farm and were impressed by the clean and hygienic conditions in which he kept his animals.

(e) Arthur Young (1741–1829)

Young was an agricultural writer who did much to publicise the new farming methods. He was in favour of enclosure in principle but he believed that the process brought about much hardship, claiming 'by 19 out of 20 enclosure bills, the poor are injured'. From 1784 he edited a farming magazine, *Annals of Agriculture*, and in 1793 the government appointed him as Secretary to a new Board of Agriculture. The Board began a survey of agricultural practices in each county and Young wrote six of the reports himself.

(f) King George III (1738–1820)

In his early life King George III was a keen farmer and he did much to spread new ideas about farming. He had his own 'model farm' in Windsor Great Park. He also wrote articles for *Annals of Agriculture* under the pen-name of 'Ralph Robinson' (the name of his farm manager).

SOURCE-BASED QUESTION: AGRICULTURE

Source A

A Visit to Robert Bakewell's Farm in 1793
The neatness of the hedge-rows and cleanness of the grounds cannot fail to attract the attention of the traveller. The different breeds of sheep kept

on the farm are brought together, put side by side, under the immediate eye of the visitor; and which after viewing alive, the carcasses of different breeds, preserved in pickle and hung up side by side, may be viewed again, to examine the thickness and flesh and fat on each.

Mr Honeybone, the nephew of Mr Bakewell, took us round the farm; we looked at the different successions of cabbages, drilled wheat and barley which are generally sown broadcast. The grand article of husbandry is the irrigated ground, about 200 acres, from a stream . . . . A mill is fed from the same source but the water is not that important in improving the lands. The dung from the yard is brought to one point and mixed with water and carried over certain fields, by which they are made so fertile that this present year some parts have been mowed twice. Beside watering the grounds the stream is formed into a narrow canal; upon which boats are constructed to carry the manure from the yard and the produce of the fields to the farm yard; and of late, the turnips have been thrown into the stream and been washed and carried down; till on their arrival at their destined port, a servant waits and scoops them onto the banks.

Mr Bakewell uses no waggons but prefers the light, single-horse carts. In the farmyard are seen ploughs and harrows; plain and spiked rollers, simple racks for feeding horses. In one pigsty are conveniences for measuring and weighing the food of hogs . . . .

(*The Gentleman's Magazine*, J. H. Urban, September 1793)

Source B

A West Country farm in about 1750

38

An East Anglian farm in 1785

1. Which animals mentioned in source A can you see in source B?
2. In source A, what is meant by
   (i) 'sown broadcast'?
   (ii) 'harrows'?
   (iii) 'carcasses'?
3. (i) What differences do you notice between the farmyard scenes shown in sources B and C?
   (ii) What similarities are there?
   (iii) How do you explain these differences and similarities?
4. What sort of crop rotation did Robert Bakewell use on his farm (source A)?
5. List *three* uses of water mentioned in source A.
6. How would a modern farm differ from the farms described and depicted in sources A, B and C?

3.6 The Wars with France (1793–1815)

In 1793 France declared war on Britain. The war and other events in Britain caused problems in agriculture. During the war, four developments helped farmers in Britain.

1. The population continued to increase, from 8.5 million in 1793 to 11.8 million in 1815. This created a demand for more food.

2. Napoleon, the French Emperor, tried to prevent food from getting to Britain by sea. The government encouraged farmers to grow as much food as they could and large numbers of Enclosure Acts were passed (see Section 3.4).
3. Developments 1 and 2 led to an increase in prices. Between 1800 and 1815 the price of wheat doubled from 40 shillings to 80 shillings a quarter.
4. Improved farming methods (e.g. crop rotations, farm machinery, marling), enclosures and better transport (canals and roads) enabled some farmers to become very rich.

3.7 The Corn Laws

When the wars with France ended in 1815, farmers were afraid that cheap foreign corn would be brought into the country. With so much grain on the market, there would be a fall in the price of British wheat. In 1815 farmers and landowners had great political power. Most M.P.s were landowners themselves. Parliament passed a law stating that no foreign corn could be brought into Britain until British grain reached a certain price. The prices were:

Wheat   80 shillings a quarter
Rye   53 shillings a quarter
Barley 40 shillings a quarter
Oats   26 shillings a quarter

(A 'quarter' was a way of measuring out quantities of corn, equal to 64 gallons or 8 bushels.)

One result of the Corn Law was that the price of bread was kept artificially high. For many people, bread was a staple diet (a basic food); they could afford few other types of food and relied upon loaves of bread as the basis for most meals. To these people the Corn Law seemed unfair. Farmers and landowners were being given special favours at the expense of others. To make matters worse, there was great social distress in Britain in the period 1815–1830. Thousands of soldiers and sailors returned home from the war to find that there were few jobs for them. Expensive bread, high unemployment and heavy taxes led to great unrest among the poor. The Corn Law was changed in 1828, when William Huskisson, President of the Board of Trade, introduced a sliding scale of duties on corn imports. The higher the price of foreign grain, the lower the duty on it.

3.8 The Swing Riots (1830)

After 1815 depressions in industry and farming in 1818, 1824–1825 and 1830–1831 meant an increase in the number of those out of work. The increase in poverty was linked to unrest and rioting. Times became so hard for starving labourers and their families that in 1830 a series of riots broke out in Kent, Sussex and Essex. In desperation groups of farm workers marched to farms and destroyed machinery, burned ricks and demanded a minimum wage of 2s. 6d. ($12\frac{1}{2}$p) a day. The farm workers claimed to be led by a mysterious 'Captain Swing'. The government sent in soldiers and the riots were stopped. Hundreds of farm workers were put on trial. Nine were hanged and 457 transported to Australia.

40

3.9 The Anti-Corn Law League

During the 1820s and 1830s British trade was improving. Factories were turning out more manufactured items and more exports were being sent abroad. Factory owners and businessmen wanted to be able to send goods overseas and to bring goods into the country without paying taxes on them — a system of *free trade* (see Section 10.3). They were also against the idea of taxing bread. They believed that the Corn Laws had caused the cost of bread to increase and had resulted in a high cost of living. Their workers were demanding higher rates of pay because they needed more money to buy bread. This had resulted in lower profit margins in industry.

Many factory owners gave their support to a free trade movement formed in 1838, called the Manchester Association. The leaders of the movement were Richard Cobden (1804–1865), a cotton manufacturer, and John Bright (1811–1889), a Rochdale factory owner. A year later the *Anti-Corn Law League* was formed. The League ran a national campaign against the Corn Laws. Speakers were sent around the country to convince people that the Corn Laws should be scrapped. Thousands of pamphlets and newspapers were printed attacking the Corn Laws. However, there was widespread opposition to the League's campaign from landowners, farmers and some M.P.s. The arguments for and against the Corn Laws are shown below.

(a) Arguments in Favour of the Corn Laws

- The British economy depended upon agriculture. If British farmers did not receive a fair price for their crops, they could go out of business. If this happened, there could be an economic depression and famine.
- The French Wars had shown the danger of Britain relying upon other countries for her food.
- The Corn Laws kept food prices stable.
- Farmers could invest the profits they made from selling their grain in farm improvements. In the long run, this would lead to cheaper food for all.

(b) Arguments against the Corn Laws

- Factory owners believed that if the price of bread was kept artificially high, they would have to: (1) pay their workers higher wages, which would have the effect of leaving manufacturers with less money to plough back into industry; (2) charge higher prices for the goods they produced; (3) lay workers off.
- The poorest people in Britain felt that the Corn Laws forced the price of bread up and made them even worse off.
- Factory owners and workers, farm labourers, the poor and unemployed seemed to be paying out money which was being used to line the pockets of wealthy farmers.
- The Corn Laws led to competition between nations rather than co-operation. Other countries would impose duties on British goods in retaliation for duties on corn.

In 1842 the Conservative Prime Minister, Robert Peel, made some changes to the Corn Laws. Peel believed in free trade and thought that the Corn Laws were stifling the economy. Three years later a disastrous potato famine hit Ireland. Peel decided that the Corn Laws would have to be changed at once so that starving people in Ireland could receive cheap grain. In June 1846 Parliament passed an Act repealing the Corn Laws. Many M.P.s predicted disaster for British agriculture. In fact, farmers were about to enjoy one of the most prosperous periods ever known.

3.10 1846–1870: The 'Golden Age' of Farming

This period was one of high profits for farmers. It is sometimes known as the period of *high farming*. Many farmers made a heavy investment in farm improvements in order to secure higher output. Why did farmers do so well in the middle years of the nineteenth century?

(a) Reasons for the Expansion and Prosperity of Farming from 1846 to 1870

(i) *Population*

There was increasing demand for food in Britain. The population increased from 17 million in 1846 to 24 million in 1874. People in the growing industrial towns of the North and Midlands were receiving higher wages and could afford to eat better-quality food.

(ii) *Railways*

The new railways carried large amounts of meat, milk and vegetables from country areas to towns. They carried fertilisers, cattle-cake and farm machinery from ports and cities to farms. The railways also took many farm workers away from the countryside and forced farmers to use labour-saving machinery for sowing, reaping, threshing and ploughing.

(iii) *Lack of Foreign Competition*

Parliament had repealed the Corn Laws in 1846 (see Section 3.9) but foreign grain did not swamp the market as some M.P.s had predicted. British farmers were able to get a good price for their grain because no foreign country had large enough surpluses to export to Britain. The U.S.A. had yet to link the great prairie lands of the Midwest to the east coast by railway. Cheap grain could not yet be shipped to Europe.

(iv) *Education*

Farmers were encouraged to take advantage of the research facilities offered by:

- the Royal Agricultural Society (1838);
- the Rothamsted Experimental Station (1842);
- the Royal College of Agriculture at Cirencester (1846).

Farmers could also learn about the latest farming techniques by reading the journals of the Royal Agricultural Society and by attending agricultural shows.

(v) *Technical Improvements*

All the time, thousands of improvements were being made to farming methods, crops and animals.

Drainage

James Smith, a farmer from Perthshire, developed a way of digging shallow trenches filled with stones. In Worcestershire James Ellington used trenches five feet deep for drainage purposes. John Reade invented tile drain pipes similar to those used today. John Fowler devised a drainage plough (or 'mole plough') which could lay clay pipes for 5 shillings (25p) an acre. All these drainage pipes became cheaper to produce. The government handed out loans to farmers so that they could lay drains.

Fertilisers

In 1840 Justus von Liebig, a German scientist, published a book, *Organic Chemistry in its Applications to Agriculture*, showing how plants benefit from certain chemicals in the soil. Three years later, Sir John Lawes started to manufacture superphosphates at his factory in Deptford. At the same time *guano* (seagull droppings rich in chemicals) was being sent to Britain from Peru. *Nitrates* were sent from Chile and *potash* from Germany. By use of these chemicals, both arable land and pasture land were enriched.

New Machines

An improved version of Tull's seed drill (see Section 3.5) became popular with farmers. A reliable reaping machine was produced in the U.S.A. by McCormick and introduced into Britain in the 1850s. Andrew Meikle's threshing machine, Henry Salmon's hay tosser and James Small's plough were also in use by 1870.

(vi) *Livestock*

There was considerable interest in pedigree cattle breeding using Bakewell's methods (see Section 3.5). New types of cattle-feed (linseed, oilseed, maize) were imported from abroad. More meat, cheese and butter became available. Many farmers grew more kale, swedes and turnips for winter fodder.

(vii) *Wages*

During this period the wages of farm workers remained low. Farmers could therefore keep their labour costs down.

3.11 The Great Depression (1870–1914)

There was a sudden depression in farming after 1870 which resulted in many changes in agriculture. Between 1873 and 1879 there was a series of wet summers and poor harvests. Foot and mouth disease and sheep liver rot followed the bad weather. Farming conditions were so bad that many farmers did not even notice a greater threat to their way of life — foreign competition.

(a) Foreign Competition in the 1870s and 1880s

(i) *Grain*

For the first time, in 1872, more imported wheat was shipped into Britain than was grown here. Imported wheat was much cheaper than home-grown grain. Prices fell from 56 shillings a quarter in 1870 to 31 shillings a quarter in 1886.

In America new reaping machines had made it possible to harvest tons of grain on the prairie lands of the Midwest cheaply and quickly. A new American railway network was used to carry the grain from the prairies to the ports. Steamships brought the cargoes of wheat across the Atlantic to Europe.

(ii) *Meat*

In 1882 the first cargo of frozen lamb from New Zealand arrived in Britain aboard a steamship with refrigerated holds, the *Dunedin*. By the mid-1880s, large cargoes of frozen meat were being imported into Britain from Argentina (beef), the USA (pork) and Australia (beef and mutton). By 1900 half the meat consumed in Britain came from abroad. However, British meat-producers did not suffer as much as the wheat farmers, because imported frozen meat was not of the best quality. Many dairy farmers went over to producing milk (which does not freeze well) rather than cheese or butter.

(iii) *Wool*

Wool prices fell sharply. The opening of the Suez Canal and improvements in steamship services to the East meant that large supplies of good-quality merino wool were soon being shipped to Europe from Australia and New Zealand. British farmers found that the prices they received for their own wool dropped dramatically.

(b) The Effects of the Great Depression

- The effects of the depression varied from region to region.

  Many farmers in the South and East began to produce food which was difficult to import. They began to grow fruit and vegetables on a large scale. Many of them concentrated on producing high-quality mutton and beef. This produce could be transported quickly and cheaply to Britain's cities by railway.

  The wheat-producing areas of the South and East were very badly affected by the depression. Farmers growing oats and barley were slightly better off.

  Pasture farmers in the North and East remained fairly well off until the end of the 1880s.

  Stock breeders all over the country benefited from low grain prices because it enabled them to feed their animals cheaply on cereals.
- Many farmers could only stay in business by cutting costs to a minimum and employing fewer farm workers. The agricultural labour force fell from over a million in 1871 to 600 000 in 1901.
- Agriculture remained in a depressed state until the First World War (1914–1918). Britain became a country which normally had to rely upon imported food to feed her people and had to pay for her food with money raised from *exports*.

- One important outcome of the depression was that the government began to play an active part in helping farmers. Parliament set up two Royal Commissions in 1879 and 1893 to look into the causes and effects of the depression. The Commissions did not come up with any clear-cut recommendations. Two Smallholdings Acts were passed in 1893 and 1907 to help farm workers buy small farms, and a government department, the Board of Agriculture, was set up in 1889.

3.12 Farm Workers' Unions (see also Section 5.10)

Throughout the nineteenth century, farm workers' wages were low. Farm workers often depended upon the goodwill of their employers to make ends meet. 'Tied cottages' (cottages which farm workers were allowed to live in as part of their condition of work) meant that few farm hands had homes of their own.

In 1872 *Joseph Arch*, a Methodist preacher and farm worker, formed a National Agricultural Labourers' Union (N.A.L.U.). By the end of 1872, membership stood at 100 000. The union met with violent opposition from farmers, landowners and magistrates, and in 1884 the union collapsed. However, in that year agricultural workers won the vote, under the terms of the Third Reform Act. The union was revived early in the twentieth century and conducted a successful campaign against the *gang system* (using women and children as a source of cheap labour on farms).

SPECIMEN QUESTION, EXAMINATION GUIDANCE AND MODEL ANSWER: AGRICULTURE

In your GCSE examination you are almost certain to get questions like this:

It is the year 1880. You are an old farm worker. You have been asked to write a newspaper article describing your life in agriculture over the past fifty years. Write the article, outlining all the changes you have seen taking place in agriculture in that time.

Planning

It is easy to let your imagination run riot here. Turn to Chapter 7, and follow the steps suggested. Use your knowledge of history and what you have learned from visits to county shows or agricultural museums to good effect. You may also have seen TV documentaries such as 'Bread or Blood' about rural life in the nineteenth century. Work out an essay plan for the empathy question above.

Dialect

In an empathy question it is inadvisable to write your answer in dialect. For one thing, it is almost impossible to reproduce the spoken idiom or accent on paper. If you do so, the results may be quite bizarre. Another point is that the examiner may suspect that you are trying to conceal gaps in your knowledge of history, spelling and grammar if you write something like this:

Oi well recall t'wat it were loik back in the 1830s. Moi good lady Martha used to bake 'er own bread and fer me breakfast oi 'ad bread 'n ale. In those days t' summers seemed to be warmer, t' winters colder . . .', etc.

Rambling scripts like this earn candidates few marks. Try to imagine what a farmer's life was really like in the nineteenth century. You can include period detail if you like, but do remember that the examiner is most interested in your *interpretation* and *understanding* of events in the past.

Possible Essay Plan
PARAGRAPH 1
Introduction — setting the scene.
PARAGRAPH 2
Swing Riots of 1830.
PARAGRAPH 3
Social order in 1830s.
PARAGRAPH 4
Living conditions for labourers.
PARAGRAPH 5
Repeal of Corn Laws, 1846.
PARAGRAPH 6
'Golden Age', 1846–1870.
PARAGRAPH 7
Great Depression, 1870.
PARAGRAPH 8
Farm Workers' Unions.

How close is this to *your* plan? Have you left anything out? The essay takes us up to the 1880s. Note the *date boundaries* which have been set by the examiner. It is pointless writing about open fields or enclosures, because this phase in agricultural history was nearly over by 1830. Likewise, it would be absurd to write about the events which took place after 1880, as the examiner has told us 'It is the year 1880' in the question. Your answer could read something like this.

Model Answer

I was born near the county town of Warwick in the year 1821. I was a youngster of 9 when I began to earn money. My first job was crow-scaring and for this I earned fourpence a day. The day was twelve hours long, so it sometimes happened that I got more than I bargained for and that was the taste of the farmer's stick when he ran across me outside the field I had been set to watch!

The 1820s were times of great hardship for farmworkers. Prices were high, wages were low and work was hard to come by. There were many men who came back from the wars against Boney who simply couldn't find work. Some farmers in Warwickshire paid starvation wages — six shillings a week! By 1830 things had come to a head. Groups of farm workers roamed the countryside by night, smashing threshing machines and setting light to ricks and crops. I suppose this was a way of drawing people's attention to their desperate plight. They said they were led by a 'Captain Swing' but I never saw him. The authorities dealt harshly with the men who were caught rioting. 644 were hanged, 20 jailed and 500 sent to Botany Bay.

We labourers had no lack of lords or masters. There was the parson and his wife at the rectory. There was the squire with his hand of iron overshadowing us all. At the sight of the squire, the people trembled. He lorded it over his tenants, the farmers. The farmers, in their turn, tyrannised the labourers. The labourers were no better than toads under a harrow. My heart used to burn when I saw how the men who worked so hard for the farmers were treated like the dirt beneath their feet.

Our living conditions were appalling. Our houses were little better than hovels, made of mud and straw, and old cast-off windows stuck in the mud walls. Inside, our furniture consisted of chairs and stools, a few boards tacked together for a table, the floor made of pebbles or bare earth. Our food consisted of bread, potatoes, cheese and root vegetables. Sometimes my father would poach a hare or deer for our supper, although if he had been caught doing this, the penalties would have been severe.

When I was between 12 and 13 years of age, I became a ploughboy. It was a proud day for me when I drove my first pair and got 18 pence a day. The farmer I worked for was extremely well off. He received a high price for the wheat and barley we harvested, on account of the Corn Law. No foreign corn was allowed into the country until the price of wheat reached 80 shillings a quarter. In practice, this meant that no foreign corn at all came into Britain and so my employer faced no competition. I will always remember the look of dismay on his face that day in 1846 when he learned that the Corn Laws had been repealed.

The years after 1846 were prosperous ones for farmers but not for us labourers. Some of the farmers called it a 'Golden Age'. The value of their land went up and they received more in rents from tenant farmers. Many of them used new machines like the McCormick reaper to harvest their crops, and phosphates and nitrates were used to improve the quality of their soil. Many began to improve the quality of their farm stock by employing the 'selective breeding' techniques pioneered by a Mr Bakewell of Leicestershire.

For most of us farm workers, however, things just stayed the same, or even got worse. In 1860 we were given a 'tied' cottage each and our wages were increased to ten shillings a week. I got married and brought up four children, three of whom are still living. Then we ran into bad times again. At the beginning of the '70s a depression hit farming. More foreign food was imported into Britain from Canada, the U.S.A. and Australia. The grain and meat from these countries was carried to Britain on the new steamships which plied the great oceans of the world. Huge quantities of beef and mutton were carried in their refrigerated holds. This had the effect of bringing about a collapse in the price of food — and a fall in our wage-rates.

To make matters worse, we had a run of bad harvests between 1873 and 1879. 1879 was the wettest summer ever recorded! In Warwickshire the cattle suffered from foot and mouth disease, the sheep from liver rot. Men found themselves out of work or on short time. But perhaps there is a ray of hope on the horizon. A fellow farm worker, Joseph Arch, from Barford, has set up a combination or union of farm workers. The idea is to put pressure on the farmers to pay their men a decent wage. I feel certain that through the new National Agricultural Labourers' Union farm workers will achieve better rates of pay, see an end to the iniquitous gang system and tied cottages, and be valued more greatly by the members of the community which they serve!

SOURCE-BASED QUESTIONS: AGRICULTURE

Source A

A few of the houses had thatched roofs, whitewashed outer walls and diamond-paned windows, but the majority were just stone or brick boxes with blue-slated roofs. The older houses were relics of the pre-enclosure days and were still occupied by descendants of the original squatters. Some of the cottages had two bedrooms, others only one, in which case it had to be divided by a screen or curtain to accommodate parents and children. Often the boys of a family slept downstairs, or were put to sleep in the second bedroom of an elderly couple whose children were out in the world. Except at holiday times, there were no big girls to provide for, as they were all out in service. Still, it was often a tight fit, for children swarmed, eight, ten, or even more in some families, and although they were seldom all at home together, the eldest often being married before the youngest was born, beds and shakedowns were often so closely packed that parents and children often had to climb over one bed to get into another.

(*Lark Rise to Candleford*, Flora Thompson, 1939)

Source B

Farm workers lived in thatched cottages built of cracked and ancient stud work [timber and plaster], containing one bedroom, one sitting room and one lean-to scullery. The bedroom in the roof, which was stopped with rags to keep out the rain, was approached by a steep ladder.

(*Rural England*, H. Rider Haggard, 1906)

Source C

In our village was a row of labourers' cottages fronting the street. In the middle of the street was an open gutter. Behind the houses were the pigsties and toilets. The filth seeping from the pigsties and toilets found its way between the cottages into the gutter so that the cottages were surrounded by streams of filth.

(*Labouring Life in the Victorian Countryside*, P. Horn, 1976)

Source D

Inside the cottage was an old table and a broken chair. There was a small piece of carpet on the floor. A few bedclothes had been dumped in one corner. At night these were handed out to members of the family who, lying about on different parts of the floor, could not possibly in cold weather get a reasonable amount of warmth.

(*The English Peasantry*, F. G. Heath, 1874)

Source E

Source F

1. (a) Describe in detail what you can see in sources E and F.
   (b) Which two sources suggest that there was overcrowding in some farm workers' cottages 100 years ago?
   (c) Which source suggests that sanitary arrangements in some villages were extremely primitive?
   (d) Why do you think farm workers put up with such appalling conditions?
2. Source E was drawn in 1871. Source F was photographed in 1892. Which source would be more useful to a historian studying social conditions in the late nineteenth century? Give reasons for your choice.
3. Describe the main differences between farm workers' cottages like those in sources A–F and farm workers' cottages in 1980.

3.13 Farming during the First World War

When war with Germany broke out, on 4 August 1914, Britain was heavily dependent upon supplies of imported food.

- *Imports of food into Britain in 1914*: meat, 40 per cent; fruit, 75 per cent; cereals, 80 per cent; sugar, 100 per cent.

Soon German U-boats (submarines) were sinking hundreds of merchant ships carrying food to Britain. By December 1916 there was a serious food shortage. The government decided to take action to increase the amount of food grown at home.

(a) War Agricultural Committees (1916)

In each county a committee was set up. The committees had the power to take over and to plough up fallow land, including parks and playing fields.

(b) Improved Efficiency

In 1916 the government bought 5000 new Fordson tractors from the U.S.A. Women drivers were trained to use them, thus releasing men for the army.

(c) Ministry of Food (1917)

Food supplies were rationed. People received ration cards entitling them to certain amounts of butter, meat and cheese each week.

(d) Women's Land Army (1917)

Thousands of male farm workers had joined the armed forces. The Women's Land Army was formed to fill the gaps in farming. The number of women at work on the land rose by 33 000. The 'land girls' were provided with a uniform consisting of boots, breeches, overalls and hat, wages of 18 shillings a week (90p) and places to stay.

(e) Corn Production Act (1917)

- Subsidies were handed out to those farmers growing wheat, oats and sugar-beet.
- A minimum wage for farm workers was introduced. The minimum wage was fixed by an Agricultural Wages Board.
- Farmers who were not making the best use of their land were evicted.
- Much pasture was ploughed up and arable farming was encouraged.

On the whole, these were prosperous times for farmers. By 1918 nearly three million acres had been added to the total amount of land under cultivation in Britain and production of wheat, barley, oats, hay and potatoes had been greatly increased. However, the days of prosperity were not to last for long.

3.14 Farming between the Wars

Two years after the end of the First World War, the prosperity enjoyed by farmers came to a sudden end. There was a world-wide depression in trade and the price of British goods abroad fell disastrously. At home the price of farm produce also fell. Many farmers went bankrupt, the price of land and grain collapsed and farm workers once again left the land in their thousands. The general policy of successive governments was *laissez-faire* (non-interference), but as time passed and the depression grew worse, the government was forced to take measures to help farmers survive the depression.

Table 3.3 Average price of corn per cwt

Year	Wheat	Oats	Barley
1920	18s. 10d.	25s.	20s. 5d.
1922	11s. 2d.	11s. 2d.	10s. 5d.

- *Agricultural Holdings Act (1923)* This gave more security to farmers who rented land.
- *Agricultural Credit Act (1923)* Farmers could apply to the government for loans to improve farm buildings.
- *Agricultural Mortgage Corporation (1928)* The Corporation handed out loans for farm improvements.
- *Local Government Act (1929)* Under the terms of the Act, farmers did not have to pay local rates on farm land and buildings.
- *Import Duties Act (1932)* After 1932 Britain ceased to be a *free trade* nation. Less foreign food was allowed into the country and the amount of meat imported into Britain was reduced by one-third.
- *Wheat Quota Act (1932)* A tax was placed on flour which had been made from imported corn. The money raised from the tax was used to guarantee British farmers 45 shillings a quarter for the wheat they produced.
- *Marketing Acts (1932–1933)* The government set up *marketing boards* to regulate the price of farm produce and to control the amount of food imported into Britain. The marketing boards controlled the amount of hops, milk, potatoes, bacon and pork on the market.

Despite the measures taken by successive governments, British agriculture remained in a depressed state until 1939. The only crop which increased its acreage was sugar-beet. Large areas of land were left fallow, but there was a slight increase in fruit, poultry and dairy farming.

(a) Technical Improvements from 1919 to 1939

Farmers used more machinery than ever before. Tractors began to replace horses:

Year	Tractors	Horses	Farm workers
1921	6 000	955 000	996 000
1939	50 000	649 000	711 000

By 1930 *combine-harvesters* were in use on many farms. These machines made harvesting faster and saved labour. They cut the wheat, threshed it and put the grain into sacks in one operation.

Milking machines also came into use. They were developed by a Scotsman, Alexander Shields, who based his designs on an earlier machine of 1892.

(b) Sources of Power on Farms

- The *internal combustion engine* provided farmers with cars, vans and lorries. This made it easier to transport produce to market. Tractors also used an engine which ran on petrol and oil.
- *Electricity* was a valuable source of power on farms. In 1926 the Central Electricity Board was set up. Thousands of miles of cable was carried on pylons to isolated farms, bringing heat, light and power to farmers, farm workers and farm animals. By 1935 more than 90 per cent of the population had the benefit of electricity in their homes.

(c) Scientific Advance

- Research stations such as Rothamsted (see Section 3.10) developed better crops.
- Farmers started to spray weed-killers and pesticides on their fields. This resulted in higher yields.
- Fertilisers were used more widely to improve the quality of the soil.

3.15 Farming during the Second World War

When war broke out in September 1939, Britain faced similar problems to those experienced during the First World War. Seventy per cent of Britain's food was imported. It was obvious that more food would have to be grown at home. The government took the following measures.

- *Agricultural Development Act (1939)* This offered a subsidy of £2 per acre to farmers willing to plough up grassland. During the war six million acres of grassland were ploughed up and turned over to arable farming.
- *County War Agricultural Committees (1940)* Once again the government set up committees to supervise each county's agriculture. The committees were made up of farmers, landowners and farm workers. They had the power to force farmers to grow certain crops. If farmers refused to co-operate, the committees could take over their land. The committees also made sure that farmers were using the right pesticides, fertilisers and cattle fodder.
- *Agricultural Improvement Council (1941)* The idea behind the Improvement Council was to apply scientific research to farming.
- *Women's Land Army (1941)* In December 1941 Parliament passed a National Service Act. This stated that all women between the ages of 21 and 30 had to join the armed forces or the auxiliary services, or work in industry or agriculture. Many women opted to join the Women's Land Army. They did the work of the thousands of farm workers who had joined the armed forces.

(a) Results of Government Measures

- By 1945 there was more land under cultivation in Britain than at any time since 1870.
- Farm workers received higher wages.
- As a result of government grants, farmers were much better off.
- There were greatly increased crop yields:

Year	Acreage of arable land in U.K.	Acreage sown to wheat	Wheat production in tons
1939	12 million	2.02 million	1.95
1945	18 million	2.93 million	2.79

- There was a substantial increase in beef production.
- More combine-harvesters, reapers, tractors and lorries were used on farms.
- By the end of the war, Britain had one of the most efficient systems of farming in the world.

3.16 Farming since 1945

In 1945 politicians were worried that agriculture might slide into depression, as it had done after the wars with France (1793–1815) and the First World War (1914–1918). The two World Wars and the depression had shown how important it was for Britain to control the amount of food imported into the country from abroad. So the government took the following steps to aid British farmers.

(a) Agriculture Act (1947)

- Farmers were guaranteed a fair price for their farm produce. The price was reviewed each year.
- Efficient farmers were given long leases or the right to buy the land they farmed. Inefficient farmers could be turned off their land.
- Grants and subsidies were handed out to farmers to encourage them to use up-to-date methods.

(b) Hill Farming Acts (1946 and 1956)

The government handed out grants of up to 50 per cent to farmers who wanted to improve farm buildings, farm workers' cottages, roads, drainage or cattle-sheds.

(c) Marketing Boards

In 1954 a Potato Marketing Board was set up. Three years later an Egg Marketing Board and a Pig Industry Development Board were established.

(d) Other Developments

(i) *Technical Developments*

Since the Second World War there has been a great increase in the number of sophisticated machines in use on farms, including new designs of combine-harvesters, milking machines and tractors. Many farmers now use *computers* on their farms to help them with feeding cattle, ordering parts for machines, checking production figures and working out farm accounts.

(ii) *Factory Farming*

Since the 1960s factory farming has become very common. Pigs, chickens and calves are kept in special units called 'batteries' or 'belsens' and reared intensively. They have warmth, light and shelter, and fatten up quickly. This is a cheap way of producing food, which saves time and labour. However, there has recently been a limited move away from intensive methods towards 'free range' farming, which provides the animals with more 'natural' conditions.

(iii) *The Common Market*

In 1973 Britain became a member of the European Economic Community (the 'Common Market'). The community's policy towards farming is known as the *Common Agricultural Policy* (C.A.P.). The policy dictates that food prices within the E.E.C. are to be kept at a fixed level by imposing tariffs (taxes) on food brought in from countries outside the E.E.C.

If the price of food within the E.E.C. falls because of over-production, the community buys up the surplus produce at a fixed price. This has the effect of keeping food prices stable. It also creates butter and wheat 'mountains' and wine 'lakes'. To many people it seems absurd that Europe is stockpiling food while a few thousand miles away, in Third World countries, millions are starving.

(iv) *Farming Today*

Today the percentage of people employed in agriculture continues to fall; in 1980 just under 3 per cent of the working population were involved in farming. Yet Britain now produces over half her total food requirements. British farming has passed through depression twice during the past 100 years and twice it has risen to the challenge of feeding an island population under wartime conditions. British agriculture is now one of the most efficient in the world — an industry whose livestock and machinery are exported to nearly every country.

'SHORT-NOTE' QUESTION, EXAMINATION GUIDANCE AND MODEL ANSWER: AGRICULTURE

Write about *four* of the following:

The 'open-field' system; the enclosure movement; Jethro Tull; the Anti-Corn Law League; Marketing Boards; the Women's Land Army.

Steps in Writing the Answer

1. Work out which four questions you can do best.
2. Split the time to answer equally between them.
3. Jot down the points you know about them very briefly, and sort out the order in which you will mention them in your answer.
4. Do not answer in note form, using abbreviations or your own distinctive shorthand style. You must write continuous prose. Make sure that you know the number of items that you are required to write about. The examiner will mark you mainly on the number of correct facts you include in your writing.
5. The order in which you write your answers is not important and you may want to begin with the one you know least about. Look at the example above. By now you should know a great deal about agriculture in the eighteenth and nineteenth centuries, but you may not have revised the twentieth century so thoroughly. So you can eliminate 'Marketing Boards' and 'Women's Land Army'. Of the four remaining, let's suppose that 'The Anti-Corn Law League' is the topic you know least about.

Model Answer

The Anti-Corn Law League was set up in 1839 in opposition to the Corn Law of 1815. The Corn Law had been passed at the end of the Napoleonic Wars, to prevent cheap foreign grain flooding the home markets. It was modified in 1828 by William Huskisson, President of the Board of Trade. In 1838 Richard Cobden and John Bright, two Lancashire textile manufacturers, set up the Manchester Association for the Repeal of the Corn Laws. A year later this association became the Anti-Corn Law League. Cobden and Bright believed that the Corn Laws hampered trade, made food prices high and created unemployment. By 1845 there were twelve Anti-Corn Law M.P.s in Parliament, including Cobden and Bright. They used leaflets, newspapers and political speakers to spread their message outside Parliament. In 1846 a dreadful potato famine in Ireland left thousands of Irish peasants on the verge of starvation. In England the Prime Minister, Robert Peel, realised that the only way to get cheap food to the Irish was by repealing the Corn Law. Against the wishes of the majority of his party, the Conservatives, Peel passed an Act repealing the Corn Laws. The campaign launched by Cobden and Bright had finally achieved success.

WORK OUT SHORT-ANSWER QUESTIONS: AGRICULTURE

1. What percentage of the working population have jobs in agriculture today?
2. In which parts of the country would you have found open-field villages in 1700?
3. How many large, unfenced fields surrounded most open-field villages?
4. What was the approximate area of a single strip in an open field?
5. Why were the strips this size?
6. Name three crops grown in the open fields.
7. What was a fallow field?
8. Who was the most important person in an eighteenth-century village?
9. What was 'glebe' land?
10. Write down *four* advantages of open-field farming.
11. How was land wasted on open fields?
12. What is meant by 'selective breeding'?
13. Name three agricultural writers who described changes in agriculture between 1768 and 1830.
14. Why did Chambers and Mingay disagree with J. H. Clapham's interpretation of how and why changes had taken place in agriculture?
15. Write down *three* causes of agricultural change.
16. Define the word 'enclosure'.
17. What were 'voluntary enclosures'?
18. Why were enclosures necessary?
19. What part did the parliamentary commissioners play in obtaining an Enclosure Act?
20. When did Parliament pass a General Enclosure Act?
21. In which decade 1750–1850 did Parliament pass most Enclosure Acts?
22. What were the main reasons for terrible hardship among the poor in the period 1790–1820?
23. Write down the three most important effects of enclosure.
24. Name two 'great lords' who promoted agricultural change.
25. Which two agricultural inventions are usually associated with Jethro Tull?
26. How did 'Turnip Townshend' earn his nickname?
27. What were 'Coke's Clippings'?
28. Why were foreign visitors so impressed with Robert Bakewell's farm?
29. Where was 'Ralph Robinson's' model farm?
30. Between which years was Britain at war with France?
31. Why did Parliament pass a Corn Law in 1815?
32. How did Huskisson modify the Corn Law in 1828?
33. How did the 'Swing Riots' get their name?
34. In which city did the Anti-Corn Law League hold its first meetings?
35. When was the 'Golden Age' of British farming?
36. How did the work of James Smith help farmers?
37. Name the author of *Organic Chemistry in its Applications to Agriculture*.
38. Who invented a mechanical reaper in the 1840s?
39. What is guano?

40. Name three types of cattle feed introduced in the 1850s.
41. What was the main cause of the 'Great Depression' of 1870–1914?
42. From which countries were we importing meat by 1875?
43. Explain what is meant by a 'tied cottage'.
44. What do the initials N.A.L.U. stand for?
45. How did the government help farmers to produce more food during the Second World War?
46. How are computers used on modern farms?
47. What is meant by 'factory farming'?
48. When did Britain join the E.E.C?
49. How does the Common Agricultural Policy work?
50. What are 'butter mountains' and 'wine lakes'?

4 Industry

Examination Guide

Industry is one of the most important topics on the GCSE Social and Economic History course and you are certain to get at least one question on industrial change in your exam. All the examining boards have a section on industry in their syllabuses. So this is one topic you can't afford to avoid!

You should remember that the term 'Industrial Revolution' (see Section 4.1) describes a process rather than a historical event. The phrase 'Industrial Revolution' was first coined by Arnold Toynbee, a nineteenth-century social reformer and economist, about 100 years ago. Many countries have had their own industrial revolutions at different times over the past 200 years. Some Third World countries are in the process of having their own industrial revolutions in the 1980s.

You should also bear in mind that some historians have argued that the word 'Revolution' is inappropriate. It suggests sudden change, and in many countries change took place very slowly. Industrial *Evolution* would probably be a better way of describing the process.

The best way of revising the industry topic is to divide it up into sections:

Sub-topic	Revise
Domestic industry	How the system worked; advantages and disadvantages
Textiles*	Machines; advantages of machines; effects of growth of industry on social and economic life; factories
Coal*	Methods of mining; problems involved in extracting coal; effects on other industries
Iron and steel*	Mining and smelting; Darby family; new techniques (e.g. puddling and rolling); effects on the economy
Steam power*	Sources of power before 1750; the need for a new source of power; James Watt; effects of steam power on industry
Pottery, chemicals, engineering, shipbuilding*	Reasons for growth; effects on the economy

Great Depression	Reasons for Great Depression; was the depression as serious as people at the time imagined?
New industries	Reasons for their growth; effects on social and economic life

*Important topics.

This is a very quick guide. For more detailed information on what to revise, look at the syllabus you are following or ask your teacher.

The types of question set on Industry will vary a great deal. Most short-answer questions will test *recall* and will be of the Who . . .? What . . .? Which . . .? variety. For some examples of these, refer to the 50 short-answer questions at the end of this chapter.

Most essay-type questions will start by asking you to *describe* some aspect of industrial change and will then ask you to write about the *effects* of industrial change on economic and social life.

4.1 Introduction

British historians use the term 'Industrial Revolution' to describe the changes which took place in British industry between 1780 and 1830. Before the Industrial Revolution most people lived in the country and worked on farms. After the Industrial Revolution most people lived in towns and worked in workshops, shops or factories. Britain was the first country in the world to go through these changes. Today countries such as India and China are going through similar changes. In this chapter we shall be looking at how and why industry in Britain has changed over the past 200 years.

4.2 Domestic Industry

'Domestic system' and 'cottage industry' are terms used to describe the process of making goods in workers' own homes. In 1750 craftsmen made goods such as pins, nails, pots, pans, cups and knives. The most important cottage industry was the production of *wool*. In many parts of the country there were cottages containing hand-looms or spinning-wheels. When there was little farm work to do, families would make woollen cloth. Table 4.1 shows how the domestic system worked in the three main wool-producing areas in 1750.

The domestic system had many advantages for workers and employees:

- Workers could work at their own pace in their own homes.
- There was no foreman or overseer standing over them, telling them what to do.
- No time was wasted travelling to and from work.
- The domestic system usually operated in country districts where food was cheaper than in the towns.

Table 4.1 The domestic system in 1750

> *East Anglia*
> The system in this area (Norfolk, Suffolk, Essex) was organised by clothiers (wool merchants) who bought up bales of wool produced by the Lincoln and Leicester breeds of sheep. Norwich specialised in worsteds (woollen yarns) and light fabrics. Suffolk and Essex produced heavier woollen fabrics. Early in the eighteenth century both these areas produced broadcloth.
>
> *The South-west*
> Merchants bought up supplies of wool and took them to workers' homes for spinning, weaving and finishing. Exeter produced large quantities of serge (a tough fabric) and much of this was sent to London, Bristol or Barnstaple.
>
> *The West Riding of Yorkshire*
> Domestic workers produced woollen goods on a small scale. They bought the raw materials they needed and sold the finished product in towns such as Leeds, Wakefield and Halifax.

- When trade was slack, spinners and weavers could work at other jobs such as farming.
- The whole family could work together as one economic unit.

However, the system also had its defects:

- Sometimes the work in the cottages was badly done or materials were lost.
- Workers often found themselves in debt to clothiers and moneylenders.
- Sometimes textile workers received 'payment in kind' (they were paid in goods rather than money)
- Workers were scattered over a wide area, so it was difficult for a merchant to make sure that the cloth was all of the same quality.
- The workers' hours of work were irregular. Many people worked an eighteen-hour day for three or four days, so that they could have time off at the weekends.
- Young children worked long hours in dirty, dangerous conditions, and there was no distinction between home life and work.

Figure 4.1 shows the main areas producing metals and textiles in about 1750.

4.3 Wool

Making woollen cloth had been Britain's main industry since the early Middle Ages. Cloth was the country's main export, and woollen goods were sent to Europe, Africa and North America. In the House of Lords the Lord Chancellor still sits on a woolsack, to show the historical importance of wool in British industry.

In 1750 woollen cloth was made in every county where sheep farming existed but was especially important in East Anglia, the South-west and the West Riding

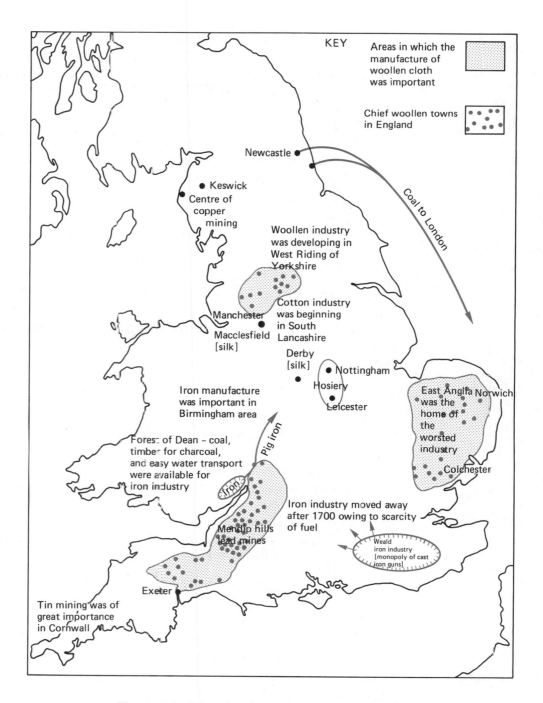

Figure 4.1 Map showing British industry in about 1750

of Yorkshire (see Table 4.1). The six main stages in the manufacture of wool were as follows:

1. *Cleaning the wool* Most people used soap and water to wash the raw wool. In Somerset stale urine was used!
2. *Carding* Carding means combing out the wool to separate and straighten the individual strands. In the early days of wool production this was done with teasles or thistles. Later, wire brushes were used.
3. *Spinning* Spinning the wool involved twisting the fibres together to make them longer and stronger. The work was done by using a distaff (spinning-stick) or a spinning-wheel. Most spinning was done by women.

4. *Weaving* To make cloth, it is necessary to pass weft thread under and over warp thread on a loom. In 1750 wool was woven on a *handloom*, usually by men. The weaver passed a shuttle from one side of the loom to the other. This meant that he could only make cloth of a limited width.
5. *Fulling* After weaving, the cloth was beaten in water containing soap or fuller's earth. This matted the fibres together.
6. *Finishing* The final stage involved *cropping* (cutting the surface of the cloth), bleaching, dyeing or printing. These processes required machinery which was too big to fit into people's homes. The work had to be done in special workshops in towns.

After the introduction of new machinery and steam power into the textiles industry, the West Country and East Anglia became less important as wool-producing areas. These two regions did not have the coal needed to power the new steam engines. By 1830 the woollen industry in both areas had almost collapsed, apart from limited production of items such as carpets and broad-cloths. Four further reasons for the decline of the woollen industry are shown below:

1. The textile industry became more dependent upon machinery in the late eighteenth century. Wool was not suited to the new machines. Its fibres are more difficult to twist and stretch on a machine than are those of cotton.
2. There were shortages of raw materials. By the eighteenth century English sheep farmers could not provide merchants with enough raw wool. So bales of wool were sent to Britain from Spain and, after 1830, from Australia.
3. There were a number of old-fashioned rules and regulations which made it difficult for the wool industry to expand. The Weavers' Act (1555) was still in force. Under the terms of the Act, country areas were only allowed to produce limited quantities of wool.
4. Competition from cloth made from a new raw material, cotton, was fierce.

In the West Riding of Yorkshire, however, where there were plentiful supplies of coal to power the new machinery, the woollen industry survived well into the twentieth century. By the 1950s the British woollen industry was concentrating on quality fabrics. These either were pure wool or were made by mixing wool with synthetic fibres.

4.4 Cotton

Cotton comes from a plant which cannot be grown in Britain, because it needs a warm climate. The raw cotton needed for British factories was picked by slaves in North America or the West Indies and sent across the Atlantic in sailing-ships to London or Liverpool.

During the late eighteenth century an important cotton industry grew up in Lancashire, for the following reasons:

- The area had an excellent port, Liverpool (see Figure 4.2), with good road and river links to the interior. Later, canals and railways helped the port to expand rapidly. Each year tons of raw cotton arrived in Liverpool from the New World.
- The Pennines (see Figure 4.2) provided the factories with water power before the days of steam power.
- Later, coal supplies provided the power source needed for steam engines in cotton mills.
- Soft water, important in the production of cotton, came from the Pennines.
- The mild, damp climate of Lancashire was ideal for stretching and twisting cotton thread.
- For many years South Lancashire had been well known for its textile goods.
- Income from farming was low in South Lancashire. There were large numbers of poorly paid people who were willing to work in factories.
- The merchants and businessmen of Lancashire were keen to invest money in, and make profits from, cotton spinning and weaving firms.

Figure 4.2 shows the main cotton towns of South Lancashire and the men linked to the growth of the cotton industry.

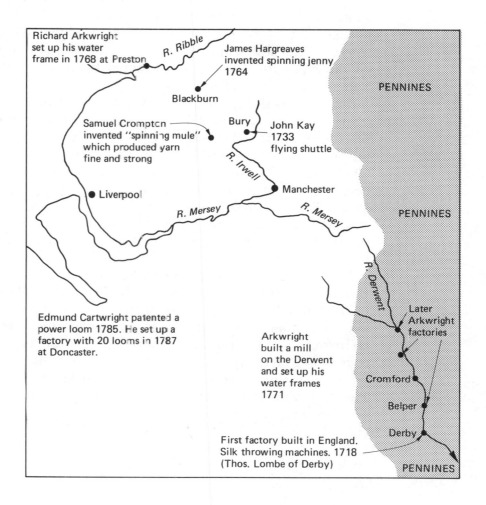

Figure 4.2 The cotton inventors

The cotton industry grew slowly before 1780. The wool producers of the West Country, East Anglia and West Yorkshire did their best to stop the cotton industry from expanding. They were worried about losing trade. Between 1780 and 1810 there was rapid expansion in the cotton industry, which soon outstripped the wool industry. Cotton was the first industry in the world to adopt the factory system.

Table 4.2 U.K. exports

	Percentage of total national exports	
Period	Cotton	Wool
1750–1759	1	48
1760–1769	2	44
1770–1779	3	43
1780–1789	7	35
1790–1799	15	30
1800–1809	39	24
1810–1819	53	16
1820–1829	62	12

By 1810 cotton cloth had become Britain's most important export. Cotton continued to hold a major place in our pattern of trade throughout the nineteenth century. One reason for this was that the early textile machines worked better with cotton than with wool. There was also a greater demand for cotton goods from people who wanted to wear healthy, lightweight clothes rather than thick woollen fabrics.

Before 1770 the spinning and weaving of cotton goods was organised on a domestic basis (see Section 4.2). Merchants went to Liverpool or London to buy raw cotton and to sell woven cloth. Work was put out to spinners and weavers in the country districts around Bury, Blackburn and Bolton. However, the new textile machines of the eighteenth century were too large to be used in people's homes. Many of them required water power, and some spinners and weavers lived miles from fast-flowing streams. It was a much better idea to put the machines in a single, large building. A water wheel would provide the power for the machines. Each day the spinners or weavers could come to the building or factory to do their work.

In 1771 Richard Arkwright (see Section 4.5) set up the first cotton mill at Cromford, near Derby (see Figure 4.2). Soon other mills were being built and in the cotton industry domestic spinning came to an end within 30 years. Huge, iron-framed mills were built by cotton manufacturers in Cheshire, Yorkshire, Derbyshire and Lancashire. Towards the end of the eighteenth century mill owners began to use steam engines to power the textile machines. In the factories employees worked set hours for regular rates of pay (see Section 4.19). The days were gone when craftsmen could sit at home spinning and weaving when they felt like it!

4.5 The Textile Machines

Between 1733 and 1785 the invention of new machines brought about major changes in the spinning and weaving of cotton. These textile machines were the result of the demands and needs of weavers, spinners and clothiers. Most of the machines did not work very well at first, and many improvements had to be made before they could be used on a wide scale. However, by 1810 the use of these machines led to a huge increase in textile production and a higher standard of living for thousands of people. Table 4.3 shows the most important textile inventions.

Table 4.3   Inventions in the cotton industry

Date	Event
1733	*Flying shuttle* John Kay, a weaver from Lancashire, invented a weaving device at a time when ways of speeding up spinning were needed. On the old hand-loom the shuttle was thrown from side to side of the cloth by hand. Kay's invention consisted of two wooden hammers which knocked the shuttle backwards and forwards on small wheels across the loom. The shuttle was not widely used until the 1760s, but it meant that wider cloth could be woven at greater speed.
1733	*Roller-spinning machine* The flying shuttle had speeded up weaving. The spinners could not provide the weavers with enough thread and there was a shortage of spun yarn. In 1733 John Wyatt invented a roller-spinning machine which speeded up spinning. Lewis Paul later made several improvements to this machine.
1765	*Spinning-jenny* James Hargreaves, a weaver and carpenter from Blackburn, invented the spinning-jenny. The machine did the same job as a spinning-wheel but it could produce more than one thread at a time. The jenny was small enough to be used in a spinner's cottage. In 1770 Hargreaves improved the machine so that it could spin 16 threads. By 1784 jennies were capable of spinning up to 80 threads.
1769	*Water frame* Richard Arkwright, a Preston businessman, patented a spinning machine similar to Paul and Wyatt's roller-spinning machine (see above). The frame was a large machine which was run by water power and used in factories. It made strong thread which could be used for warp as well as weft. For the first time, British manufacturers could produce pure cotton cloth.
1779	*Mule* Samuel Crompton, a Bolton weaver, produced a spinning-machine which he called a mule. It used the rollers of the water frame and the spindles of the spinning-jenny. Crompton called it a mule because the machine was a cross between a jenny and a water frame, just as a mule is a cross between a horse and an ass. The mule made yarn which was strong and fine. The first mules were hand-operated but later models were powered by water and steam. By 1810 it was the most important of all the spinning-machines. Four million of them were in use by 1811.
1785	*Power loom* Edmund Cartwright, a clergyman from Manchester, produced a large, clumsy, mechanical loom which needed two strong men to work it. By 1787 Cartwright had set up a power loom factory in Doncaster. The looms in the factory were powered by a bull but later machines were powered by steam. The power loom did not catch on immediately and was only widely used in the cotton industry after 1825.

4.6 Textiles, 1850–1979

By 1850 Britain was 'the clothes shop of the world'. British cotton goods were sent to the four corners of the globe and textile products made up 60 per cent of our exports. Between 1861 and 1865 there was a civil war in America. The anti-slave states of the North prevented raw cotton from the southern states reaching Europe. This created a cotton famine in Britain. Mills had to be closed down because of the shortage of cotton. In some parts of Britain the cotton industry never recovered from this shortage of raw materials.

Between 1875 and 1890 the price of cotton goods on world markets fell sharply. Countries such as India were beginning to produce cotton fabrics which were just as good as British textiles. Despite this foreign competition, cotton production in Britain kept increasing until 1920 (Table 4.4).

Table 4.4 Cotton production and imports

Period	Raw cotton imports (thousand pounds)	Exports (million yards)
1880–1889	1 473 000	4575
1890–1899	1 556 000	5057
1900–1909	1 723 000	5649
1910–1919	1 864 000	5460
1920–1929	1 498 000	4239

During the First World War (1914–1918) German submarines prevented supplies of raw cotton from reaching British ports. Cotton production fell dramatically. Merchants all over the world started buying cotton goods from India and Japan rather than Britain. India and Japan had plentiful supplies of raw cotton and cheap labour. They could sell their cotton goods at much lower prices. After the First World War Britain's cotton trade never really recovered. Other reasons for the decline of the British cotton industry are as follows:

- British firms had supplied the world with textile machinery. By the 1920s these machines were producing enough cotton to compete with British markets.
- Countries to which we had previously sent cotton goods — the Far East, India, the Balkans — were producing their own textiles.
- There were too many small British firms competing against each other.

During the 1920s a depression in trade and industry hit Britain. Mills closed and hundreds of workers lost their jobs. The decline in cotton production continued throughout the 1920s. In 1929 a Lancashire Cotton Corporation was set up. The corporation closed down unprofitable mills and made other mills more efficient. Seven years later (1936) a *Cotton Industry Reorganisation Act* set up a Spindles Board, which aimed to cut down on wasteful spinning processes. By 1939, 78 mills had been closed by the Board. In the same year Parliament fixed minimum prices for cotton goods, and in 1940 a Cotton Board was set up to control production and distribution.

During and after the Second World War (1939–1945) there was a revival in the British cotton industry. The destruction of German and Japanese factories gave Britain the chance to recapture the markets she had lost. Unfortunately, the chance was lost — the owners and managers of the textile factories did not expand their businesses and went on using out-of-date machinery. The decline of

British cotton continued throughout the 1950s. Between 1954 and 1959, 25 per cent of British cotton firms went out of business. The government passed a *Cotton Industry Act* in 1959 which gave redundancy payments to workers who had lost their jobs and provided funds for new machinery.

Since 1959 millions of pounds have been spent on developing new machinery. Yet the decline of our cotton industry goes on. Japan, India and China can produce cotton goods much more cheaply than can Britain. There has also been strong competition from *synthetic* fibres (man-made fibres such as nylon, rayon and Terylene). In 1966, 79 mills closed down. A year later 50 more had closed. Table 4.5 shows the decline in the number of workers in the cotton industry betwen 1914 and 1980.

Table 4.5   The decline in textile employment — cotton

Year	Number of workers
1914	710 000
1960	200 630
1970	109 600
1980	56 800

The wool industry has experienced similar problems. Competition from abroad and from synthetic fibres resulted in falling prices and factories closing down. But the woollen industry is in better shape than the cotton industry. Wool manufacturers have concentrated on making high-quality woollen goods from tweeds and worsteds. Even today, one-quarter of the world's trade in wool is made up of British goods.

EXAMINATION GUIDANCE: DOMESTIC INDUSTRY AND TEXTILES

(a) Domestic Industry

You may get pictures showing cottage industries and the factory system, and a question asking you to compare and contrast working conditions and different methods of production. The assessment objectives being tested here are continuity and change, and similarity and difference. You should be aware of the *disadvantages* of the domestic system. Don't paint too rosy a picture of cottage life in the eighteenth century. For thousands of cottage workers life was extremely harsh.

(b) Textiles
Whoever says Industrial Revolution says cotton.

(E. J. Hobsbawm)

Most of these questions will be based on the period 1760–1820 and will deal with textile machines, why they were introduced and what effects they had on social and economic life. You should be able to pinpoint the main textile-producing areas in 1750 and you should be able to explain *why* these areas had become the centres of the cotton and wool industries. A typical question might look like this:

1. Name the three most important spinning inventions of the eighteenth century and the men who invented them.

2. In what ways were these machines an improvement on the old method of spinning?
3. How did changes in the production of textiles affect the lives of ordinary people in the eighteenth century?

It is unlikely that you will get many detailed questions on the textiles industries in the twentieth century, although you should be able to write about the reasons for the decline of the cotton industry and the results of government intervention.

4.7 Coal-mining in the Eighteenth Century

Eighteenth-century coal mines were small-scale organisations compared with modern pits. They were often run as family businesses or by small companies. There were three main methods of getting the coal out of the ground (Figure 4.3).

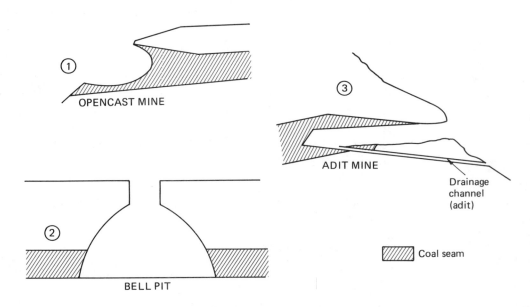

Figure 4.3 Methods of mining in 1700

In 1700 coal was put to many uses, but the most important of these was for heating people's homes. Coal was also used for brewing, soap- and brick-making and sugar-refining, and for the production of metals. During the eighteenth century the demand for coal increased. Table 4.6 shows why.

The main coal-mining area was Northumberland (see Figure 4.4). There were many important coal mines close to the rivers Tyne and Wear. Horse-drawn carts were used to move the coal to the rivers along wooden 'tramways' or 'waggon ways' (see Section 9.12). Once the coal had reached the rivers, it was loaded onto keels (river-boats) and taken downstream to the sea. It was then placed in sea-going ships called colliers, which sailed down the east coast of Britain to London. In London coal from Northumberland was therefore known as 'sea-coal'.

Other important coalfields were to be found in the Midlands, the North-west and Wales. Coalbrookdale, the heart of the iron industry, was based on a coalfield. Figure 4.4 shows the main coal-mining areas in 1750.

Table 4.6 The increase in demand for coal in the eighteenth century

1. The population increase produced a demand for more coal.

   Population statistics: 1700 — $6\frac{1}{2}$ million people
   1800 — $10\frac{1}{2}$ million people

2. The iron industry was expanding. Both Abraham Darby's method of smelting iron using coke (1709) and Henry Cort's 'puddling and rolling' process (1784) required coal.

3. The country was running out of timber and in great need of a new source of fuel.

4. More coal was needed for the following steam engines. By 1800 steam was the main form of power for industry. (See also Section 4.18.)

   (i) Thomas Savery's steam engine (the 'miner's friend') (1698) — the first steam pump
   (ii) Thomas Newcomen's steam engine (1709) — a more reliable pump
   (iii) James Watt's rotary engine (1780s) — the first engine with a separate condenser and rotary motion

   N.B.: Both the Savery and Newcomen engines used up large amounts of coal.

5. Distillers, glass-makers, and pottery, soap and nail manufacturers also needed coal.

4.8 Improvements in the Coal Industry

(a) Dangerous Gases

In the nineteenth century methane gas or 'fire-damp' caused many disasters down coal mines. Huge explosions underground killed hundreds of miners. Methods of dealing with fire-damp were very dangerous. Sometimes a 'fireman' would crawl along underground galleries with a long pole. At the end of the pole was a lighted candle. When the fireman reached a pocket of gas, he would thrust the candle into it and ignite the gas. This job was unpopular but highly paid!

Another dangerous gas was carbon dioxide. Miners called it 'choke-damp' because the gas made it difficult for them to breathe. They would try to get rid of 'choke-damp' by shaking a jacket or blanket to and fro. A far more dangerous gas, carbon monoxide or 'after-damp', was left in a coal mine after an explosion or fire. The effect of this gas was to make miners giddy or sleepy. Without fresh air they went into a coma and died.

One way of making sure the air was fresh was to take a canary down the mine. A small bird is affected by gas more quickly than people. Sir Humphry Davy (1778–1829), a famous scientist, thought up a better way of helping miners to detect dangerous gases. In 1815 he produced a miners' safety lamp in which the flame was protected by wire gauze. The heat from the flame was reduced by the gauze, so that any fire-damp present could not explode. George Stephenson, the famous railway engineer (see Section 9.14), produced a similar lamp called the 'Geordie lamp'.

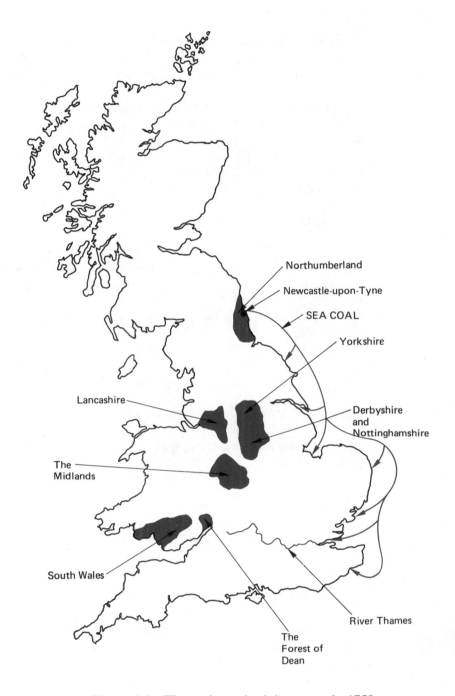

Figure 4.4 The main coal-mining areas in 1750

Ventilation down coal mines was later improved by digging ventilation shafts or by using giant exhaust fans. John Buddle (1760–1818), a mining engineer from Hebburn Colliery near Newcastle, invented a mechanical fan which drew 'bad' air up a ventilation shaft by suction. Buddle's *exhaust fan* enabled the owners of coal mines to sink deeper shafts to seams which had once been too dangerous to mine.

(b) Flooding

A second serious problem facing miners was flooding. Water seeped through the rock where men were working and flooded the mine. This problem was solved as follows:

- At first, water was scooped up in leather buckets and carried to the surface by hand.
- Later, drainage channels were dug to drain away the water. This only worked if the coal seam was close to the surface.
- By 1750 horse 'gins' were being used. These consisted of a chain of buckets wound up and down the mine shaft by horse-power.
- In 1698 Thomas Savery invented a small steam pump (see Section 4.18). This design was improved by Newcomen and Smeaton. James Watt's steam engine (see Section 4.18) was used to pump water from greater depths.
- After 1881 powerful electric pumps were used in most pits.

(c) Pit Collapse

A third problem facing miners was pit collapse. In the nineteenth century most accidents in coal mines were caused by the roof of the mine collapsing while coal was being cut out from the seams. There were two main methods of holding up the roof. In the *pillar and stall* (or *room and pillar*) method, miners cut away the coal and left pillars of uncut coal supporting the roof. In the *longwall* method, wooden posts or *pit props* were used to prevent the roof caving in. The space behind the props (the *goaf*) was filled in, leaving only a single tunnel or *road* running to the shaft. Nowadays steel pit props are used.

The increase in the size, depth and number of coal mines in the nineteenth century, aided by these improvements, led to a big increase in coal production, as the statistics in Table 4.7 suggest.

Table 4.7   Coal output, 1800–1900

Date	Output (millions of tons)	% Exported
1800	11.0	2.0
1810	14.3	2.3
1820	17.4	1.4
1830	22.4	2.2
1840	33.7	4.8
1850	49.4	6.8
1860	80.0	9.2
1870	110.4	13.4
1880	146.8	16.3
1890	181.6	21.3
1900	225.3	25.9

4.9   Coal-mining in the Twentieth Century

Before the First World War (1914–1918) there was a big demand at home and abroad for British coal. In 1913 the coal industry employed $1\frac{1}{4}$ million men in 3000 collieries. But many of the most productive seams had been exhausted and the cost of getting the coal out of the ground was rising. Unlike the industry in other countries, British coal-mining remained largely a 'pick and shovel'

Source A

Source B

72

74

Source C

Source D

11 August 1756 At about 2 a.m. a dreadful accident happened at Chatshaugh Colliery, on the Wear. The foul air in one of the pits ignited, by which four men were instantly killed and torn to pieces. The explosion was so violent that a corf full of coals was blown up the shaft from a depth of 180 yards into the open air.

1 April 1765 A terrible explosion took place at Walker Colliery, near Newcastle. The workings of this mine were about 180 yards below the surface of the earth. The foul air fired in an instant and the explosion which followed made a noise as loud as thunder. There were no lives lost but the workmen were in a most miserable condition, being scorched and burnt. On the day following, several over-men and others went down to examine the state of the mine, when it fired a second time, and killed eight persons and 17 horses, who were all burnt in a shocking manner.
(*An Account of the Losses in the Northumberland Pits*, R. Edwards, 1780)

Source E

Fatal Colliery Accident
A fatal colliery accident took place on Saturday morning last, by which seven persons met their deaths at a mine known as the Bellfield Colliery. The depth of the shaft is 75 yards. It appears that men and coals are wound up and down upon an iron platform which is 4' 6" long and 3' wide. Fixed over the centre is an iron bar which serves as a handle for the men to hold

75

when descending the shaft. In this position seven men and boys were placed on Saturday morning. When the props beneath the platform were removed, the men appear to have felt a giving way and immediately called out. The engineers instantly jerked the platform up again but both it and the men were thrown to the bottom of the pit, all being killed on the spot. An inquiry as to the reason for this disaster informed us that one of the links in the chain supporting the platform had broken.

The following persons were killed:

Thomas Sheppard, age 24
James Sheppard, age 11
David Sheppard, age 9
James Wilson, age 24
John Brierly, age 13
Thomas Marsden, age 22
Thomas Wild, age 18.

(*The Times*, Tuesday, 14 November 1854)

Source F

I saw quite a few accidents. One man had his leg cut off with a coal cutter and Len Church bound up the stump and saved his life. He went back to work on top of the pit with a cork leg and a walking stick. I got away with my life a few times. I'll tell you one incident that happened. They used to allow you to come up half an hour early if you were going to a funeral or had some excuse. I asked to come up early. There was a landing at 400 yards where the cage stopped for coal to be loaded, and I got in the cage with the surveyor who happened to be there at 500 yards. As we passed the landing at 400 yards, 30 trucks full of coal came away and came down the shaft. We just missed that lot. That was a lucky escape. It held up work for half a day.

On another occasion I was riding on a waggon. We used to have leather curtains across the road to divert the air. You weren't supposed to ride on the waggons but at the end of the shift sometimes, if you had a sympathetic engine driver, he'd let you ride through the curtains sitting down in the waggons. On this particular day I went to duck my head down but I caught my head in a hole in the curtain and I nearly got strangled.

(A. G. Church, quoted in *Collier's Way — The Somerset Coalfield*, Peter Collier, 1986)

1. Briefly explain *why* the accidents shown in sources A–C and described in sources D–F occurred.
2. Name *two* dangerous gases which were probably present in the mines shown in sources A and C.
3. Source B shows three tubs of coal colliding in a mine shaft in 1854. How would these tubs of coal have been raised and lowered up and down the mine shaft?
4. (i) According to source D, how many men were killed on 1 April 1765 at Walker Colliery?
   (ii) According to source E, how many juveniles [children under the age of 16] were killed at Belford Colliery on Saturday, 11 November 1854?
   (iii) How do the accidents described in source F differ from those in sources A and D?

(iv) Which of the sources A–F suggests that pit-ponies were used in some coal mines?

(v) Which source refers to the depth of coal mines?

5. Which of the sources A–F would you say is least reliable? Give reasons for your choice.

6. Why are there fewer accidents in modern coal mines than in eighteenth- and nineteenth-century mines? You can refer to information in sources A–F if you wish.

4.10 The Iron Industry in 1700

The iron industry was of great importance in the eighteenth century. The Industrial Revolution could not have taken place without great advances in the quality and quantity of iron, which was needed in factories, workshops and mills for machines and machine parts. Without machine parts which could be replaced, there would have been no Industrial Revolution. Such parts had to be made from metal cast in moulds or metal milled to the same shape and size. Iron, not wood, was the vital basic material.

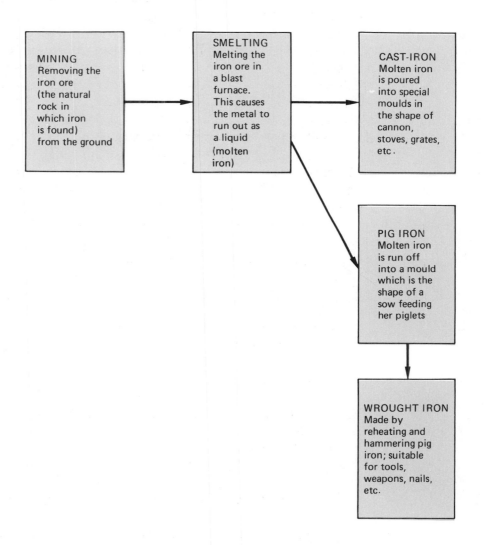

Figure 4.6 The different stages in the production of iron

77

In the early eighteenth century the British iron industry was backward. By 1800, however, Britain had become the centre of iron production. By the mid-nineteenth century, Britain had earned herself the title 'workshop of the world'.

Iron had been made in Britain since Roman times. During the Middle Ages (1066–1485) the iron industry had expanded. Figure 4.6 shows how iron was made.

The main mining and smelting areas were found in places where there were good supplies of charcoal (for smelting), iron ore and fast-flowing rivers. Figure 4.7 and Table 4.8 show the main iron-producing areas in 1750.

In 1700 there were three main problems facing the British iron industry. These problems were a shortage of fuel for smelting, the transport of iron ore and iron goods, and the power blast in the furnace.

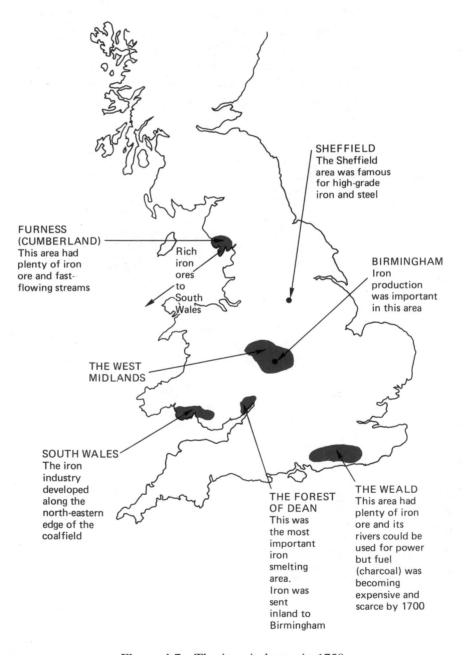

Figure 4.7 The iron industry in 1750

Table 4.8 The main iron-producing areas in 1700

- The Forest of Dean (Gloucestershire and Herefordshire).
- The Weald (Sussex and Kent).
- The West Midlands. Birmingham was famous for its iron. Locks, pins, swords, buttons, bolts and nails were made in workshops by small family businesses.
- Sheffield was famous for its steel goods, which included cutlery, scissors, hammers and files.
- South Wales, the Wrekin district of Shropshire and the Furness district of Cumbria also produced iron goods.

The fuel used for smelting was *charcoal*. To make charcoal, many tons of wood were needed. Timber was in short supply, for it was the main raw material for all industry. It was used for many other purposes, including ship-building, houses, coaches and machinery. So many forests had been cut down in the sixteenth century that the Elizabethan Parliament had passed a law preventing people from chopping down trees for charcoal-burning. Without greater quantities of charcoal or an alternative source of fuel for smelting, the iron industry could not expand. So in the eighteenth century hundreds of tons of iron were imported into Britain from Sweden, Russia and the American colonies.

Iron was difficult to transport over land. Most roads in 1750 were in poor condition and wagons laden with iron ore or iron goods often got stuck in potholes or ruts.

The third problem was keeping the iron at the right temperature during smelting. The industry depended upon water power to drive the bellows which ironmasters used to make the furnaces hotter. Water wheels were also used to work heavy hammers. But fast-flowing streams were not always to be found near quantities of iron ore or timber. In winter the rivers froze; in summer they dried up.

Thus, in 1750 iron-smelting was a small-scale, slow process. Iron producers and manufacturers such as the Darby family began to think of ways of speeding up the production of iron in Britain.

4.11   The Darby Family

Abraham Darby (1677–1717), a Quaker ironmaster, owned a firm in Bristol which made brass and copper cooking-pots. In 1708 he moved his firm to Coalbrookdale in Shropshire. Coalbrookdale was a good place for making iron, because there were plentiful supplies of iron ore, coal and wood close together. A small tributary of the River Severn, the Cole Brook, had cut a deep valley through coal seams forty feet thick and iron-ore beds twenty-four feet thick. The River Severn provided a navigable waterway from Bristol to Shrewsbury (see Figure 4.8).

In 1709 Darby made one of the most important discoveries of the eighteenth century. He designed a smelting furnace which used *coke* as fuel. Coke, like charcoal, is almost pure carbon. As a result of this breakthrough in iron production, Darby's firm was soon producing large boilers, garden rollers and castings for steam engines. Unfortunately, the iron produced by Darby's coke furnace was only suitable for making cast-iron items.

Following the death of Abraham Darby, the family business was run by his wife Mary. In 1732 Darby's son, Abraham Darby II (1711–1763), became manager of the Coalbrookdale Ironworks. Abraham Darby II was not happy

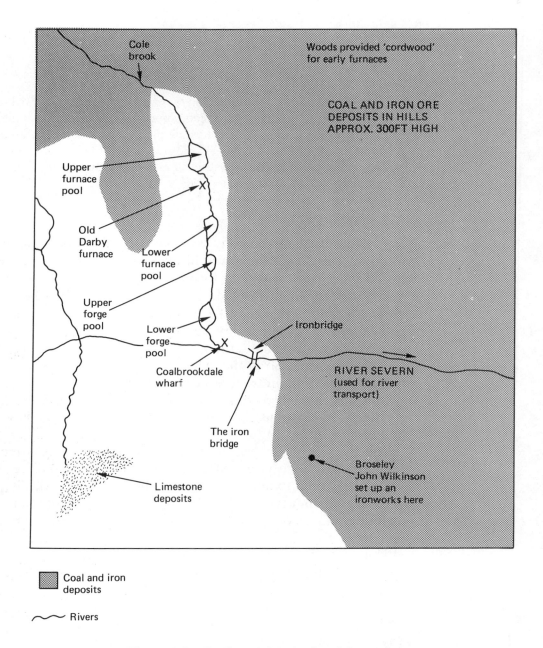

Figure 4.8 Coalbrookdale in the eighteenth century

with his father's method of making coke in heaps (like charcoal-burning). Instead he used coking ovens, which produced better-quality coke. He also increased the power of the blast in the Coalbrookdale furnaces by strengthening the bellows.

The problems of providing fuel for smelting and strengthening the blast in the furnace had been partially solved. The problem of transporting iron goods remained. Abraham Darby II tried to improve transport in the Coalbrookdale area. In 1767 he laid cast-iron rails along roads between the furnaces and the River Severn. These made it easier for laden wagons to travel to and from the ironworks.

Darby's son, Abraham Darby III (1750–1791), became manager of the ironworks in 1768. He carried on the work of his father. By now, cast-iron was so plentiful and cheap that it was being used for building purposes rather than wood, lead or brass. With the help of John Wilkinson (see Section 4.13), Abraham Darby III built the world's first iron bridge across the River Severn south of Coalbrookdale. It was made entirely of cast-iron and was eight yards wide and 100 yards long. A small town grew up close to the bridge, which became known as Ironbridge (see Figure 4.8).

Darby family tree:

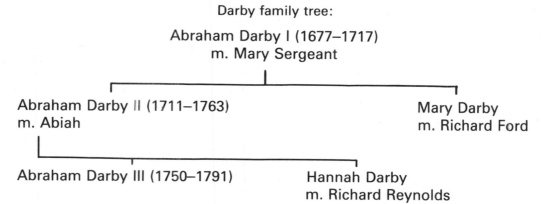

Abraham Darby I (1677–1717)
m. Mary Sergeant

Abraham Darby II (1711–1763)
m. Abiah

Mary Darby
m. Richard Ford

Abraham Darby III (1750–1791)

Hannah Darby
m. Richard Reynolds

4.12 Puddling and Rolling

Darby's coke-smelting process had made it possible to produce pig-iron on a large scale. The next stage of the iron-making process — changing pig-iron into wrought-iron — was slow in comparison.

The reverberatory furnace was one way of turning pig-iron into wrought-iron quickly and cheaply. This furnace was first developed by two brothers, George and Thomas Cranage, in 1766. By 1783 Peter Onions of Merthyr Tydfil had improved the design of the furnace. Onions's work interested Henry Cort (1740–1800), an ironmaker from Hampshire. Cort supplied iron goods to the navy. He realised that British iron was of poor quality compared with iron from other countries, and decided to try to improve ironmaking methods by experimenting with various types of iron.

By 1784 Cort had made a great breakthrough in the production of wrought-iron. The breakthrough was the *puddling process* for converting pig-iron into wrought-iron using coal. Like the Cranage brothers, Cort used a reverberatory furnace, and like Onions, he stirred the metal with iron bars until it became spongy. However, Cort carried the process a stage further. The spongy iron was taken to a *rolling-mill*, where the hot iron was passed between grooved rollers. The rollers were formed in such a way that the iron took the shape of the space left between them. Thus, an iron bar or sheet could be made quickly and cheaply from pig-iron.

Cort's process brought immediate improvements in the iron industry. Among the first to use it were Richard Crawshay of Cyfarthfa, Samuel Homfray of Penydarren and William Reynolds of Coalbrookdale (see Section 4.11). Crawshay was able to increase his production of bar iron from 55 tons a year in 1787 to 10 000 tons a year 25 years later. Many other industrialists benefited from the cheap iron. It also helped engineers, farmers, textile inventors and shipbuilders. As the iron industry now depended on coal rather than charcoal, forgemasters began to site their ironworks near coalfields rather than woods. There are very few coalfields in the South of England and after 1850 very little iron was made in the South.

4.13 The Ironmasters

During the eighteenth century a number of men made large sums of money out of the production of iron. They became known as 'Ironmasters' or 'Iron Kings'. The most important ironmasters were:

(a) John Wilkinson (1728–1808)

As a young man, Wilkinson expanded the small iron business his father had set up. He could see no limits to the uses to which iron might be put. He built an iron barge (1787), an iron chapel, an iron ship, an iron lavatory and an iron bridge (1779). He owned iron mills at Broseley (Shropshire), Bradley (Staffordshire) and Bersham (near Chester). He also had business interests in several French ironworks, tin mines in Cornwall and copper mines in South Wales. During the Seven Years' War (1756–1763) he was asked to supply the government with cannon. To carry out this contract, he developed a method of boring the barrels of cannon very accurately. This process was later used to make cylinders for James Watt's steam engines (see Section 4.18). He was one of the first businessmen to use steam power in industry and he was the first ironmaster to use steam engines to drive bellows, hammers and rollers. Wilkinson's energy and skill made Britain one of the world's greatest iron-producing nations. When he died, 'Iron Mad' Wilkinson's iron coffin was buried below an iron monument. Figure 4.9 shows Wilkinson's 'Empire' in 1808.

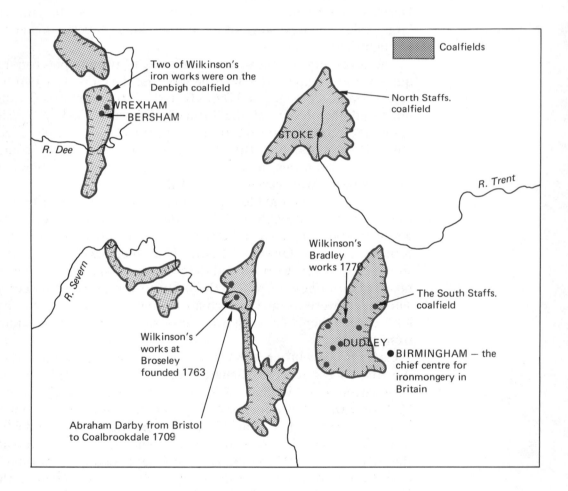

Figure 4.9 John Wilkinson's works in the West Midlands

(b) Richard Crawshay (1762–1811)

Crawshay was born in Yorkshire. As a young man he went to London, where he found a job selling household goods. He married his boss's daughter and became a partner in the Cyfarthfa Ironworks near Merthyr Tydfil in South Wales. He was one of the first to use Cort's methods (see Section 4.12) and by 1800 he was employing 2000 workers. Merthyr Tydfil grew from a village to an industrial town. By 1807 Crawshay's ironworks had six blast furnaces, two rolling-mills and four steam engines, and produced 200 tons of iron a week. By the 1840s the Crawshays' business was described as 'the largest in the kingdom'.

(c) Samuel Walker (1715–1782)

Walker started off in life working in a nail-shop. By 1780 he had built up a huge business in Rotherham, Yorkshire. His 'Rotherham plough', with its cast-iron cutting piece, was of great value to farmers all over Britain.

(d) John Roebuck (1718–1794)

During the Seven Years' War (1756–1763) Roebuck made a large amount of money out of selling the government weapons and cannons. His ironworks at Carron, near Falkirk, were close to large quantities of coal and iron ore. The Firth of Forth, nearby, was an important waterway and provided Roebuck with a method of sending iron goods to other parts of the country and places abroad. In 1773 Roebuck went bankrupt but his ironworks were taken over by the Carron Company and continued to do well.

ESSAY QUESTION, EXAMINATION GUIDANCE AND MODEL ANSWER: THE IRON INDUSTRY

Explain the changes in techniques, organisation and location of the iron industry during the eighteenth century.

Always plan your essays carefully before writing them. It will help you to sort out your ideas and it will certainly impress your teacher/examiner. My plan for the essay above looked like this:

PARAGRAPH 1
How iron was produced in 1700 — changes in technology — investment.
PARAGRAPH 2
The location of the industry.
PARAGRAPH 3
The demand for more iron.
PARAGRAPH 4
How the problems facing the iron industry were solved.
PARAGRAPH 5
The ironmasters.
PARAGRAPH 6
Puddling and rolling.
PARAGRAPH 7
Increased production, 1790–1810.

In 1700 English ironmakers used fairly simple methods to produce iron. Iron ore was smelted in open-topped blast-furnaces made of brick or stone. Charcoal was used for fuel. The second stage of the ironmaking process was carried out by blacksmiths in small forges or workshops. With continued heating and hammering they produced *wrought-iron*. However, changes were beginning to take place in iron production. Blast furnaces were getting bigger and water power was being used for driving bellows and hammers. There was more money being invested in iron production.

The main mining and smelting areas were places where plenty of timber for charcoal was available. As the woodlands of Sussex and Kent became exhausted, new areas of production developed in the Forest of Dean, the West Midlands and the Sheffield area. Poor transport facilities meant that furnaces had to be situated close to supplies of fuel. The use of coal in forges and workshops meant that some small ironworks were already based on the coalfields of South Yorkshire, West Lancashire and Tyneside.

The growing need for iron goods such as nails, bolts, pins, buckles and agricultural tools led to a demand for greater quantities of iron. In 1720 the country used about 50 000 tons of wrought-iron a year. Nearly half the iron had to be imported from Sweden and Russia, as a result of a shortage of charcoal for smelting.

The difficulty in finding a substitute for charcoal was solved by Abraham Darby I at Coalbrookdale in 1709. Darby used coke rather than charcoal for smelting iron ore. The pig-iron produced in this way was not of very high quality but it could be used for making cast-iron. Abraham Darby's son, Abraham II, increased the strength of the blast in the furnace and by 1750 small quantities of coke-smelted iron were being hammered into bar-iron in Shropshire forges.

At this time an increase in population, an increase in the country's wealth and the military demands of the Seven Years' War (1756–1763) led to a steady growth in the demand for iron. Ironmakers began to use Darby's coke-smelting techniques, Newcomen steam pumps and John Wilkinson's cannon-boring machines at their works. Wilkinson was a remarkable ironmaster who broke many rules. He invested heavily in large-scale production rather than smaller ironworks, and established a number of important industries on or near the coalfields. Wilkinson was typical of a group of ironmasters who succeeded in satisfying the demand for iron goods. John Roebuck opened up the huge Carron Ironworks in Scotland; Matthew Boulton built up the Soho Works at Birmingham; Richard Crawshay became the 'Iron King' of South Wales.

The other major difficulty facing the iron industry in the late eighteenth century was that the increase in pig-iron production led to a 'bottleneck' in the production of wrought-iron. Reheating and hammering pig-iron to make wrought-iron was a slow, laborious process. A breakthrough came in 1784, with Henry Cort's 'puddling and rolling' process. Pig-iron was heated in a reverberatory furnace in which the iron was kept separate from the coal by a bridge. A 'puddler' stirred the iron until the impurities were burnt off, and the purified 'loops' were taken to the rolling-mill and shaped into bars or girders. It had previously taken a blacksmith about 12 hours to forge one ton of bar-iron. Now the same amount could be rolled in half an hour. The price of bar-iron fell by a half between 1750 and 1820.

Towards the end of the century there was an increased demand for wrought- and cast-iron goods as a result of the war with France, 1793–1802. The problems facing iron producers in 1700 had largely been solved and the industry was able to expand dramatically. Production of pig-iron increased from 68 000 tons in 1788 to 125 000 tons in 1796 and 250 000 in 1805.

4.14 Hot Blast and Steam Hammer

The combined efforts of the great ironmasters had led to Britain having the largest iron industry in the world by the 1790s. In the first half of the nineteenth century there were two further improvements in iron production.

(a) The Hot Blast (1828)

As blast furnaces became bigger, the strength of the air-blast from the bellows had to be increased. James Neilson, the manager of Glasgow Gas Works, decided to heat air *before* it went into the furnace. This cut down coke consumption and increased the force of the blast.

(b) The Steam Hammer (1839)

James Nasmyth, a Manchester engineer, invented a steam hammer which was used to forge large objects such as the crankshaft of a paddle steamer. A heavy iron hammer was driven downwards by steam and the force of gravity. This meant that blows of great force could be delivered.

4.15 Steel Production in the Eighteenth Century

Steel is a mixture of wrought-iron and carbon. Mixing the two substances makes a metal which is tough yet springy. Today steel has largely replaced iron as the chief metal used in homes, offices and factories. In 1750, however, steel was expensive and quite rare.

The centre of the British steel industry for centuries has been the Sheffield area. In the eighteenth century Sheffield steelmakers produced a type of steel known as *blister steel*. To make blister steel, workers packed bars of good-quality iron and pieces of charcoal into clay boxes. The boxes were heated for ten days. When the steelmakers removed the bars, they had been turned into steel which was covered in blisters. The steel was uneven in quality, being harder on the outside than in the middle. This blister steel had to be reheated and hammered in a forge to turn it into high-grade steel. The whole process was known as *cementation*. This method took about three weeks to make a small quantity of steel.

Benjamin Huntsman (1704–1776), a clockmaker from Doncaster, became interested in finding a better way of making steel. He had difficulty in finding steel suitable for the springs and pendulums of his clocks. After many experiments in Doncaster, he moved to Sheffield in 1740. Shortly after his arrival in Sheffield, he developed a new method of making steel — the *crucible process*.

Huntsman put a little charcoal and pieces of blister steel into clay pots or 'crucibles'. Next he burned away all the impurities at a very high temperature in a coke-filled furnace. After three hours, workmen lifted the crucibles from the furnace and poured the steel into moulds of the shape and size required. The *cast-steel* produced in this way was ideal for articles such as clock springs, razor-blades, cutlery and farm tools.

During the 1750s and 1760s the demand for Sheffield cast-steel increased. In 1770 Huntsman built a new factory at Attercliffe, north of Sheffield. Later in the century steelmakers discovered that high-grade steel could be made simply by fusing good-quality wrought-iron and charcoal in crucibles. By 1860 nearly all Britain's steel was made in Sheffield by the Huntsman method.

4.16 Bessemer, Siemens and Gilchrist-Thomas

Until 1856 all steelmaking was slow and very expensive. Steel could never replace iron in industry until large amounts of it could be made quickly and cheaply. In the second half of the nineteenth century three outstanding men discovered ways of doing this.

(a) Henry Bessemer (1813–1898)

Bessemer, the son of a French refugee, was an amazing inventor. He devised a machine for putting perforations on postage stamps, a method of making gold powder, a sugar press, a way of making imitation velvet and a new method of making plate glass.

During the Crimean War (1854–1856), he became interested in the production of iron and steel. The government asked Bessemer to produce a new type of cannon which would not shatter under the force of a shell being fired from it. Bessemer decided to make a gun which combined the best qualities of wrought-iron and cast-iron — a gun made of steel. The 'crucible process' (see Section 4.15) was slow and expensive, and so Bessemer started working on a cheap, reliable way of making steel. He came up with the idea of a *converter* (1856). This was a long, pear-shaped container which looked a bit like a huge cement-mixer. Molten pig-iron was poured into the converter and a blast of hot air was blown through its base. The oxygen in the air combined with impurities in the pig-iron. The impurities were driven out in the form of burning gases or turned into slag. In about twenty minutes the iron was pure, and small amounts of carbon and manganese were added to it to produce *mild steel*. This type of steel is neither as brittle nor as hard as ordinary cast-steel. It is ideal for making such things as steel girders, rails, tools or wire ropes.

The converter reduced the price of making steel by 75 per cent. Mild steel could now be produced cheaply and in huge quantities. However, the converter had three drawbacks:

1. Some of the steel produced was 'wild steel' (full of holes), as it had taken in too much oxygen. This problem was solved by Robert Mushet, from the Forest of Dean, who showed that by adding manganese after the 'blow', the quality of the steel could be greatly improved.
2. Much heat was wasted and some of the iron was carried away with the blast. Later, William Siemens (see below) produced a furnace which did not do this.
3. The converter could only be used with iron containing very little phosphorus. Unfortunately, most of Britain's iron contained phosphorus. This problem was not solved until Gilchrist-Thomas's 'basic' process was developed in 1879 (see below).

Despite these drawbacks, the converter was one of the greatest inventions of the nineteenth century. Soon steel was being used for making ships, bridges and machine-tools.

(b) William Siemens (1823–1883)

Siemens was born in Germany but came to live in England. He designed a furnace which used recycled heat to make iron. This *open-hearth furnace* was modified by two French brothers, Pierre and Emile Martin, in 1863. Three years later Siemens set up his own furnace at Llandore in South Wales. The converting vessel was a long, narrow trough which held over 300 tonnes of pig-iron and scrap metal. Preheated air and coal gas were burned over it to melt the iron and to drive out any impurities. It took about ten hours to produce 350 tonnes of steel. During this time, the temperature of the furnace reached 1650 degrees Celsius.

At first many steel producers preferred to stick to the Bessemer process rather than switch over to the open hearth. After a while, however, it became obvious that Siemens' process was better, for two reasons:

1. Large amounts of scrap metal could be converted into mild steel, because of the high temperature of the furnace.
2. The metal could be inspected and temperatures could be controlled while the steel was being made.

Like the Bessemer process, only non-phosphoric ores could be used in the open-hearth process. Today, some open hearths are still in use in steelworks, although they are being gradually phased out.

(c) Sidney Gilchrist-Thomas (1850–1885)

Gilchrist-Thomas was a clerk in a police court in London. In his spare time he studied chemistry. He realised that if someone could solve the problem of using phosphoric ores in the converter or open hearth, a fortune could be made. He set to work in a backyard workshop. By 1879 he had come up with a solution to the problem. He lined a Bessemer converter with dolomite limestone. The limestone combined with the phosphorus in the iron to produce slag (calcium phosphate), which could subsequently be used as a fertiliser by farmers. This became known as the 'basic' process and most steel produced today is *basic steel*.

In 1879 Gilchrist-Thomas demonstrated his new discovery in Middlesborough. He used iron ore from the nearby Cleveland Hills, which had large amounts of phosphorus in it. To the surprise of many onlookers, the system worked well. Gilchrist-Thomas became internationally famous. Phosphoric iron from Lorraine in Germany and Lake Superior in the U.S.A. could now be converted into steel.

Mild steel became so cheap and plentiful that engineers used it instead of iron for boilers, machinery, buildings and guns. Railway companies bought it in large quantities for steel rails. One steel bridge built after the inventions was the Forth Railway Bridge (1882–1889). The bridge required 50 000 tons of steel. The manufacture of steel plates made it possible to build larger, stronger steamships. In the building industries, steel girders were used to strengthen concrete. The statistics in Table 4.9 show the sudden growth of the steel industry during the period 1850–1960.

Table 4.9 Steel production in Britain

Date	Quantity (tons)	Date	Quantity (tons)
1850	60 000	1900	5 000 000
1870	250 000	1950	18 240 000
1880	2 000 000	1960	24 300 000

4.17 Iron and Steel in the Twentieth Century

By 1900 many items that had previously been made of iron were being made of *steel*. Britain had led the world in ironmaking but soon the U.S.A. and Germany overtook our steelmaking industry as Figure 4.10 suggests. Both the U.S.A. and Germany had large deposits of iron ore and coal.

Steel became very important for making weapons and battleships in the period before the First World War (1914–1918). Germany was able to produce about twice as much steel as Britain. During the First World War the demand for ships and weapons led to a massive expansion of the iron and steel industries. However, during the war many foreign markets were lost to British exporters. During the 1920s a world-wide slump badly affected both industries. Many British ironworks and steelworks were run on old-fashioned lines and production costs were high. Thousands of steel workers lost their jobs.

In the 1930s tariffs (taxes) were placed on many iron and steel goods brought into the country. The demand for iron and steel rose, with the recovery of the motor-car, engineering and shipbuilding industries. The steel towns of Scunthorpe and Corby grew up based on local iron ore. New steelworks were built in South Wales and Middlesborough. By 1937 steel output had reached a record level of 12.9 million tons.

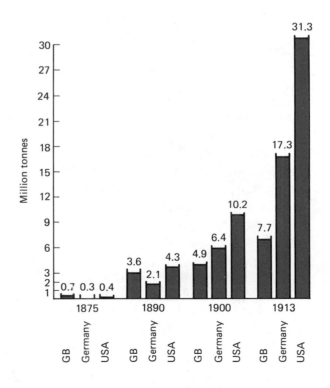

Figure 4.10 Steel production in Great Britain, the U.S.A. and Germany

During the Second World War (1939–1945) the iron and steel industries expanded. When the war ended, a Labour government nationalised (took over) the steel companies, as steel production was vital to the nation's economic well-being. This was not popular with some people, as private companies were making huge sums of money out of steel production. In 1953 a Conservative government handed back the industry to private owners. Fourteen years later (1967) a Labour government re-nationalised the industry and set up a *British Steel Corporation*.

Since 1967 there have been many improvements in the industry. Today the main steelmaking method is the *basic oxygen process*. Computers and automation have been used to increase iron and steel production, but the British Steel Corporation has found it increasingly difficult to compete in world steel markets. During the 1980s there were big cuts in manpower and output. The present government is planning to sell off a profit-making steel industry to private investors.

EXAMINATION GUIDANCE: IRON AND STEEL

Be prepared for iron and steel together in one question. Questions on iron will cover the period up to 1830. You need to be able to describe the changes in methods of making iron and you must be able to explain *why* the production of cheap, plentiful iron was so important. Questions on steel generally cover the period 1850–1914, but you should also know how 'crucible steel' was produced. You may get an empathy-type question on an ironmaster or steelmaker — for example, Darby, Wilkinson, Cort, Bessemer.

Specimen Questions

1. Why did many ironmasters move their businesses away from the South of England in the mid-eighteenth century?
2. Describe the contribution to the iron and steel industry of *two* of the following:

Abraham Darby I	John Roebuck
John Wilkinson	Henry Bessemer
Henry Cort	William Siemens

3. Which other industries were helped by the success of the steel industry in the late nineteenth century?

4.18 Steam Power

Steam power was the key to the Industrial Revolution. The change-over from domestic industry to making things in factories could not have taken place without a new source of power. For industry to expand, factory owners needed a form of power they could use *wherever* and *whenever* they wanted it.

Before 1750 water was the main source of power for machinery. Britain has plenty of fast-flowing streams and high rainfall! However, in some years there was too much rain in winter and too little in summer. During the winter months water-wheels often froze up.

Other sources of power in the eighteenth century included animal power, human muscle power and wind power. These also had their disadvantages.

Between 1700 and 1780, engineers developed a new source of power — the steam engine. The chief need for such an engine was to drive pumps to keep mines free from water, so that rich deposits of copper, coal and iron could be mined at lower levels. The three most important engineers to work on steam engines were as follows.

(a) Thomas Savery (1650–1715)

Savery, an inventor who lived in Devon, succeeded in making a machine which pumped water by steam. His invention was not really an engine, as it had no moving parts. Savery designed the pump to drain mines, but it had so many drawbacks that few mine-owners used it. It had limited power and burnt a large amount of fuel. The pump could not be used down deep mines. The boiler had no safety valve and the pumps sometimes blew up!

(b) Thomas Newcomen (1663–1729)

Newcomen, an ironmonger and engineer from Dartmouth, often visited the tin and copper mines of Cornwall as part of his business. The miners used pumps worked by men or horses to drain their mines. Newcomen designed a more effective pump which worked by atmospheric (air) pressure. The pump had a cylinder and a piston. Newcomen filled the cylinder with steam and then sprayed cold water over the cylinder. This created a vacuum (absence of air) in the cylinder. Air pressure then forced the piston down the cylinder. You can still see a real Newcomen engine at the Science Museum in London.

The Newcomen pump was a tremendous achievement. It relied on low steam pressure and there was little to go wrong. However, Newcomen pumps did have their drawbacks:

- Early engines were clumsy and inefficient. It was impossible to make close-fitting parts, and power was lost through inaccurately bored cylinders and ill-fitting valves.
- The pumps burned a large amount of fuel and were not widely used in areas a long way from coalfields.
- The pumps could only produce reciprocating (up and down) motion. They could not be used to turn a wheel.

(c) James Watt (1736–1819)

James Watt was a maker of mathematical instruments at Glasgow University. In 1765 he was asked to repair a model of a Newcomen engine. He realised that it used up a great deal of fuel because the cylinder had to be heated and reheated at every stroke of the engine. Watt decided to try to improve the Newcomen engine. Between 1765 and 1788 he made five improvements to the steam engine:

1. *The separate condenser* (1765) Watt's condenser was connected to the side of the cylinder by a tube. After each upward thrust of the piston, steam could be drawn from the cylinder. The result was a great saving of steam and fuel.
2. *Rotary motion* (1781) Watt had developed a useful pumping machine, but factory-owners needed a steam engine which could turn a wheel.

Somehow reciprocating motion had to be converted to a rotary movement. Watt fixed the outer end of the beam to a crank with a rigid connecting rod which turned a flywheel. This *sun and planet gear* was probably Watt's most important invention.

3. *The valve-box* (1782)   Watt fixed an airtight cover onto the top of the cylinder and used steam to force the piston up and down the cylinder. A valve-box injected steam on both sides of the piston alternately.

4. *Parallel motion* (1784)   A system of levers which allowed the piston rod to move up and down in a straight line and, at the same time, pushed and pulled the end of the beam.

5. *The governor* (1788)   This device simply controlled the supply of steam to the piston and kept the engine going at a regular speed.

(d) The Impact of Steam Power

The steam engine had an impact on many aspects of the economy:

- *Industry*   Rotary motion (see above) meant that steam power could be used in a wide variety of industries. Rotary engines were first used to drive bellows, hammers and rollers in the iron industry (see Section 4.11). In 1785 the first steam engines were used to power textile machines in Nottinghamshire. By 1800 Watt's company had installed steam engines in sugar-refineries, breweries, flour-mills and forges. Coal production increased dramatically, as rotary engines could be used to haul coal and people from the coalface to the surface.

- *Transport*   In 1784 William Murdoch, the foreman at the Soho Ironworks in Birmingham, designed a model of a steam-powered locomotive. By 1800 Trevithick and Hedley (see Section 9.13) were building full-size steam locomotives. Steam-powered boats first appeared in 1802.

- *Engineering*   Steam-powered machines were used to make locks, tools, scientific instruments and machine-parts.

- *Factories*   There were many more factories containing machines and engines powered by steam (see also Section 4.19). The decline of the domestic system continued.

- *The location of industry*   Steam power relied on coal. Many factories and businesses (e.g. soap-making, brewing) became based on or near coalfields.

- *Other forms of power*   Water, wind and muscle power became less important. Industry became less dependent on weather conditions!

Figure 4.11 shows the links between different industries and steam power.

EXAMINATION GUIDANCE: STEAM POWER

You may be asked to identify the working parts of Newcomen and Watt steam engines (see Source-based Question). Usually you are given a diagram showing a steam engine, with certain words on the diagram missing. Alternatively, you may be expected to draw a diagram of a steam engine from memory as part of an essay-type answer.

Steam power questions generally go up to about 1830 and fall into five categories:

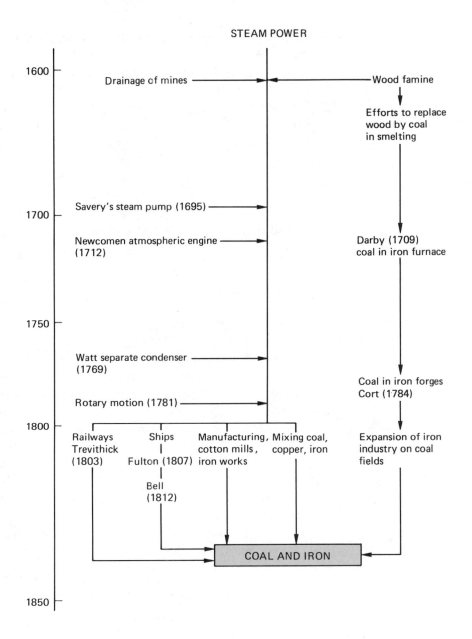

Figure 4.11 The link between the different industries and steam power

1. How and why the steam engine was developed in the eighteenth century.
2. How the steam engine helped industry.
3. Steam power and factory life.
4. The importance of Boulton and Watt.
5. The decline of steam power and the development of other forms of energy.

Do make sure you know how a steam engine works. You should certainly be able to tell a piston from a cylinder and a Newcomen engine from a Watt engine! You should also be aware that the development of the steam engine was not the work of one man but of many engineers over a long period:

The steam engine was far from being the work of brilliant individual inventors. The names that have reached the textbooks are those few out of a large crowd who were feverishly working on every one of the major inventions.

(*The First Industrial Nation*, Peter Mathias, 1969)

You should also be prepared for questions on the steam engine which are linked to other topics — for example, factory conditions, textiles, steamships and locomotives and coal.

Specimen Questions

1. How did developments in steam power affect the coal-mining and textiles industries?
2. Why did steam power become less important in the second half of the nineteenth century?

You may be asked to write a biography of James Watt — for example:

Assume you are James Watt near the end of his life in 1817. Write a letter to a young relative describing the main events in your life. You should mention the most important decisions you had to take and what you think the long-term effects of your work will be.

SOURCE-BASED QUESTION: THE STEAM ENGINE

The steam engine in the picture (page 94) was erected near Dudley Castle in 1712.

1. Name the Devon blacksmith who designed this type of steam engine. Briefly describe how it worked.
2. What were the disadvantages of using this type of steam pump?
3. Is this a primary or secondary source? Give reasons for your answer.
4. How did this steam engine help iron-, tin-, copper- and coal-producers?
5. What modifications [changes] did James Watt make to this type of steam engine between 1765 and 1800? Illustrate your answer with drawings and diagrams if you wish.

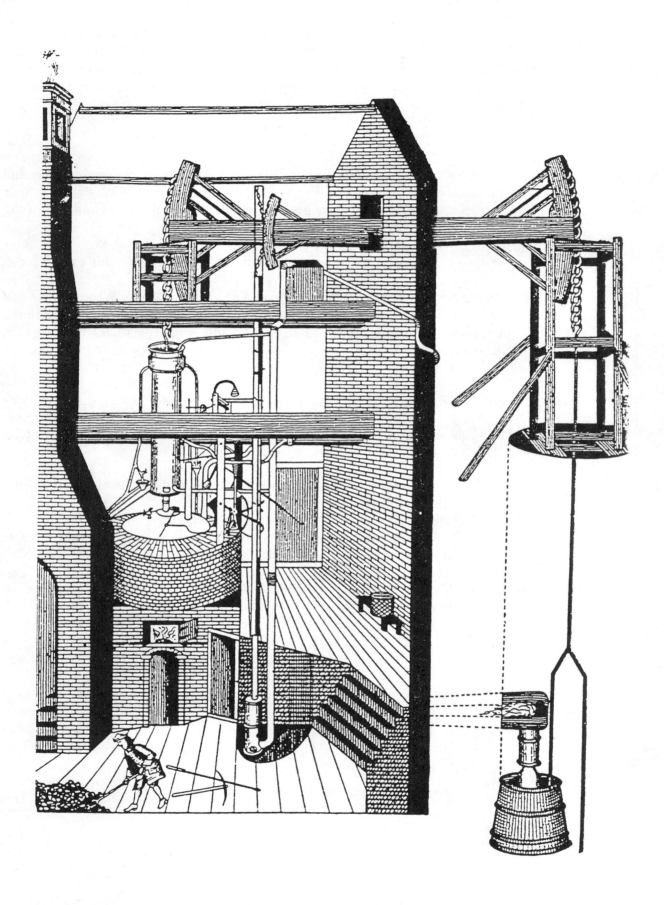

4.19 The Factory System

In the late eighteenth century there were very few large factories in Britain. Early factories were often built in remote, hilly places where there were good supplies of water power, such as Cromford, near Derby. There were a few large spinning-mills; in 1816 Arkwright's son employed 2000 people at Cromford and Robert Owen employed 1600 at New Lanark. However, factories using steam power in the towns were much smaller.

By the early nineteenth century many factory-owners were making huge sums of money out of the textiles industry. Many factory-owners gave little thought to the welfare of their workers. Some employees worked a fourteen-hour day for very low rates of pay. There was harsh discipline. Thousands of women and children were employed in mills and factories because they were good at delicate work and would accept lower rates of pay than men. Youngsters were given dangerous jobs such as crawling under machines to collect fluff or working with chemicals. As machinery became more complicated and as steam engines became more widely used, more skilled and literate adults were needed. But in many parts of the country child labour continued well into the nineteenth century, as struggling families needed their children's wages in order to make ends meet.

In the long run, many people benefited from the factory system. Domestic industry had many drawbacks (see Section 4.2). The earnings of farm workers were well below those of miners and cotton workers. Not all factory-owners were cruel tyrants, and men such as Benjamin Gott and Robert Owen (see Section 5.4) showed that it was possible to make large profits while treating their workers humanely. The Factory Acts passed between 1833 and 1878 (see Section 6.7) led to major improvements in working conditions.

4.20 Pottery, Chemicals and Engineering

(a) Pottery

In the early eighteenth century most earthenware jugs and pots were made in Tunstall or Burslem in Staffordshire. In 1759 Josiah Wedgwood (1730–1795), the son of a Burslem potter, opened a pottery, where he made cream-coloured china known as *Queensware*. To make large quantities of Queensware, Wedgwood brought in a system of *division of labour*. He divided up all the traditional skills of the potter — mixing, shaping, firing and glazing — and gave each job to specialist workers. He later introduced steam engines for heavy jobs such as mixing clay and grinding flint.

For the pottery industry to expand, Wedgwood needed to get his pots safely to market. He was one of the keenest supporters of the Grand Trunk Canal. The canal linked the Potteries to Liverpool, and the rivers Severn and Trent. In 1769 he built a new factory on the banks of the canal near Burslem. He called the factory 'Etruria' because he admired the pottery of the Ancient Etruscans. Wedgwood was a clever salesman, and set up showrooms in Bristol and London. He looked after his workers well, and built them cottages, chapels and schools. It is mainly due to Wedgwood that the area around Stoke-on-Trent has been the main centre of the pottery industry for over 200 years.

(b) Chemicals

In 1750 the shortage of cheap chemicals was causing major problems for the textiles and glass industries. The cotton industry needed huge quantities of bleach and glass-makers needed potash.

In 1746 John Roebuck (1718–1794) invented the lead chamber process. This produced sulphuric acid, a useful ingredient of bleach. Later Claude Berthollet (1748–1822) developed the use of chlorine as a bleaching agent. By 1789 Charles Tennant was making liquid bleach from chlorine and slaked lime.

By the end of the eighteenth century a chemical industry had grown up to meet the demands of other industries for acids, soda, tars and alkalis. Newcastle upon Tyne, Glasgow and Merseyside became centres of the chemical industry and remain important today. In the nineteenth century many more industries began to use chemical products. Large chemical works were built to meet the demands of industry. In 1856 W.H. Perkin accidentally made a purple dye from coal tar. Soon a whole range of colours were being made from coal products.

Between 1918 and 1939 the chemical industry expanded in England. In 1926 four large firms came together to form I.C.I. (Imperial Chemical Industries), one of the biggest chemical firms in Europe. More firms started to produce plastics, disinfectants, drugs and artificial fibres. The chemical industry played an important part in the development of rayon made from cotton and cellulose.

Since 1945 the chemical industry has continued to expand. Many types of Cellophane, Terylene and polyester are made by British firms. Chemicals remain one of our most successful industries.

(c) Engineering

The engineering industry was one of Britain's fastest-growing industries of the nineteenth century. *Machine-tools* (machines which are themselves tools) were replacing the old hand-tool methods of engineering. Machine-tools made objects which were all the same size and shape, thus cutting out craftsmen's errors. For the first time the parts of machines in factories were made to a standard size. Without this change there would have been no factories filled with identical machines.

The machine-tool industry was based on the work of a number of brilliant engineers and craftsmen. Table 4.10 shows who they were and what they achieved.

4.21 Shipbuilding (see also Sections 9.12 and 9.31)

In the eighteenth century thousands of shipwrights, carpenters, smiths and nail-makers worked in dockyards along the River Thames and the South Coast. By the early nineteenth century shipbuilding was one of Britain's most important industries. But changes in the industry took place slowly. Until 1850 most shipwrights and sailmakers worked in small yards and most boats were made of wood. During the 1870s and 1880s Britain's ships dominated the world's trade routes. British shipbuilders had gained many advantages over their competitors abroad. Great quantities of cheap iron and steel were available for making ships. There were new sources of power — compound engines and turbines. Making new steamships was a large-scale task involving thousands of engineers, crafts-men and shipwrights and huge sums of money. Both the technical skills and the money could be found in Britain. The main shipbuilding centres became Belfast,

Table 4.10

Name	Machine
John Wilkinson (1728–1808) (see also Section 4.13)	Machine-tools which could bore cylinders and make parts for steam engines
Joseph Bramah (1748–1814)	The water closet, a beer pump and an unpickable lock
Marc Brunel (1769–1849)	Block-making machinery for naval dockyards
Henry Maudslay (1771–1831)	The screw-cutting lathe, the slide rest and the micrometer
Joseph Clement (1779–1844)	The water-tap, a new lathe and a calculating machine
Joseph Whitworth (1803–1887)	Lathes, measuring devices, and machines for planing, drilling, slotting and shaping
James Nasmyth (1808–1890) (see also Section 4.14)	A 'steam arm' shaping machine, the safety ladle and the steam hammer
Richard Roberts (1789–1864)	A new lathe

the Clyde, Liverpool, Barrow-in-Furness and the River Tyne area. By 1902 the British were building over two-thirds of all the world's ships!

Thousands of British ships were sunk during the First World War (1914–1918). There was a short boom in shipbuilding after the war and then a serious slump. Other countries began to build their own ships rather than ordering them from British shipbuilders. Little effort was made to modernise British dockyards and Britain soon lagged behind Germany and America. Firms decided that the only way to save the industry from total collapse was to buy up the oldest yards and then close them down! In 1935 the government introduced a *scrap and build* scheme. Shipowners were encouraged to scrap old ships and build new ones.

In the late 1930s the British government decided to build more warships, to combat the growing threat of Hitler's navy.

After the Second World War, British shipyard-owners were busy replacing ships sunk by enemy aircraft and U-boats. By this time many of our shipyards were out of date and could not compete with Japanese, Polish and Russian firms. Over the next twenty years, orders for British ships fell steadily. Many of the shipyards in Belfast, Liverpool and Clydeside closed. In 1977 the government took over the industry and renamed it *British Shipbuilders*. However, the shipbuilding industry is still in the doldrums. The recessions of the 1970s and 1980s have placed the industry in an even worse position than it was in the 1930s.

4.22 The Great Exhibition (1851)

The Great Exhibition of 1851 was a chance for Britain to show off her industrial and technical achievements to the rest of the world. Thousands of iron, steel, textile and other goods were on display to visitors from Britain and the Continent.

The main events leading up to the Great Exhibition were:

1. Prince Albert, Queen Victoria's husband, had the idea of putting on an exhibition to display the latest British industrial and scientific achieve-

ments. He believed that an exhibition would help to promote trade and develop peace between nations.

2. Albert found a sixteen-acre site on the south side of Hyde Park which he thought would be suitable for the exhibition. The exhibition planning committee held a competition for a design for a building to house the exhibition. Two hundred and forty-five entries were submitted but none was suitable. Joseph Paxton, a head gardener, came to the committee's rescue with a plan for a building made of glass and iron. This later became known as the *Crystal Palace*.

   There was a great deal of opposition to the scheme, people objecting to the shape and size of the building. Colonel Sibthorpe, M.P. for Lincoln, believed that people would be robbed and murdered by hordes of foreigners! There were also fears of riot and revolution.

3. Work began on the Crystal Palace in the autumn of 1850. More than 2000 men put up the iron framework to the building. Glassmakers then fitted 300 000 panes of glass. The main section of the building was crossed by a huge dome 108 feet high. The dome was large enough to cover three fully grown elm trees! The building was nearly a third of a mile long.

4. Inside the Crystal Palace British exhibitors displayed 7381 items and there were 6556 items from other countries. The British exhibits were divided up into five classes: metals and ceramics; textiles; 'fine arts'; machinery; raw materials. There were steam engines, textile machines, steam hammers, steamboats and machine-tools. You could also see railway locomotives, bridges, telescopes, cameras, barometers, furniture and jewellery.

5. Between May and October 1851 over six million people visited the Exhibition. On some days tickets were sold for only one shilling (5p), so that working-class people could look around. The Exhibition made a large profit, which was used to buy the land where the Science Museum, the Royal College of Art and the Victoria and Albert Museum now stand. The Crystal Palace was dismantled in 1852 and re-erected at Sydenham in South London. On 30 November 1936 the Crystal Palace was destroyed by fire.

(a) **Effects of the Great Exhibition**

- The Exhibition showed that British industry had a clear lead over that of all other countries.
- Many people had the chance to visit London for the first time. They travelled by exhibition train, paying excursion rates. Traders in London benefited from the huge number of visitors.
- The Exhibition brought together people from different social classes. Middle-class Victorians were surprised to see working-class visitors from the North behaving in a sensible, responsible manner. There were few robberies or violent acts.
- The Crystal Palace showed the tremendous technical possibilities of buildings made from iron and glass.
- The Exhibition did not improve British trade to any great extent, nor did it promote the cause of world peace. In 1854 the Crimean War broke out between Britain and France and Russia!

4.23 The Great Depression (1870–1900)

The period between 1870 and 1900 has been known as *The Great Depression*. However, recent research has suggested that many businessmen and factory-owners in new types of businesses and industries such as chemicals and electricity prospered during this period. The iron and steel, metalworking, shipbuilding and farming industries were the main ones affected by the Great Depression.

Britain's share of world trade was declining while other countries such as Germany and the U.S.A. were taking on a more important role as trading nations. The result in Britain was a period of *boom and slump*. During some years British industry and agriculture did well but during others factory-owners and farmers were making very small profits or none at all.

(a) Industry

Factory-owners found that prices were falling sharply and that they were making smaller profits (Table 4.11). To offset this fall in prices, a big increase in sales was necessary. Orders for British goods were more difficult to obtain, because foreign firms were increasing the quantity and improving the quality of their output. In Britain output per person increased much more slowly than in Germany, France and the U.S.A. There was high unemployment in the 1880s, and people began to leave the large cities of the North to search for work in the Midlands and the South-east. Factory-owners began to form trade associations in order to cut down on wasteful competition between themselves.

For all the talk of 'depression', there were signs of growing national prosperity. People employed more domestic servants than ever before. The fall in prices meant cheaper food, and the working classes could buy more tea, sugar, vegetables and meat. The fall in textile prices meant cheaper clothes.

Table 4.11

Product	1874	1883
Steel rails	£12.00 a ton	£5.38 a ton
Iron rails	£9.90 a ton	£5.00 a ton
Pig-iron	£4.88 a ton	£1.66 a ton

(b) Agriculture

There was certainly a 'Great Depression' in British agriculture. The cause of the depression was not inefficiency or old-fashioned farming practices but foreign competition (see Section 3.11).

(c) The Effects of the Great Depression

- After 1880 Germany and the U.S.A. became major industrial competitors with Britain.
- Some businesses closed down and many farmers were ruined. Farm workers left the land to seek work in towns and cities.

- After 1896 prices tended to rise, and for twenty years trade improved.
- The British economy became more dependent on manufactured goods and less dependent on agriculture. We began to *import* more food and *export* more factory-made items.
- Britain's four basic industries — textiles, coal, iron and steel, shipbuilding — recovered from the depression, although during the period 1900–1914 growth in these industries was slower than in Germany and the U.S.A.
- Britain started to produce more manufactured goods such as bicycles, toys, cars, chemicals and electrical goods to sell abroad.

4.24 Gas and Electricity

(a) Gas

The first person to experiment with coal gas was William Murdoch (1754–1839). He used gas to light his home in Redruth, Cornwall. In 1798 he got a job as Matthew Boulton's foreman at the Soho Ironworks, near Birmingham. Within months Boulton's firm was making retorts, gas-holders and pipes. Gas was used to provide the Soho factory with lighting.

In 1804 Albert Winsor established a National Light and Heat Company, and by 1812 his Gas Lighting and Coke Company was providing street lighting in London. By 1830 there were 200 different gas companies. Consumers used gas mainly as a source of light. People rarely used gas for heating or cooking.

By the mid-nineteenth century the gas industry was employing thousands of workers. The industry remained a major employer until the 1960s, when the government closed many gasworks as part of the clean air programme. Today most of our gas is *natural gas*, piped to our homes from under the North Sea.

(b) Electricity

Scientists had been experimenting with electricity since the late eighteenth century, but it was only in the late nineteenth century that inventions were developed for the use of electricity in our everyday lives. In 1809 Michael Faraday (1791–1867) invented an electric battery, but the only widespread use of electricity before 1875 was in the electric telegraph (see Section 9.2). Table 4.12 shows the main developments in the use of electrical power between 1878 and 1926.

In 1926 the Central Electricity Board set up a national network of power lines known as the *National Grid*. Huge power stations were linked up by a network of cables which carried electricity to every part of the country. The power stations were owned by private companies or town councils, but the C.E.B. controlled the supply. The National Grid made it possible to build factories away from the coalfields (see Section 4.27). Dozens of light engineering firms were set up in the Midlands and the South-east. There were also many new industries producing electrical goods for use in the home.

In 1947 the electricity supply industry was nationalised. All electric power came under the control of the Central Electricity Generating Board. The C.E.G.B. produced the power, and local electricity boards distributed it. During the 1950s and 1960s most power stations used coal to produce electricity, but a

Table 4.12 The development of electrical power

Date	Development
1878	Joseph Swan (1828–1914), a Gateshead inventor and electrician, invented a light bulb
1879	Thomas Edison (1847–1931), an American, developed a similar bulb. 'Ediswan' light bulbs sold to the public
1881	The first electricity generating plant was built by the Siemens Company in Godalming, Surrey
1884	Charles Parsons (1854–1931) invented the steam turbine. This could be used to generate electricity
1900	First electric tube train in London
1905	Hydroelectric power used in Scotland
1914	Five hundred electricity generating stations in Britain
1926	*Electricity Supply Act* A Central Electricity Board was set up to standardise different voltages. Some small power stations closed down

growing number used oil, gas or water. From the 1960s onwards the C.E.G.B. began to build more nuclear power stations. There has been great public anxiety over whether nuclear power stations are a safe way of generating electricity.

4.25 The Effects of Two World Wars

(a) The First World War (1914–1918)

The First World War forced the British Government to be heavily involved in planning and running industry. It was the first major war to be fought with tanks, aircraft and machine-guns. Much industry went over to producing goods needed for the war effort. Thousands of extra men were needed in the armed forces, and women workers were brought into factories and businesses to do men's work.

The government took over the railways (see Section 9.18). Steelworks started making bombs and shells, and hundreds of factories were built or modernised with government aid. The government took over parts of the chemical industry and started producing medicines. There was a new government Department of Scientific and Industrial Research. The war gave a boost to the aircraft, wireless and motor industries. The government also tried to improve electricity supplies to industry. Some electricity companies were given government money to build factories to meet the demand for electric power.

The government's role in industry helped win the war for Britain. At the end of the war, in 1918, most industries and companies were handed back to private owners.

(b) The Second World War (1939–1945)

The government took over the running of the British economy much more quickly than during the First World War. Ernest Bevin, a trade union leader (see Section 5.17), left his job as Secretary of the Transport and General Workers' Union and became Minister of Labour. He organised five million people to work in the forces, the Land Army and munitions factories. Miners became key industrial workers in the fight against Hitler. Twenty-two thousand 'Bevin boys' were conscripted into the mines to help miners dig more coal.

Most factories went over to war work, making arms or essential goods. Aircraft production, for example, shot up from 2800 planes in 1939 to 26 000 in 1944. The government paid for the steel industry to build electric furnaces to smelt the highest-quality steels. Thousands of new machine-tools produced accurate, high-calibre weapons.

Luxury goods virtually disappeared from the shops. There were fewer imports, and items such as chocolate, cigarettes and oranges were hard to obtain. Food rationing began on 8 January 1940.

Women played an important part in keeping industry running. An extra 750 000 women worked in engineering and 110 000 more worked on farms (see Section 11.9).

4.26 The Growth of New Industries

Since the end of the Second World War some sections of industry have expanded so quickly that historians have talked about a 'Second Industrial Revolution' in Britain. The most important of the new industries are as follows:

- *The petrochemical industry* has produced a new range of fertilisers and insecticides, and a new plastics industry.
- *Atomic energy* has been developed for peaceful purposes under the direction of the Atomic Energy Authority.
- *Motor engineering and aero engineering* have benefited a great deal from automation and computer technology (see below). 'Automation' is the term used to describe the production of goods by machines with very little human supervision.
- *Computers* The first calculating machine was produced by Charles Babbage (1792–1871) in 1823. During the Second World War, electronic-valve computers were built as codebreakers. After the war, in 1948, Tom Kilburn built the first modern computer at Manchester University. It was so big that it filled up three rooms! However, the invention of the transistor and the integrated circuit meant that much smaller computers could be developed. In the 1980s the microchip brought the size and price of computers within the reach of most firms and many households. Today computers are used in most industries. In 1986 the Stock Exchange was computerised. Computers are also used for printing, weather forecasting and production control in factories.
- *Radio and television* These industries have supplied consumers with a whole range of equipment and have produced a 'social revolution' in the home. Radio links via satellite have greatly improved global communications, and most ships and aircraft use radar to help them navigate. Short-wave radios are used by police, security guards and the armed forces.
- *North Sea gas and oil* On 14 August 1959 a Dutch drilling rig discovered a vast field of natural gas below the North Sea. British oil companies found so much natural gas that it was piped ashore to domestic and industrial users. The first large oilfield to be discovered was Ekofisk (1969). By 1971 British Petroleum had successfully exploited the huge Forties and Brent oilfields. Britain became a major oil producer in the decade 1971–1981.

- *The service industries* These include the medical, education, transport, communication and information technology industries. Today people expect a wider range of services than ever before, and in the South-east they have the money to pay for them. The only service industry to decline in recent years is domestic service, although there are signs that more servants and 'nannies' are being employed in the more prosperous parts of the South. Table 4.13 shows the number of employees in service industries 1961–1980.

Table 4.13 Employees in service industries (thousands)

Job	1961	1971	1980
Transport and communication	1 678	1 568	1 500
Distributive trades	2 767	2 610	2 790
Insurance, banking, finance	684	976	1 258
Professional service	2 124	2 989	3 717
Public service	1 311	1 509	1 596
All service industries	10 382	11 597	13 379

4.27 Changes in the Location of Industry

Four factors have caused a change in the location of industry since 1918:

1. There has been a decline in Britain's 'basic' industries (steel and iron, textiles, shipbuilding, coal). These were all based on or near coalfields. After the economic depressions of the 1920s and 1930s these industries never regained their importance. Thousands of workers looked for jobs in other parts of the country. They moved to the Midlands and the South-east to find work in light industry or service industries.
2. The use of electric power and nuclear power meant that electricity could be transmitted over great distances quickly and cheaply. One result of this has been that industry has grown most rapidly in London and the South-east.
3. London's large population needs services such as shops, transport and luxury goods.
4. With improvements in the road and motorway networks, many businessmen have built factories on or near the motorways around London. By 1981 over 20 per cent of England's population lived in the London area. Other towns in the South-east have expanded as a result of new industries — for example, Luton (Vauxhall Motors), Milton Keynes (information technology), Watford (aircraft production).

4.28 Government Intervention

Until the First World War in 1914 the government took little part in the running of industry. Most politicians supported a policy of *laissez-faire* (government non-intervention). People felt that it was not the job of central government to tell factory-owners and businessmen how to run their industries. The First World

War forced the government to take an active part in running industry. After the war, a series of trade depressions meant that the government had to carry on helping British industry. Government aid to industry took various forms. A grant of £9.5 million was given to shipbuilders, a Spindles Act (1936) assisted the cotton industry and the coal industry received government subsidies during the 1920s and 1930s. Local government received subsidies for council-house building and most industries were derated (paid low rates) in 1929. The government set up the British Broadcasting Corporation (B.B.C.) in 1926, the Central Electricity Generating Board (C.E.G.B.) in 1927 and London Transport (L.T.) in 1933.

After the Second World War, the Labour government favoured a policy of nationalisation (government ownership of industry) between 1945 and 1951. The Conservatives campaigned against nationalisation, but when they returned to power in 1951, they denationalised very few industries. The steel industry and road transport were partially denationalised, but other industries remained under public control. The Labour Party renationalised the steel industry in 1966.

By 1972 the Conservatives were directing and controlling the siting of factories, particularly in depressed areas of the country. Four years later (1976) a Labour government forced through proposals to nationalise the shipbuilding and aircraft industries. There was strong opposition to this and the ship-repairing industry remained in private hands.

The importance of the transfer of industry to public ownership is *economic* rather than *political*. The government is now the largest employer of labour in the country *and* the largest consumer! The Welfare State (see Chapter 7) required the government to take a major part in the running of the economy. Industry asked the government to provide it with conditions which would help it to grow. These included cheap power and good roads. Industry also expected government help if it began to lose money. In the 1980s this situation has changed, and the government now expects business to stand on its own two feet. To help make business more efficient the government has also sold off to private investors many state-owned industries, such as British Telecom. This represents a radical shift in the policies of all governments since 1945.

ESSAY-TYPE QUESTIONS: INDUSTRY IN THE NINETEENTH AND TWENTIETH CENTURIES

On your GCSE papers you will almost certainly find essay-type questions like the ones below:

1. In which industries was the steam engine used between 1800 and 1830? What problems had to be overcome by the builders and users of steam engines during this period?
2. Why did the cotton industry grow more rapidly than the woollen industry in the early nineteenth century?
3. Describe the changes in methods of producing steel between 1850 and 1900. What effects did these changes have on the economy?
4. Describe the main developments in British industry in the second half of the twentieth century. In your answer you should refer to: new products; new sources of power; new types of transport. Can these developments be regarded as a second Industrial Revolution?
5. Describe the different ways in which Britain's industries and patterns of trade changed in the first half of the twentieth century.

N.B.: The questions on twentieth-century industry are often difficult to answer successfully, and it is best to avoid them if possible!

WORK OUT SHORT-ANSWER QUESTIONS: INDUSTRY

1. What is meant by the phrase 'Industrial Revolution'?
2. What was 'cottage industry'?
3. Name England's most important cottage industry in 1750.
4. Name the three most important wool-producing areas in 1750.
5. How were some domestic workers swindled by clothiers?
6. What is 'carding'?
7. Explain the difference between spinning and weaving.
8. Why did the wool industry decline in the early nineteenth century?
9. Name South Lancashire's chief port.
10. Which range of hills provided South Lancashire with plenty of fast-flowing streams?
11. When did Richard Arkwright build an important cotton mill at Cromford?
12. Name the weaving device invented by John Kay in 1733.
13. Who invented the first roller-spinning machine?
14. What was the importance of the spinning-jenny?
15. How did the spinning-mule get its name?
16. Why did many Lancashire mills close down between 1861 and 1865?
17. Where was a Cotton Corporation set up in 1929?
18. What are synthetic fibres?
19. Why is the British woollen industry of the 1980s in better shape than the cotton industry?
20. What was an adit mine?
21. Give three reasons why there was an increase in demand for coal in the eighteenth century.
22. Name the most important coal-mining area in 1750.
23. What were 'keels' and 'colliers'?
24. Name one explosive gas found in eighteenth-century coal-mines.
25. Why were canaries taken down coal-mines in the 1790s?
26. Who were the 'Bevin boys'?
27. Why was so little iron produced in Britain in 1700?
28. Where was the world's first iron bridge built?
29. What type of furnace was used for puddling iron?
30. Who invented (i) the hot blast? (ii) the steam hammer?
31. With which invention do you associate Henry Bessemer?
32. Why did steel-producers prefer to use Siemens' 'open hearth' rather than the Bessemer process?
33. What are tariffs?
34. What was the main source of power for machinery before 1750?
35. Why did Watt decide to improve the design of the Newcomen engine?
36. Write down *three* improvements Watt made to the Newcomen engine.
37. What was the name of Wedgwood's famous cream-coloured china?
38. Who developed the use of chlorine as a bleaching process?
39. What do the initials I.C.I. stand for?
40. Who invented the micrometer?
41. Name Britain's four main shipbuilding centres in the 1870s.
42. Why was a Great Exhibition held in Hyde Park in 1851?
43. When was the 'Great Depression'?
44. Name Britain's four basic industries in 1900.
45. Name the Cornish inventor who first used coal-gas to light his home in Redruth.
46. Who invented the steam turbine in 1884?

47. What is the National Grid?
48. Write down the names of three 'new' industries which have grown up in Britain over the past 40 years.
49. What are the 'service industries'?
50. Explain what is meant by the phrase *laissez-faire*.

5 Working-class Movements

Examination Guide

The topic of working-class movements tends to be popular with examiners and unpopular with many students. Perhaps this reflects an interest on the part of examiners in labour relations and working-class movements. Pupils, on the other hand, often find the trade union topic rather daunting.

A good starting point for your revision is to revise trade unions, using columns like those below. Some pupils find it easier to cope with revision when they can see exactly what each section of a topic involves. Try filling in the three remaining columns when you have read through the chapter. Questions on trade unions will be set within the date boundaries mentioned in your syllabus. The SEG syllabus, for example, requires candidates to have covered trade unions from 1866 to 1914. Check these dates carefully. You can see that you would be wasting your time learning about the Combination Acts for SEG!

Trade clubs	Combination Acts, 1799–1800	N.A.P.L.	G.N.C.T.U.
Mainly skilled workers			
Met in pubs			
Subscriptions			
Social benefits			
Legal in 1793			

There is a tendency for questions on the nineteenth-century unions to be descriptive ('Describe the main developments and changes in trade unionism between 1868 and 1914'), or descriptive and explanatory ('Describe and explain the reasons for the collapse of large trade unions in the 1830s and 1840s').

The different requirements of different boards are analysed below.

(a) Northern Examining Association

Theme 3 is called 'Responses to Industrialisation'. In Paper 2 candidates have to answer a question on either (1) or (2) (below):

1. Trade unions
   (i) New model unions and the emergence of the T.U.C.
   (ii) New unionism
   (iii) Trade unions and the law, 1871–1927
   (iv) The General Strike
   (v) The changing nature of trade unions from 1970

2. Political representation
   (i) Chartism
   (ii) The rise of the Labour Party to 1923
   (iii) The extension of the franchise, 1867–1928

It is probably easier for you to score high marks on topics 1 (i), (ii) and (iv) and 2 (i) than on the others, but this is really a matter of personal interest and taste.

Questions on Chartism may consist of structured questions based on a picture or document. You may be asked to explain the growth and decline of Chartism and the long-term impact of the movement on politics. Make sure you know the six points on the charter and *why* the Chartists wanted them to become law. You should also be aware that recent research has suggested that O'Connor was a competent leader of the movement and not the arrogant demagogue portrayed in some history books. It is also important to remember that few contemporary accounts of Chartism were written by the Chartists themselves. Can you think why?

Questions on 1 (ii) and (iii) may be based on documents. It is likely that the language level will be quite difficult here. You may come across legal terms you do not understand. It is also difficult to remember the terms of all the Acts passed between 1871 and 1927 (e.g. was 'peaceful picketing' legal in 1871 or not?). Only attempt questions on 1 (iii) if you have carried out a detailed study of this period.

(b) London and East Anglian Board

Schemes A, B and C all contain topics on trade unions. Scheme A covers 'Working-class movements, 1760–1870'; Scheme B, 'Labour in the economy since 1870'; and Scheme C, 'Working-class movements, 1760–1870' and 'Labour in the economy and society since 1870'. Paper 1 will contain short-answer questions and structured essay questions. Paper 2 will test your understanding of historical evidence relating to trade unions.

(c) Midland Examining Group

'Trade unions and working-class movements' is an optional topic in Paper 2. Most questions will be based on pieces of source material. Again there will probably be stimulus material on the Chartists, new model unions and the General Strike.

5.1 Introduction

In the Middle Ages many workers and employers set up guilds to protect the interests of their trades. In times of sickness or hardship workers could turn to these guilds for help. By the seventeenth century guilds were on the decline. Changes in trade, business organisation and the economy meant that the guilds no longer served any useful purpose. Instead workers set up *trade clubs*. You may have a pub near your home with a name such as The Jolly Porters or The Bricklayers Arms. The pub probably gets its name from the workers who met there. The clubs would help members who were sick or out of work. Such clubs might also negotiate hours and conditions of work, wages, prices and the numbers of apprentices. These trade clubs or 'friendly societies' were the forerunners of modern trade unions.

By the 1750s some of these trade clubs had become quite powerful. Groups such as the Hatters, the Sailmakers and the Weavers enrolled thousands of members. In theory trade clubs were illegal. In practice Parliament allowed them to continue. In 1793 *Rose's Act* gave trade clubs legal recognition for the first time. The Act allowed clubs to raise funds and hand out benefits. By 1799, however, Parliament's attitude had changed. M.P.s feared that the French Revolution (1789–1799) would spread to Britain. The British Government believed that the trade clubs were plotting the overthrow of the state. A group of London master millwrights persuaded Parliament to pass the *Combination Acts* making *combinations* (workers combining together) illegal.

5.2 The Combination Acts

The Acts (1799–1800) made it easier and quicker to prosecute workers who combined together to improve their conditions of work or pay. The Acts also stated that combinations of *employers* were illegal.

In practice the Combination Acts were difficult to enforce, although they led to the closing down of most trade clubs. Some trade clubs decided to meet secretly. Others broke up. In some parts of the country, unions carried on as before. In Lancashire two Bolton weavers were put in prison for setting up a trade club. There were strikes in Portsmouth in 1801, in Manchester in 1810 and in Scotland in 1812. In each case the organisers of the strikes were put in prison for up to two years. In 1810 print workers on *The Times* were put on trial and sent to prison. The millwrights, on the other hand, carried on with their union activities. They obtained a minimum wage and shorter working hours from their employers.

(a) The Repeal of the Combination Acts

In the 1820s the government changed its attitude towards trade clubs. Francis Place (1771–1854), a London tailor, launched a campaign against the Combination Acts. He organised meetings and wrote articles in newspapers pointing out that the Acts were bad for labour relations and for masters and workmen. He persuaded Joseph Hume, an M.P., to talk Parliament into setting up an enquiry into the Combination Acts. The witnesses who appeared before the enquiry convinced M.P.s that the Combination Acts should be scrapped. In 1824 Parliament repealed the Acts. Immediately afterwards there was a wave of strikes all over the country. In 1825 Parliament passed another Act. Workmen *could* form trade unions and bargain for better conditions, but they were not allowed to make threats against employers or fellow-workers. Trade unions were now legal, but there were many restrictions and regulations limiting their activities.

5.3 The N.A.P.L.

After the repeal of the Combination Acts, a number of large unions were formed. In 1829 John Doherty (1788–1854) formed a union of Lancashire cotton spinners, the *Grand General Union*. In 1830 Doherty started the National Association for the Protection of Labour (N.A.P.L.). Unions representing 20 different trades supported the N.A.P.L. and within a year Doherty claimed to have over a million members. The union published its own newspaper, *The Voice of the People*.

In 1832 the N.A.P.L. ran into trouble. John Hynes, the secretary, ran off with the union's funds and there were arguments among members representing different trades. The union fell apart in 1832.

5.4 Robert Owen and the G.N.C.T.U.

Robert Owen (1771–1858) was a cotton-mill owner from New Lanark, Scotland. Owen believed that it was his duty to look after his workers well. He provided good houses, schools and shops for his employees. At his cotton mill, spinners worked a shorter day and earned higher wages than in other factories. Owen believed that men and women would only be happy if they worked together (co-operation) rather than working against each other (competition). He also believed that contented workers would produce more goods and make greater profits. Owen's long-term aim was to change the whole nature of society. To this end he set up a huge union in 1834, the Grand National Consolidated Trades Union (G.N.C.T.U.). In a few months the G.N.C.T.U. had 500 000 members. Groups of miners, bakers, tailors and gas workers joined the union.

The growth of the G.N.C.T.U. worried the government and many employers. They believed that the union wanted revolutionary change. Some employers forced workers to sign 'the document', which stated that an employee was not a member of a union. Other employers refused to let union members into work — a *lock-out*. The worst lock-out was in Derby in 1833, where 1500 members of the G.N.C.T.U. had refused to sign 'the document'. The G.N.C.T.U. tried to support its members, but union funds soon ran out. The employees had to return to work on the employers' terms. In 1834 six Dorset labourers, the 'Tolpuddle Martyrs', were transported to Australia for trying to form a branch of the G.N.C.T.U. This was a further blow to Owen's union. By

August 1834 the G.N.C.T.U. had collapsed. The reasons for its failure are as follows:

- The Tolpuddle case put many men off the idea of joining the G.N.C.T.U.
- The union relied upon subscriptions from unskilled workers whose wages were not very high, so the G.N.C.T.U. soon ran short of money.
- 'The document' (see above).
- The G.N.C.T.U. was poorly organised.
- Many members were more interested in local issues than national ones.
- The G.N.C.T.U. was too big to succeed.
- Unemployment was on the increase and workers therefore found themselves in a weak negotiating position.

5.5 Chartism (1837–1848)

After the collapse of the G.N.C.T.U. (see above) many workers left their unions. During the 1830s a new movement, Chartism, sprang up. The movement got its name from the *People's Charter*, which contained six points:

- Manhood suffrage (all males having the vote).
- Annual Parliaments.
- Voting by secret ballot.
- Equal electoral districts.
- Payment of M.P.s.
- The abolition of property qualifications for M.P.s (so that anyone could be elected).

There were four reasons for these demands:

1. In the 1830s bad harvests and high food prices led to much distress. People believed that they could improve social conditions by getting the vote.
2. The Poor Law Amendment Act (1834) (see Section 8.5) had made poverty worse in some parts of the country.
3. Ordinary people believed that the 1832 Reform Act had done nothing for them. Under the terms of the Act very few working-class males had the vote.
4. There was a genuine desire to obtain equal voting rights for all adult males.

There were four main Chartist leaders. *William Lovett, Francis Place* and *Thomas Attwood* believed that Chartists should use peaceful means to achieve their goals. *Feargus O'Connor* believed that in the last resort the Chartists might have to use violence.

There were three phases of the movement.

1. *1836–1840* In 1836 William Lovett, a London cabinet-maker, set up the London Working Men's Association (L.W.M.A.). Lovett and Place drew up the charter containing the six points (see above). A year later, Feargus O'Connor, an Irish journalist, founded *The Northern Star*, a Chartist newspaper. The two groups joined together in 1838. In 1839 the first Chartist petition was presented to Parliament. It contained 1 280 000 signatures. Parliament rejected it by 235 votes to 46. In the

same year there was a Chartist rising in Wales. This fizzled out almost before it had begun. By 1840 there was an improvement in trade and living standards and Chartist activity died down.

2. *1842* In 1842 there was another industrial depression. The Chartists presented a second petition to Parliament, containing over three million signatures. It was rejected by 287 votes to 49. There were strikes and riots in Scotland, Wales, Yorkshire and the Midlands. In Lancashire Chartists removed the plugs from the boilers of steam engines as a form of protest (the 'Plug Plots'). The government sent troops to all the trouble spots and many Chartist leaders were put in prison.

3. In 1848 there was yet another industrial depression. A third Chartist petition was presented to Parliament. The Chartists claimed that it contained over five million signatures. Feargus O'Connor took the petition to the House of Commons after a mass meeting on Kennington Common. A Select Committee examined the petition. They found that fewer than two million people had signed the petition and that many of the signatures were forgeries. The petition was rejected by 222 votes to 17 and Chartism was laughed out of existence.

The reasons for the failure of Chartism were:

- A revival in trade began in 1848 and continued throughout the 1850s. Britain became 'the workshop of the world'. There were more jobs and higher wages. Working men rejoined their trade unions (see Section 5.7).
- The Chartist leaders were too ambitious in their aims and failed to attract middle-class support.
- The government used police and troops to prevent Chartist meetings getting out of hand.
- Other movements were more popular and effective — for example, the Ten Hours Movement, the Anti-Corn Law League and the Co-operative Movement (see Section 5.6).
- The Chartists were often short of money.

However, since 1848 five of the six points on the charter have become law:

- Reform Acts in 1867, 1884 and 1918 gave more adult males the vote.
- In 1872 the Ballot Act introduced secret voting.
- In 1911 M.P.s received payment for their work.
- In 1867 and 1884 a redistribution of parliamentary seats led to electoral districts of equal sizes.
- In 1874 Parliament abolished the property qualification for M.P.s.

In the short term, therefore, Chartism failed. In the longer term, the movement was more successful.

SPECIMEN QUESTIONS: CHARTISM

1. You can expect structured questions requiring an essay-type response here — for example:
   (a) Write down the six points on the charter; then explain *why* the Chartists wanted the six points made law.
   (b) What sort of tactics did the Chartists use to promote their cause?

(c) Would you say that the Chartists were successful or unsuccessful in the long term?
2. It is 1848 and the third Chartist petition has just been rejected. Write two letters to *The Times* newspaper; *one* from an M.P. who supported the petition and *one* from an M.P. who voted against it. In your answer you should mention:

the reasons for the revival of Chartism in 1848; Feargus O'Connor; the meeting on Kennington Common; the bogus names on the petition; why Chartism fizzled out in 1848.

5.6 The Co-operative Movement

Robert Owen (see Section 5.4) set up a co-operative shop at New Lanark in 1813. The shop sold high-quality goods at fair prices. From 1815 many workers set up *co-operative societies* (groups of co-operative businesses). Shopkeepers bought goods at wholesale (cost) prices and resold to members of the public for less than the retail price. Members received a share of the profits made by the society. By 1832 there were 500 co-operative societies. However, none of these survived for more than two or three years.

In 1844, 28 Lancashire flannel-weavers set up the Rochdale Society of Equitable Pioneers. They each put £1 into a fund. With this money they rented a store in Toad Lane, Rochdale. They bought good-quality food and clothing from local merchants. They then sold the goods at fair prices. The shop soon made a profit, which was handed back to the shoppers in proportion to the amount of money they had spent in the shop. This share-out of profits is known as a *dividend*.

Many other unions and groups of workers followed the example of the 'Rochdale Pioneers'. The co-operative movement grew rapidly, as the statistics in Table 5.1 show.

Table 5.1

Date	Members	Funds	Profits	Business done
1844	28	£28	–	–
1845	74	£181	£22	£710
1848	149	£397	£117	£2 276
1851	630	£2 785	£990	£17 633
1854	900	£7 172	£1 763	£33 264
1857	1 850	£15 142	£5 470	£79 789
1860	3 450	£37 710	£15 906	£150 063

In 1864 the Co-operative Wholesale Society was set up and the movement started to make its own products. By 1970 the co-operative movement controlled 8 per cent of Britain's retail trade.

The importance of the movement is shown by the following points:

- The movement helped to improve the standard of living of working people. The shops sold pure food at reasonable prices.
- The shops led to the end of the truck system, in which employers sold their workers poor-quality goods.

- The movement gave ordinary people the chance to run their own businesses.
- The societies provided education for poor people and encouraged workers to save.
- The co-ops gave working men the chance to stand for Parliament.

5.7 The New Model Unions

During the 1850s and 1860s the British economy was expanding. The growth of the railway system created jobs in many industries. Skilled men could earn high wages in the iron, steel and engineering industries. Between 1850 and 1870 a new type of trade union emerged. These unions were more like the old friendly societies (see Section 5.1) than the N.A.P.L. or G.N.C.T.U. These new unions became known as *new model unions*.

The leaders of the new model unions did not want to change the whole of society. Their main aim was simply to protect the interests of their own members. Groups of joiners, boiler-makers, carpenters, bricklayers and shoe-makers made up the new unions. They were skilled men who could afford to pay high subscriptions (union fees) to their unions.

The most famous of the early new model unions was the Amalgamated Society of Engineers (A.S.E.). This union was an amalgamation (joining up) of many smaller craft unions. William Allen, the General Secretary of the A.S.E., believed that industrial disputes could be settled without strikes or disagreements. He would only support strikes which stood a good chance of success. Unlike the G.N.C.T.U., the A.S.E. was well organised. The union had an elected executive council which made major decisions and a staff of salaried clerks.

Other new model unions followed the example set by the A.S.E. Robert Applegarth founded the Amalgamated Society of Carpenters and Joiners (A.S.C.J.); Daniel Guile, the National Association of Ironfounders (N.A.I.); Edwin Colson, the Bricklayers Union; and George Odger, the Boot and Shoe Workers' Union. These trade union leaders became skilled negotiators. They earned the respect of their members and of the public at large.

5.8 The Trades Union Congress

Many of the leaders of the new model unions living in London used to meet at the Old Bell Inn in Newgate to discuss policy and compare notes. Opponents of this group called them 'The Dirty Pack' but supporters of trade unions called them 'The Junta'. In 1860 members of the Junta formed the London Trades Council. Eight years later the first Trades Union Congress was held in Manchester. The Junta did not send delegates to the Congress, because they were suspicious of the other unions. However, most unions and the Junta attended the third T.U.C. meeting, held in London in 1871.

5.9 Trade Unions, 1866–1875

(a) The Sheffield Outrages (1866)

A group of cutlers tried to force 'blacklegs' (non-union men) to join their union. The cutlers damaged the blacklegs' tools and dropped a can of gunpowder down the chimney of a 'blackleg' saw-grinder. No one was hurt but the house was blown to pieces! These activities led to a wave of anti-union feeling.

(b) The Second Reform Act, 1867

This gave skilled workers in towns the right to vote. The Act led to a great increase in trade union power. More union members could elect M.P.s sympathetic to their cause.

(c) Hornby v. Close (1867)

The Bradford branch treasurer of the Boilermakers' Society stole £24 from union funds. The Boilermakers' Society took the treasurer to court. The judge ruled that union funds were not protected by law. He argued that the union money *might* be used for illegal purposes. This was a serious blow to the unions. If their money disappeared, it would be almost impossible to get it back!

(d) Royal Commission of 1867

Parliament set up a Commission (an enquiry) to look into trade union activities. The unions came out well from the enquiry. The Commission reported that most union leaders were responsible men. The government passed two new laws based on the Commission's findings (see e and f below).

(e) Trade Union Act (1871)

The Act stated that a union's funds could be protected by law from dishonest officials. It also allowed unions to register as friendly societies, and enabled them to invest in property and bring court actions.

(f) Criminal Law Amendment Act (1871)

Peaceful picketing and intimidation (threatening non-union members) were made illegal.

(g) Conspiracy and Protection of Property Act (1875)

The Criminal Law Amendment Act (see above) was repealed. Peaceful picketing was now legal.

5.10 Joseph Arch and the N.A.L.U. (see also Section 3.12)

In the 1860s farm workers in many parts of the country worked long hours for low rates of pay. They often lived in squalid conditions. In 1872 Joseph Arch, a Warwickshire farm worker, started a National Agricultural Labourers Union (N.A.L.U.). Within a year there were 100 000 members. The union organised a successful strike for higher wages. For two years the farm workers campaigned for better living and working conditions. In 1874, however, farmers and landowners hit back at the union with a lock-out. They sacked union members and evicted them from their cottages. In 1876 there was a slump in agriculture and wages fell back to their old levels. The union was unable to support members who were on strike, and by 1880 membership had dwindled to 20 000. The N.A.L.U. increased its membership in the 1880s, but the 1890s was a decade of great hardship and by 1896 the union had collapsed altogether. However, interest in the union revived in the early twentieth century, and today many farm workers are members of the National Union of Agricultural and Allied Workers.

5.11 Unions for Unskilled Workers

In the 1880s a new type of union emerged. The 'new model' unions (see Section 5.7) had been for skilled men earning high wages. By 1888 a number of unskilled workers' unions had grown up in London. Three important strikes took place at this time.

(a) The Match Girls' Strike

In 1888 match girls working for Bryant and May formed a union to demand better pay and conditions. The girls worked under appalling conditions for as little as 40p a week. They often contracted 'phossy jaw' (a form of gangrene) from the phosphorus used to make the matches. A journalist, Annie Besant, took up their cause and wrote newspaper articles describing their plight. Seven hundred girls went on strike in 1888. Within two weeks all the girls' demands had been met. Bryant and May were obliged to increase wages and improve conditions.

(b) The Gas Workers' Strike

In 1889 Will Thorne, a tough labourer from Birmingham, organised his fellow-workers into a National Union of Gasworkers and General Labourers. The union demanded an eight-hour day instead of a twelve-hour one. Rather than face a long strike, the employers gave way to this demand. Will Thorne later became M.P. for West Ham.

(c) The London Dock Strike

One of the men who had set up the Gasworkers' Union (see above) was Ben Tillett, a dock worker. In 1889 Tillett organised a Tea Workers and General Labourers Union. The London dockers worked anti-social hours for low rates of pay. Sometimes they were taken on for short periods and then laid off. Tillett, assisted by Tom Mann and John Burns, organised a strike. The Union demanded that no docker should be taken on for less than four hours and that wages should be 6d. an hour, with 8d. an hour for overtime.

For nearly four weeks the strikers paralysed the port of London. The dockers seemed to have a good case and many members of the public supported them. At one point it seemed as though the strike would collapse because of shortage of money, but Australian trade unions saved the day with an unexpected gift of £30 000. After five weeks the employers gave in. The dockers got their sixpence an hour (the 'dockers' tanner'). They set up a new union, The Dock, Wharf, Riverside and General Labourers Union, which soon had 30 000 members.

Following the success of these three strikes, other unskilled and semi-skilled workers formed unions. From 1892 to 1900 membership rose from 1 500 000 to 2 000 000.

5.12 Keir Hardie and the Rise of the Labour Party

By the 1880s some trade union members believed that the union movement needed to campaign for political power. They believed that only through state action could the poor hope to improve their standard of living. There were few M.P.s willing to put this message across in Parliament.

In 1887 Keir Hardie, a Scottish miner, asked the T.U.C. to support working-class candidates standing for Parliament. The T.U.C. threw out the idea. In 1889 Scottish workers formed their own Independent Labour Party. Three years later this movement had spread to England. Four working-class M.P.s, including John Burns and Keir Hardie, were elected to Parliament. From 1900 to 1906 Hardie helped to build the *Labour Party* out of various socialist (left-wing) groups and trade unionists. The modern Labour Party, therefore, has its roots firmly embedded in the growth of trade unionism.

5.13 Some Important Legal Decisions, 1901–1913

(a) The Taff Vale Judgement (1901)

In 1901 a strike took place on the Taff Vale Railway in South Wales. The Taff Vale Railway Company lost money as a result of the strike. The company sued the railwaymen's union, the Amalgamated Society of Railway Servants (A.S.R.S.) for damages. The case went to the House of Lords and the courts found the A.S.R.S. liable for damages. The union had to pay the railway company £23 000 in compensation.

The Taff Vale case was a major setback for the unions. Clearly no union would be able to call a strike if it was going to have to pay for employers' losses.

(b) Trades Disputes Act (1906)

The newly elected Liberal government of 1906 took steps to reverse the Taff Vale decision. The Act stated that '. . . no civil action shall be entertained against a trade union in respect of any wrongful action, committed by, or on behalf of, the union'. The Act meant that trade union funds could not be used to pay damages and that a union member could not be sued for breach of contract in respect of a strike. The Act became known as 'The Charter of Trade Unionism'.

117

(c) The Osborne Judgement (1909)

W. V. Osborne, a branch secretary of the A.S.R.S., was a member of the Liberal Party. He objected to the system whereby a part of his union subscription was handed over to the Labour Party. These subscriptions provided a large part of Labour Party funds. Osborne took his case to court. After lengthy legal proceedings the House of Lords decided in favour of Osborne. In future no part of trade union funds was to be handed over to any political party. This ruling was a serious threat to the existence of the Labour Party.

(d) Trade Union Act (1913)

The Act stated that trade unions could use their funds to support a political party so long as a majority of union members supported the idea. Members who did not support their union's politics were to be free to 'contract out' (they did not have to pay the part of the *union* subscription used for supporting the political party).

5.14 Unions during the First World War (1914–1918)

During the war the unions gained many members. There were many workers earning high wages in armaments factories. The T.U.C. declared a ban on all official strikes. Most trade unionists supported the war effort, and thousands of union members volunteered to serve in the armed forces.

The mines, shipyards and railways were brought under state control. The government introduced a special tax on firms making money out of the war. Strikes became illegal. Women and unskilled labourers were brought in to replace skilled men who were doing other war work.

In 1917 the truce between the T.U.C. and the government began to wear thin. Prices doubled, wages fell and many trade unionists began to question the way in which the war was being run. When peace came in 1918, relations between the T.U.C. and the employers looked hopeful. There were six reasons for this:

1. During the war workers and managers had co-operated together successfully.
2. Neither the T.U.C. nor the employers wished to return to the bitter class struggles of the 1890s.
3. The government set up a Ministry of Labour. The T.U.C. believed that this showed that the government wished to take an active part in settling trade disputes.
4. There had been national agreements on pay and conditions during the war.
5. Nationalisation (state control) of the mines, railways and shipyards led workers to believe that the government was interested in supporting essential services.
6. Collective bargaining (unions negotiating with employers over pay and conditions) had become more common during the war. The government set up councils of management and labour, and these organisations made negotiations flow more smoothly.

5.15 1919–1925

By 1919 trade union membership had increased to over eight million. Before long the hopes of good relations between workers and employers (see Section 5.14) were shattered. High inflation (money losing its value) had led to demands for big pay increases. Many workers demanded sweeping political changes, such as nationalisation and a greater degree of workers' control.

The government, however, was determined to restore the control of industry to private ownership. It decided to return mines, railways and shipyards to private employers. The unions knew that this would mean an end to nationally agreed settlements. They also feared that return to private ownership might lead to cuts in wages. To strengthen their hand, the miners, the railwaymen and the transport workers formed a 'Triple Alliance' in 1919. The unions agreed to take joint action against the employers if any single union felt under threat.

In 1921 wage negotiations between the miners and the employers broke down. The miners came out on strike on 15 April but the other members of the Triple Alliance refused to support them. The humiliation of the miners became known as 'Black Friday'. The miners' strike dragged on for a few weeks, but the men eventually returned to work on 1 July 1921, having gained very little.

The mine owners proposed further wage cuts in 1925. The Miners' Federation argued that it was 'stripped to the bone' and that its members could not accept a lower standard of living. This time the Triple Alliance stood firm. The Prime Minister, Stanley Baldwin, realised that the only way to avoid a nationwide strike was for the government to *subsidise* (make up) miners' wages to their previous level. On 31 July the government offered the Miners' Federation a state subsidy of £24 million. The money was to be used to offset the mine owners' wage cuts. The Triple Alliance called this success 'Red Friday'. However, both the unions and the government realised that there was bound to be trouble as soon as the subsidy was withdrawn.

5.16 The General Strike (1926)

In 1926 a Royal Commission reported that the coal industry should be reorganised, that wages should be cut and that working hours should be made longer. The mine owners and the government accepted the findings of the report. The miners' leaders rejected it because they could not accept the idea of cuts in pay. A. J. Cooke, the Miners' General Secretary, coined the slogan 'Not a penny off the pay, not a minute on the day!'

The government set up an Organisation for the Maintenance of Supplies (O.M.S.) in preparation for a *general strike* (a strike supported by all the unions). The O.M.S. asked for volunteers who would be willing to keep services running in the event of a general strike. Many of the volunteers were middle-class young men. Union members poured scorn on the idea of a bunch of middle-class volunteers running the country during a strike. The unions themselves made few detailed plans for a long, drawn-out strike.

In April 1926 talks were arranged between the T.U.C. and the government in the hope of settling the miners' dispute. The talks broke down when some printers who were working for the *Daily Mail* refused to print an article attacking the trade unions. When government ministers heard about the printers' action, they broke off negotiations with the T.U.C., claiming that union leaders were trying to muzzle the press. At midnight on 3 May the T.U.C. called a general strike.

On the first day of the strike most of Britain's transport system ground to a halt. The government brought in O.M.S. volunteers to get people to work and to transport food to places where it was needed. Troops and police protected the O.M.S. volunteers from angry strikers. There were some clashes between strikers and O.M.S. volunteers, but on the whole the strike was a good-humoured affair. At Plymouth police played strikers at football. The strikers won 2–1!

The government printed its own newspaper, *The British Gazette*. The paper was used to publish propaganda against the T.U.C. and the miners. The T.U.C. responded with *The British Worker*, which put across the unions' point of view.

After nine days, the strike was called off. The T.U.C. leaders announced that they had been 'given assurances that a settlement of the mining problem could be reached'. However, the miners were dismayed to find that the government and the mine owners had made very vague promises to the T.U.C. The miners were left to fight on alone for another six months. They returned to work only when their families were starving.

There were six main consequences of the General Strike:

1. Some coal-mining areas never recovered from the strike. Many pits were closed. Two hundred thousand miners lost their jobs.
2. In 1927 the government passed a Trade Disputes Act which made general strikes and sympathetic strikes illegal.
3. The unions ran short of money. The General Strike had cost them £4 million.
4. Half a million workers left their unions, either because they felt that they had been let down by the T.U.C. or because they had lost their jobs.
5. During the strike Britain lost some of its overseas markets.
6. Trade unions became unpopular with the general public.

5.17 The Depression

In 1928 prices and wages all over the world began to fall. There was a major economic crisis in America when the Wall Street stock market collapsed and thousands of investors were ruined. Over the next two years trade slumps and high unemployment spread throughout Western Europe. Britain did not escape from the economic crisis. Thousands of workers lost their jobs in the early 1930s, as the figures in Table 5.2 show.

The trade union movement supported the ideas put forward by J. M. Keynes, an economist. He believed that a huge increase in state spending would solve the

Table 5.2 Total numbers of registered unemployed in Great Britain, 1927–1940 (thousands)

Year	Number	Year	Number
1927	1088	1934	2159
1928	1217	1935	2036
1929	1216	1936	1755
1930	1917	1937	1484
1931	2630	1938	1791
1932	2745	1939	1514
1933	2521	1940	963

problem of high unemployment. The trade unions also supported the idea of *nationalisation* (state ownership) of the steel, cotton and coal industries. In these 'old' industries unemployment levels were very high. However, many workers found jobs in the 'new' industries, such as chemicals, motor vehicles and electrical engineering. There were also more workers employed in *service* industries, such as insurance, entertainment and distribution.

From 1935 onwards the British economy began to recover. Hitler's rise to power in Germany led to massive rearmament and created thousands of jobs in the arms industries. Many workers rejoined their unions. Under the influence of Ernest Bevin, the highly respected leader of the Transport and General Workers Union, the unions tried to establish better relations with the government. In 1936 the government reorganised the cotton industry. Ministers asked the union leaders for their help and advice. As the threat of war with Nazi Germany loomed closer, the government consulted the T.U.C. about keeping certain key workers in industry in the event of war. Once again the unions and the government seemed to be in the process of forging a working partnership.

5.18   The Second World War (1939–1945)

During the Second World War the trade union movement co-operated more closely with the government than ever before. In May 1940 Winston Churchill formed a coalition government (a government made up of all three parties). Several leading members of the Labour Party became ministers. Ernest Bevin (see Section 5.17) became Minister of Labour.

The coalition government followed a policy of 'war socialism'. The state took over the running of important industries. There was strict rationing of clothes, food and petrol. Anyone could be called up into the armed forces or into industry. The government made wealthy people pay higher taxes, and manufacturers of weapons had to contribute a share of their profits to the war effort. Workers on low incomes, such as miners, farm labourers and dockers, had their wages increased.

The T.U.C. wanted these policies to continue after the war. Union leaders supported the Labour Party's plans for nationalisation of key industries, full employment and a fairer distribution of the nation's wealth. There were plans for a Welfare State (see Section 8.9) with a free National Health Service and increased social security payments.

Before the end of the war, in 1945, there was a general election. Winston Churchill had become a national hero during the war but people did not want a return to the unsuccessful Conservative economic policies of the 1930s. The election resulted in a huge parliamentary majority for the Labour Party.

5.19   1945–1960

The newly elected Labour government, led by Clement Attlee, quickly repealed the 1927 Trade Disputes Act (see below). The government went on to pass a series of Acts designed to set up a number of state-run industries. The most important of these Acts are listed below.

- *Trade Disputes Act (1943)* Picketing and 'sympathetic' strikes were now legal. Union members who did not wish to donate money to a political party could 'contract out'.

- *Coal Industry Nationalisation Act* (*1946*) National Coal Board set up to run mines.
- *National Insurance Act* (*1946*) Compulsory insurance for all workers.
- *Civil Aviation Act* (*1947*) Two publicly owned firms, BOAC and BEA, were set up to run Britain's air transport industry.
- *Transport Act* (*1947*) Nationalisation of railways, harbours, canals, road haulage services. The nationalisation programme disappointed some trade unionists. The new managers of the nationalised industries were not always sympathetic towards their workers' political views. Despite these disappointments, many workers still felt they were better off working for the state than for private firms.

The increase in union power after the war was not welcomed by everybody. Some people believed that the union movement was too large, cumbersome and old-fashioned. David Low, a famous cartoonist, drew pictures portraying the unions as a lumbering carthorse (see source-based question below). Low believed that the whole trade union movement lacked direction. How could the T.U.C. pretend to speak for all the unions when powerful groups such as the T.G.W.U. and the A.U.E.W. often acted on their own? Some unions were so powerful that they introduced the principle of the 'closed shop'. This meant that no one except a trade union member could be employed in that 'shop' or place of work. These practices gave the whole union movement a bad name.

In 1948 the trade unions fell out with Attlee's government over pay restraint. Attlee had called for a period of low pay increases so that the government could pay for social welfare schemes. But as prices increased, many workers demanded large pay increases. It became clear that some groups of workers were asking for more money in wages than they were earning in output.

The problem of high wage demands dogged British industry throughout the 1950s and 1960s. To create jobs, to feed people and to improve the standard of living, Britain had to sell more goods abroad. This meant that goods had to be produced cheaply at home to compete with overseas markets. Both Labour and Conservative governments tried to persuade unions not to make high wage demands. These appeals fell on deaf ears. Higher wages led to higher prices and *inflation* (money losing its value). Some politicians came to the conclusion that it might be necessary to *legislate* (pass laws) to force the unions to change their ways.

SOURCE-BASED QUESTION: TRADE UNIONS AFTER THE SECOND WORLD WAR

Source A

In 1945 the union movement had won the power it had so long fought for but it showed many signs of ill-health. It was large and cumbersome, set in its ways and old-fashioned in outlook. It was often portrayed as a lumbering cart-horse, sturdy and reliable but sadly out of date and not very efficient. The movement lacked effective central guidance. The T.U.C. could not easily speak for unions as a whole when its most powerful members, such as the Transport Workers (T.G.W.U.) and Engineers (A.U.E.W.) often preferred to act on their own. The General Council represented the older manual unions rather than the newer unions with growing membership.

(*The British Trade Unions*, Elizabeth Gard, 1983)

Source B

The Transport and General Workers, with its enormous membership, was especially vulnerable to agitation directed against its official policies. Among the dockers in particular there had been a serious revolt in the form of an unofficial strike in 1945; and a 'National Port Workers' Defence Committee' was set up to represent the unofficial movement. This committee, which had a number of Communist members, was involved in fresh strikes in 1948, 1949, and 1950.

(*A History of British Trade Unionism*, Henry Pelling, 1963)

Source C

Trade union membership and trade disputes, 1940–1950 (thousands)

Year	Total number of unions	Total number of union members (*thousands*)	Working days lost each year (*thousands*)
1940	1004	6613	940
1941	996	7165	1080
1942	991	7867	1527
1943	987	8174	1808
1944	963	8087	3714
1945	781	7875	2835
1946	757	8803	2158
1947	734	9145	2433
1948	735	9319	1944
1949	726	9274	1807

(Source: *A History of British Trade Unionism*, Henry Pelling, 1963)

Source D

"NOW, ARTHUR, YOU KNOW WHAT TO DO"
"YES, BUT DOES THE HORSE KNOW?"

MARGATE OLYMPICS

1. In source A, what do the initials T.G.W.U. and A.U.E.W. stand for?
2. Calculate the percentage increase in
   (i) union members
   (ii) working days lost each year between 1940 and 1949 (source C).
3. What is the correct chronological [date] sequence of sources A–E?
4. (i) Which two sentences in source A confirm what is suggested by sources D and E?
   (ii) How does source C contradict what is suggested by source E?
   (iii) How does source B confirm what is suggested in source E?
5. Which of the sources A–E would you say is *least* coloured by personal opinion? Give reasons for your choice.
6. How have public attitudes towards trade unions changed since 1945?
7. If you were asked to write a history of the trade union movement between 1945 and 1950, what other sources of information would you want to look at?

5.20   Trade Unions Today

Relations between the unions and successive governments since 1960 have often been strained. During the 1960s improvements in the economy led to many people in Britain becoming better off. Unions demanded higher wage increases for their members. Workers elected strong-willed union leaders to put their case for higher wages. There were many strikes.

Both Labour and Conservative governments introduced measures to try to control high wage demands. In 1962 the Conservatives set up a National Incomes Council to control prices and wages. The T.U.C. refused to co-operate with this. In 1964 a Labour government passed a Prices and Incomes Act. This aimed to restrict wage increases by force of law. Five years later the Labour Prime Minister, Harold Wilson, presented a plan called 'In Place of Strife', designed to restrict *unofficial* strikes (strikes which do not have the backing of a union). Most trade unionists opposed this plan. After months of argument Wilson agreed to scrap 'In Place of Strife' on condition that the T.U.C. took measures of its own to stop unofficial strikes.

In 1970 the Conservatives won a general election. A year later the government passed an *Industrial Relations Act*. The Act set up a new Industrial Relations Court which had the power to send strike leaders to prison. The Act met with a great deal of opposition from trade unionists. The law had been designed to cut down the number of strikes but it had the opposite effect. In 1972, 24 million working days were lost, the highest number since the General Strike of 1926!

In 1974 the miners demanded a large pay increase. The government told the National Coal Board not to pay the increase. The miners came out on strike. Shortages of fuel resulted in industry working a 'three-day week'. Edward Heath, the Prime Minister, decided that the country was 'ungovernable' and called a general election. The Conservatives lost the election and Harold Wilson formed a Labour government. Later in 1974 Wilson came to a voluntary agreement with the unions, called the 'social contract'. Under the terms of the social contract the T.U.C. agreed to try to control wage demands. In return, the government agreed to scrap the Industrial Relations Act and to improve social conditions.

The social contract did not work well. In January and February 1979, 'the winter of discontent', the country suffered a series of strikes by hospital workers, local government workers, ambulancemen and teachers. Prime Minister James Callaghan was forced to call a general election. The Conservatives won the 1979 election and later passed three Acts designed to reduce the power of the unions:

- The *Employment Act* (*1980*) restricted picketing, gave legal protection to workers who opposed the closed shop (see Section 5.19) and provided money for unions to hold secret ballots.
- The *Employment Act* (*1982*) made it illegal to sack a worker for not belonging to the closed shop.
- The *Trade Union Act* (*1984*) made secret ballots compulsory and changed the rules affecting the election of union officials.

Between 1984 and 1985 a second miners' strike took place. This time the issue was not pay but pit closures. After a year on strike, the miners had to return to work. They had gained very little. Many people believed that the government had got its revenge for the election defeat of 1974.

SPECIMEN QUESTIONS: TRADE UNIONS

1. Show the importance of each of the following in the development of trade unions:
   (a) Robert Owen
   (b) Joseph Arch
   (c) The Match Girls' Strike
   (d) The Taff Vale Case
2. Write an account of *either* the Match Girls' Strike *or* the Dockers' Strike as if you were a working-class man or woman who supported the strike.

In your answer you could mention why the strike was called; what happened during the strike; the long-term consequences of the strike.

3. (a) Describe the different types of union which had emerged by 1890.
   (b) Why was it so difficult for unskilled workers to form unions?
   (c) How and why did the trade union movement put pressure on the government and the employers in the period 1900–1914?

ASSESSMENT OBJECTIVES: TRADE UNIONS

In the GCSE national criteria, assessment objective 4(b) refers to 'detecting bias' (deciding whether historical evidence has been written from a particular point of view).

Detecting bias is one of the most important skills on the GCSE History course. You can find bias in books, magazines, comics, TV programmes and newspapers. Knowing what bias is and being able to detect it is an invaluable skill which will help you pass your History examination and will be of value to you in later life.

What is bias? Some writers give their writing a particular slant — they want to present their writing in a particular way. They often want to influence their readers politically. It is possible to be biased against women (sexism) and black people (racialism).

In your own writing try to avoid bias. The study of history and historical evidence should help you to write *objectively*. Try to see both sides of any argument and to achieve balance in your writing.

It is difficult to avoid bias when writing about trade unions (can you detect any bias in this book?). The reason for this is that most people have *preconceived* ideas about the role of trade unions and either love them or hate them! A typical middle-class view of trade unions is that they are full of left-wing agitators who are hell-bent upon wrecking British industry. Many working-class people believe that unions have fought long and hard for social democracy, better working conditions, an improved standard of living and higher wages. They therefore feel that trade unions deserve their support. The truth about trade unions probably lies somewhere between these two extremes.

When writing history answers or essays, do bear in mind that the examiner or teacher marking your script may also have strong opinions about the events you are describing. If you give your writing — left-wing or right-wing — slant, the examiner may not agree with your views. He may not feel like awarding you many marks. Try to hedge your bets!

The passages below are extracts from history books about the General Strike. Read them through carefully and then attempt the questions below.

Source 1

In one way the failure of the General Strike strengthened the trade union movement. The idea of overthrowing the established order by the withdrawal of labour lost its hold on the rank and file. The more moderate aim was the only practicable one at a time of mass unemployment which coincided with a Labour Party weakened because of Macdonald's national government. The outbreak of war in 1939 saw co-operation between the unions' management and the government in the face of the common enemy.

(*The Age of Industrial Expansion*, A. J. Holland, 1968)

Source 2

The government and the employers won a complete victory. Many workmen were victimised for going on strike. They were given worse jobs or lower wages, had their pension rights cut or had to leave their unions. The strike cost the unions £4 000 000. Baldwin's government drove its victory home with the Trade Disputes Act of 1927. This struck a deliberate blow at the working-class political action. The whole episode left memories of defeat and betrayal in the minds of many working-class men.

(*British Economic and Social History 1700–1975*, C. P. Hill, 1977)

Source 3

The General Strike had failed: there could no longer be any serious fear of a 'red revolution' in this country. Unemployment continued and trade union membership declined. Although no one realised it at the time, 1926 was the end of an era. There were to be many strikes in the future — even a naval mutiny in 1931 — but there was never again to be a direct confrontation between capital and labour.

(*Economic and Social History of England 1770–1970*, R. B. Jones, 1971)

1 (a) In which source is there a reference to political events in Russia?
  (b) Which source provides the most optimistic view of the outcome of the General Strike?
2. (a) On which points do the three writers agree?
  (b) On which do they disagree?
  (c) How do you explain this?
3. (a) What bias can you detect in the three sources?
  (b) How do you explain the fact that one account seems more biased than the other two?
  (c) Which source would you describe as right-wing in tone? Which would you say is left-wing?
4. Can you find any words or phrases in the sources which a historian might look for if he wanted to find examples of bias?

WORK OUT SHORT-ANSWER QUESTIONS: TRADE UNIONS

1. Why were the Combination Acts passed in 1799 and 1800?
2. Name the two men who campaigned against the Combination Acts.
3. Why were the Tolpuddle Martyrs transported to Australia?
4. What was 'The Document'?
5. Name the four most important leaders of the Chartist movement.
6. When was the third Chartist petition presented to Parliament?
7. What were the 'Plug Plots'?
8. How many points on 'The People's Charter' have become law since 1848?
9. What do the initials C.W.S. stand for?
10. What was the main difference between the G.N.C.T.U. and a 'New Model' union such as the A.S.C.J.?
11. Name the first General Secretary of the A.S.E.
12. Who were the 'Dirty Pack' or the 'Junta'?
13. Why did the Sheffield Outrages (1866) give the unions a bad name?
14. Write down one of the terms of the Criminal Law Amendment Act of 1871.

15. Name the Warwickshire farm labourer who set up a National Agricultural Labourers Union.
16. Who were the 'match girls'?
17. What was the 'dockers' tanner'?
18. Why was the Taff Vale Judgement a setback for the unions?
19. Who was W.V. Osborne and why was he important?
20. What is meant by 'collective' bargaining'?
21. What were 'Black Friday' and 'Red Friday'?
22. Name the three different groups of workers who formed the Triple Alliance in 1919.
23. Name the General Secretary of the Miners Union in 1926.
24. How long did the General Strike last?
25. Who was responsible for printing *The British Gazette*?
26. What were the terms of the 1927 Trade Disputes Act?
27. Name three of Britain's 'old' industries which were in decline by the 1930s.
28. What is meant by 'nationalisation'?
29. Who was Minister of Labour during the Second World War?
30. Write down three key industries which were nationalised after the war.
31. Why did the trade union movement fall out with Attlee's government in 1948?
32. What is meant by 'inflation'?
33. Which Act did Parliament pass in 1962 designed to restrict high wage increases?
34. What is an unofficial strike?
35. Who produced a plan called 'In Place of Strife' in 1969?
36. When was the Industrial Relations Act passed?
37. What was the 'Three-day Week'?
38. Why did a miners' strike take place in 1974?
39. Which groups of workers took industrial action during the 'winter of discontent'?
40. Write down *two* of the Acts passed by Conservative governments, 1980–1984, which were supposed to cut down the power of the unions.

6 Social Change

Examination Guide

This is a popular topic. You can expect to find at least one question on some aspect of social change on your exam paper. All the main examining consortia refer to urbanisation (the growth of towns) and housing and working conditions on their syllabuses. Be prepared for questions which link up topics or sub-topics — for example, the Poor Law and public health, prisons and police, religion and the slave trade. You should know the terms of the Mines Act (1842), the Factory Acts and the most important Education Acts (see Section 6.4). If you have difficulty remembering the terms of each Act, try writing the main points down on a postcard. You can then test yourself on them whenever you have a free moment.

(a) Guide to Questions

Essay-type questions may vary a great deal. Do try to answer them in as much detail as possible. It is very easy to produce answers on housing and working conditions which say a lot about dirt, squalor, disease, rats and overcrowding but contain few credit-worthy facts. Avoid bland generalisations about housing and sanitation — for example, 'All nineteenth-century towns were riddled with disease and decay'. They weren't!

You can expect questions on *why* towns grew so quickly in the nineteenth century and *what* was done to improve housing conditions. Refer to the section on the Public Health Movement (7.8) for more information on this. Be prepared for evidence questions in the form of pictures, documents and statistics on housing and public health.

Questions on *education* normally cover the period 1750–1900. You need to know the terms of the Education Acts of 1870, 1902 and 1944 in detail. Examiners usually set fairly straightforward questions on education of the 'Describe and explain . . .' variety, and you can expect to see more questions on the education of the poor than on the education of rich people.

Police and prisons are interesting areas of study but relatively few exam questions are set on the 'law and order' topic. However, if you have been studying law and order as an optional topic, you can expect some short-answer questions on Mrs Fry, John Howard and Robert Peel.

It is rare to find essay-type questions which deal solely with *religion*. Again you will find references to religion in short-answer questions and/or structured essay-type questions.

Immigration is a crucially important area of study, and most boards are likely to set detailed questions on population movement (Why? When? Where? . . .).

6.1 Introduction

Historians and sociologists (people who study society) are always trying to find out more about the way society has changed over the past 200 years and what has caused these changes. This helps them to make more sense of the world we live in today.

Most social change in Britain has taken place as a result of:

- Economic change (the Industrial Revolution).
- Political ideas.
- The growth of towns.
- The increase of population.
- Improvements in the standard of education.

This chapter is intended to help you to understand the causes and effects of social change and the problems created by change.

6.2 Prisons

(a) Prisons in 1750

Before the nineteenth century prisons were not places of punishment where criminals served long sentences. Many of the prisoners were debtors, who stayed in prison until their debts were paid off. The remainder were people under arrest or awaiting whipping, hanging or transportation. Transportation meant being sent to America or Australia as a prisoner for a number of years.

In theory all prisons belonged to the Crown. In practice they were run by the County Sheriffs, town councils or private individuals. The governor of the prison was known as the gaoler and the warders were called turnkeys. The gaolers were not paid any wages, so they charged prisoners for food, drink, bedding and furniture.

Most prisons were damp, unhealthy places. A few were purpose-built but in a small town the prison might be in a castle, a gatehouse, a stable or a pub! Many prisons were in ruins and prisoners were often chained up to stop them escaping. There were no proper beds, no sewers and a primitive system of water supply. Disease was common and thousands of prisoners died of typhus or 'gaol fever', a disease spread by lice.

(b) John Howard (1726–1790)

John Howard, High Sheriff of Bedfordshire, made the first attempts to improve prison conditions. He toured the whole country, looking at one prison after another. He measured the height, width and breadth of cells with his tape measure, and weighed out prisoners' rations on a tiny pair of scales. He noted down every detail about how each prison was run, and refused to leave until he had inspected every part of it.

In 1777 he wrote a book called *The State of the Prisons*. Many people were shocked to read about the bad state of Britain's prisons. Howard carried on inspecting prisons until he died. Today the Howard League is a pressure group which campaigns for better prison conditions.

(c) Elizabeth Fry (1780–1845)

Elizabeth Fry, a Quaker, was a woman of strong religious beliefs. In 1813 she visited Newgate Prison and was shocked to see women prisoners shouting, swearing and fighting. From 1817 onwards she worked hard to improve conditions in prisons. She wanted less harsh discipline, better food and the abolition of cruel punishments. Above all, she wanted to see prisoners taught religion. Her aim was to *reform* people rather than *punish* them.

At Newgate she set up a school for the children of prisoners, arranged sewing classes and provided prisoners with books to read. She persuaded the governor to draw up a new set of rules for the prison. A Committee of Visitors was set up to make sure the rules were obeyed.

Mrs Fry travelled up and down the country, inspecting prisons, arguing in favour of reforms and pleading for better conditions. By 1823 she had persuaded the Home Secretary, Robert Peel, to carry out a number of reforms. Under Peel's *Gaol Act* gaolers were to be paid wages and not to charge fees; female prisoners were to have female turnkeys; and prisoners could not be chained up without permission from magistrates.

(d) Prisons 1823–1980

Mrs Fry's work and Peel's Act had been designed to improve prison conditions, but in the second half of the nineteenth century prisons became harsher, more unpleasant places. Prisoners were forced to do hard labour in silence. Some were kept in solitary confinement. The most important developments between 1835 and 1948 are shown in Table 6.1.

6.3 Police

(a) The Eighteenth Century

In the eighteenth century there was no national police force. In London part-time constables and watchmen patrolled the City. Outside the centre of London, parish constables and night watchmen policed over 100 separate parishes. The night watchmen were often old men who were too feeble to do any other kind of work.

In 1748 Henry Fielding became chief magistrate for Westminster. Fielding realised that London needed a better police force. In 1750 he recruited six special constables. They worked full-time and were paid a wage. This small force became known as the Bow Street Runners, as Fielding's offices were in Bow Street, London.

(b) The Nineteenth Century

By the early nineteenth century it was clear that the watchmen, the parish constables and the Bow Street Runners were not capable of providing an adequate police service. Cities were growing at an alarming rate. There was widespread poverty, unemployment and starvation. There were no social services to help people and many turned to crime.

Table 6.1 Prisons, 1835–1948

Year	Development	Importance
1835	Prisons Act	The Home Secretary to appoint prison inspectors. The inspectors had to check that the laws governing the management of prisons were obeyed
1850	Dartmoor Prison reopened	The prison had originally been built for French prisoners during the Napoleonic Wars. Now it was used to house British criminals
1852	Australia refused to accept any more convicts	More prisons had to be opened in Britain
1853	Penal servitude introduced	Convicts started their sentences in prison, then did hard labour and were finally released on probation ('ticket of leave prisoners')
1877	Prisons Act	*All* prisons became the property of the government. They came under the control of the Home Secretary
1898	Prisons Act	The Act abolished cruel practices such as the crank, the treadwheel and hard labour
1908	Probation Act	Probation service set up for adults and juveniles
1923	Wakefield Prison experiments	Prisoners allowed to socialise more freely. There was more in the way of education and recreation provided for them
1948	Criminal Justice Act	Abolished penal servitude (see above). The Act set up detention centres and corrective training centres

In 1828 Robert Peel set up Britain's first proper police force. By the *Metropolitan Police Act* (*1829*):

- In London the system of the Bow Street Runners, watchmen and parish constables was abolished.
- A new Metropolitan Police Force was set up, with uniformed foot police patrolling individual beats.
- The new police force was to consist of 3000 men under the control of two Commissioners of Police responsible to the Home Secretary.

With more policemen on the streets, there was a drop in the crime rate. However, many people disliked the idea of an active police force in London. At first the 'peelers' were very unpopular. People called them 'blue devils' or 'Peel's bloody gang'.

By the 1830s public attitudes had started to change. People began to accept that the police force was a way of keeping law and order in London. But the crime rate remained high in other areas. In 1835 Parliament passed the *Municipal Corporations Act*. This Act changed the way in which towns and boroughs were run. In future towns and boroughs were to be controlled by *corporations*. Each corporation could set up its own police force, based on the London model.

Many were slow to act. By 1838 only half of the new corporations in England and Wales had police forces. Table 6.2 shows the measures taken between 1839 and 1919 to provide the whole country with an efficient force.

Table 6.2   The police, 1839–1919

Year	Event
1839	Metropolitan Police Act: • The Metropolitan police area was extended 25 km in all directions from Charing Cross • All the old police offices, including Bow Street, were abolished
1839	County Police Act: Magistrates had the power to organise police forces in their counties and to use the rates to pay for them
1856	Rural Police Act: • It became compulsory to have police forces everywhere • The Home Secretary was to appoint inspectors to make sure that this was done
1878	Criminal Investigation Department (CID) formed
1888	County Councils Act: Each council to set up a group of people responsible for running the police force
1901	First use of fingerprints in detective work
1905	Police patrolling in cars rather than on horseback
1909	Police using bicycles
1910	Motor boats first used by the Thames Division of the Metropolitan Police. First use of wireless radio to catch a criminal (Dr Crippen)
1916	First full-time policewomen
1918–1919	Two police strikes. The government promised better pay, pensions and allowances. These were put into effect in the 1919 *Police Act*

(c) The Twentieth Century

After the First World War, police mobility and communications improved. The introduction of telephones meant that police officers could get in touch with their stations much more quickly. By the 1920s some police cars were using radio. In 1923 the Metropolitan Police started using two-way wireless, and by 1926 wireless was being used for communication between police stations. Today all police cars have radio contact with headquarters and officers on the beat carry personal sets.

The modern police force is broken up into divisions, which are based on areas of land or population. These divisions contain a number of sub-divisions. Each sub-division is responsible for the day-to-day policing of a small area. A sub-division will have inspectors, sergeants and constables. Most will also have CID detectives, traffic wardens, typists and technicians to support the policemen on patrol.

In many areas patrols consist of a policeman in a 'panda' car. There have recently been attempts to get policemen back onto foot patrols so that they can talk to people more easily and get to know the community better. This policy is known as 'community policing', and may be one way of combating the growing crime rate.

SPECIMEN QUESTION: PRISONS AND POLICE

1. What were conditions like for most prisoners in the early nineteenth century?
2. How did John Howard and Elizabeth Fry try to improve prison conditions?
3. What changes did Robert Peel introduce into prisons and how did he improve the efficiency of the police force, 1823–1829?

Part 1 is a *descriptive* essay, part 2 is *explanatory* and part 3 tests your understanding of *continuity and change*. To answer the question successfully, you need to know a great deal about the work of John Howard, Elizabeth Fry and Robert Peel.

SOURCE-BASED QUESTION: PRISONS AND POLICE

Read through the three sources below. Then answer the questions.

Source 1

I send you the Report of last year on the London Police. In 1822 there were 2539 crimes committed; in 1825, 2902; in 1828, 3516. This is a strong proof of the great increase in crime and the need to take action to stop this increase. In 1822 there were 12 convictions for house-breaking; in 1825, 23; and in 1828, 102.

There are many parishes in which the watch establishment is not working properly. In one parish there are 18 different boards for the management of the watch, each acting without concert with the other! In some parishes there is no watch at all. Think of the state of Brentford and Deptford with no sort of police by night!

My Bill allows the Secretary of State to abolish all the existing watch arrangements and to substitute in their place a police force that shall act by night and day under the control of two magistrates. I propose to substitute the new policy gradually for the old one, not to attempt too much at first . . ..

(Letter from Robert Peel to the Duke of Wellington, 29 May 1829)

I am very glad to hear you think well of the police. It has given me from the first to the last more trouble than anything I have undertaken.

I want to teach the people that freedom does not consist in having your house robbed by organised gangs of thieves, and in leaving the main streets of London in the nightly possession of drunken women and layabouts.

The chief danger of the failure of the new system will be, if it is made a job, if gentleman's servants and the like are placed in the higher offices.
(Letter from Robert Peel to Wellington, 5 November 1829)

Source 3

No doubt three shillings [15p] a day will not give me all the virtues under heaven, but I do not want them. I have good reason for thinking that one of my police constables, can find out of his pay of a guinea a week [£1.05]: (1) lodgings, (2) medical attendance, (3) comforts at his mess, (4) clothing, and can, after finding these, save out of his pay ten shillings [50p] a week.
(Letter from Robert Peel to J. W. Croker, M.P., 10 October 1829)

1. (a) What was the weekly pay of a policeman in 1829?
   (b) How much did Peel expect one of his officers to pay in total for lodgings, medicine, subsistence and clothing each week?
2. Work out the percentage increase in crimes committed in London between 1822 and 1825, and between 1825 and 1828.
3. What reasons does Peel give in sources 1 and 2 for setting up a Metropolitan Police Force?
4. Why do you think Peel intended to change the system of policing 'gradually' (source 1)?
5. In source 2 Peel writes: 'It [the police] has given me . . . more trouble than anything I have undertaken.' What sort of trouble did Peel run into when setting up the Metropolitan Police?
6. Why do you think Peel was concerned about 'gentleman's servants' being placed in higher offices (source 2)?
7. Source 3 was written in reply to a letter from an influential M.P. to Robert Peel. What do you think Croker wrote in his letter to Peel?

6.4 Education

(a) Schools for the Poor, 1700–1900

In the eighteenth century there was no such thing as a state school. Poor people relied on the church or charity to provide them with a basic education. Thousands of working-class people received no education at all. There were six types of school available to the poor.

(i) *Charity Schools*

From about 1699 the Church of England tried to raise money for charity schools through the S.P.C.K. (Society for the Promotion of Christian Knowledge).

Sometimes a rich man would provide the money for one of these schools in his will. The charity schools usually had a uniform, and each school was known by its colour.

(ii) *Sunday Schools*

Sunday schools were the first schools to provide large numbers of working-children with some form of education. Their aim was to teach children how to read the Bible and how to 'respect their betters'.

The first Sunday school was set up in 1780 by Robert Raikes, a Gloucester newspaper editor. He opened his school because he was shocked by the bad manners and language of local children. Many of the pupils who attended his schools were tired and poorly fed. They had been at work in factories for six days of the week and were in no mood for lessons. Sunday school pupils were not taught to write, because it was not thought necessary for poor people to be able to write. Many of the Sunday school teachers themselves could hardly write!

(iii) *Dame Schools*

Dame schools were simply places where young children were looked after by old women or old men while their parents were at work. Few dame schools provided children with a worth-while education.

(iv) *Monitorial Schools*

Monitorial schools first appeared in the early nineteenth century. Joseph Lancaster, a Quaker, and Andrew Bell, a vicar, believed that it was possible for one teacher to control several hundred children with the help of *monitors*. The monitors were the older and brighter children. They came to school early in the morning and the teacher taught them the day's work. Later in the day the monitors would teach the same work to the younger children.

Unfortunately, Bell and Lancaster quarrelled over how religion should be taught in monitorial schools. In 1811 Bell set up a number of *national schools* for the sons and daughters of members of the Church of England. In 1814 Lancaster's supporters formed the *British and Foreign Schools Society*. This was open to children of all religions. Later in the nineteenth century attempts to set up a national system of education were blocked by the rival groups. They feared that a national system would harm their own schools and would conflict with their ideas about religious teaching.

(v) *Ragged Schools*

In 1820 John Pounds, a London cobbler, set up the first school for homeless children, in a small workshop. Pounds managed to teach up to 40 children at a time. His ideas about helping poor children spread. Teachers joined up their schools to form a *Ragged Schools Union*, which received help from reformers such as Lord Shaftesbury and writers such as Charles Dickens.

(vi) *Factory Schools*

Mill owners such as Robert Owen (see Section 5.4) provided schools for children working in their factories. These schools were purely voluntary. However, the first Factory Act (1833) stated that children working in factories should receive two hours' schooling a day. Four full-time inspectors were appointed to visit factories to make sure that this was done.

(b) Schools for the Rich, 1700–1900

(i) *Public Schools*

In the eighteenth century the sons of rich landowners went to fee-paying public schools such as Eton, Winchester and Harrow. The boys studied Latin and Greek at these schools. Teaching methods were dull and laborious. The boys fought and bullied each other, and the teachers were not much better. They kept the boys under control with savage beatings. Sometimes the boys rose up in mutiny. In 1808 there was a rebellion at Harrow, and ten years later soldiers had to put down a riot at Winchester.

(ii) *Grammar Schools*

Some parents could not afford to send their sons to public schools. An alternative was the grammar school. Grammar schools also taught mainly Latin and Greek grammar. Many of them had been set up in the sixteenth century to educate boys from all social classes. By the eighteenth century, however, many grammar schools were charging fees.

(iii) *Academies*

The best academies were run by Nonconformists. Academies gave children a general education designed to help them enter the world of business. Boys learned book-keeping, science and natural history, as well as English and classics. In many academies the standard of education was very poor. Two dreadful academies are described in Charles Dickens's *Nicholas Nickleby* and Charlotte Bronte's *Jane Eyre*.

(c) Elementary Education, 1811–1870

During the nineteenth century the government became more involved in educating working-class children. Table 6.3 shows the most important developments between 1811 and 1870.

(d) Secondary Education

The 1870 Act (see Table 6.3) had set up a state-run system for 5–11-year-olds. However, by the 1890s Britain needed men and women with a higher level of education to work in factories and offices. Between 1902 and 1973 the government took the steps listed in Table 6.4 to provide *all* pupils with some form of secondary education.

Table 6.3 Education, 1811–1870

Year	Event
1811	National Society founded (see page 136)
1814	British and Foreign Schools Society set up
1833	First government grant (£20 000) paid to the church schools
1839	Committee for the Privy Council for Education set up. This was the origin of the Department of Education and Science (DES)
1840	First training college for teachers set up in Battersea
1846	Government grant to church schools increased to £100 000. Pupil-teacher system set up. Head-teachers were paid a grant to train their best pupils as teachers
1858	The *Newcastle Commission* reported that less than one-half of Britain's children went to school. Of these, only one-half learned reading and writing successfully. The Commission recommended that government grants should be based on examination success – 'payment by results'
1870	Education Act ('Forster's Act'): • School boards were to be set up in each district. The boards could build *board schools* to provide elementary schools for the 5–11 age range • Religious education in board schools was not to be compulsory • The church schools were to carry on as before • Low fees could be charged by school boards but payment was not compulsory • Education was to be made compulsory in some areas

Table 6.4 Secondary education, 1902–1973

Year	Event
1902	Education Act: • School boards abolished and their duties handed over to Local Education Authorities (LEAs) • LEAs to build elementary and secondary schools and train teachers
1918	Education Act ('Fisher Act'): School-leaving age raised to 14
1926	The *Hadow Commission* recommended that secondary education should be available to all
1944	Education Act ('Butler's Act'): • Education should be in three stages — primary, secondary and further. Secondary education to remain as grammar, technical and 'modern'. Primary education to be 'infant' and 'junior' • The school-leaving age was to be raised to 15 and later to 16 • Fees in all state secondary schools were to be abolished • There should be provision for school meals, free milk and medical services
1965	A Labour government introduced schemes for *comprehensive* schools throughout the country
1973	School-leaving age raised to 16

1.

2.

The three photographs on page 139 show children from class 3 at Snowfields School, London, in 1894, 1924 and 1952. Study the photographs carefully and then answer the questions below:

1. What similarities do you notice between the three photographs? What differences are there?
2. How do the children in source 3 differ from the children in the school you attended when you were 11?
3. Why were many working-class children unwilling to attend school in 1894?
4. Are these photographs primary or secondary sources? Give reasons for your answer.
5. If you were writing the history of Snowfields School between 1894 and 1952, what other types of historical evidence would you want to look at? List as many different types of evidence as you can.
6. What problems might you come across when collecting these pieces of evidence?

SPECIMEN QUESTION

> **How and why did government interest in education increase in the period 1832–1870? You could refer to: government grants; the Newcastle Commission; 'payment by results'; the 1867 Reform Act; the 1870 Education Act.**

In this question you should note that you are asked to write about the period 1832–1870. Ignore these date boundaries at your peril! You will gain no marks for including information on Sandon's Act (1876) and Balfour's Act (1902). You should also note that the question states 'you *could* refer to . . .' the facts and dates listed in the question. You do not have to refer to all the facts and can include other material if you wish. Avoid the temptation to rewrite all the facts you are given in wordy sentences in the hope that you will gain credit for regurgitating written information. The examiner will realise that you are merely redrafting the information given on the paper and you will receive very few marks.

6.5 The Growth of Towns

(a) Introduction

The increase in population in the late eighteenth century (see Chapter 2) led to a rapid growth in the size of Britain's towns and cities. Table 6.5 shows the growth of five cities in the nineteenth century.

The sudden growth in the size of towns meant that builders had to put up many houses very quickly. The houses had to be cheap, as workers were paid low wages and could not afford to rent expensive houses. Most houses cost about £50 to build.

Cheap houses were often badly built. To make matters worse, there were no controls on building and no planning regulations. Governments and local councils did not think that it was their job to interfere in the building of houses or

Table 6.5 Population growth in five cities, 1801–1901 (thousands)

City	1801	1851	1901
London	1117	2685	6586
Birmingham	71	223	522
Leeds	53	172	429
Sheffield	46	135	381
Manchester	75	303	645

the planning of towns. They believed that it was best to leave town planning in the hands of private companies. This is known as a policy of *laissez-faire* (see Section 10.3).

The policy of *laissez-faire* resulted in houses being built back-to-back without water supply, drains or sewers. One pump often supplied water to 50 houses. In parts of Manchester there was only one lavatory for 215 people! In some towns water was bought from carriers who toured the streets. This water was often drawn from polluted streams or wells. There was also dreadful overcrowding. Whole families lived in a single room or part of a single room. When people could not find a room to live in, they moved into cellars. In 1842 there were 39 000 cellar-dwellers in Liverpool alone.

(b) Government Reports

In 1831 there was a very serious outbreak of cholera (see Section 7.4) in many towns and cities. At least 18 000 people died from the disease. A second epidemic in 1837 was so serious that the government asked Dr Southwood Smith, of the London Fever Hospital, and Dr Kay Shuttleworth to write a report. The doctors visited the terrible slums of Bethnal Green and Whitechapel. Their report on filthy living conditions shocked middle-class Victorians. Edwin Chadwick, a lawyer and social reformer, decided that there was a need for a longer, more detailed report into conditions in the rest of the country.

Chadwick used the Medical Officers of the Poor Law Unions to gather in the information he needed. He sent out long questionnaires asking the medical officers for information about their areas; he also visited the worst places himself and talked to hundreds of people.

Chadwick's report revealed grim conditions. Thousands of families were living in waterlogged cellars. There was terrible overcrowding in damp, dingy houses surrounded by unpaved streets full of refuse and muck. In most towns there was no proper drainage and no system of sewage disposal. In London the River Thames was used for drinking and sewage-disposal.

Chadwick's report was finished in 1842, but the Poor Law Commissioners refused to publish it, because they thought it would annoy too many people. Chadwick published the report under his own name. It was a great success. People were so shocked that the Home Secretary was forced to appoint a Royal Commission, the *Health of Towns Commission* to look into the state of the towns. The Commission's report, published in 1844, confirmed the findings of Chadwick's report. In 1848 Parliament passed a Public Health Act (see Section 7.8).

6.6 Food

(a) The Eighteenth Century

In 1750 most people ate locally produced food. Grain was the most important part of the daily diet in England and Wales. Most homes had an oven and people made their own bread. Potatoes were the main food in Ireland and some parts of Scotland.

Meat was a luxury, and only wealthy townspeople could buy meat, which arrived at market 'on the hoof'. The most common meat was bacon, because pigs were cheap to look after. They were kept in backyards and fed scraps, or they were allowed to root around on commons or in woods. Pigs were killed at home, and the bacon was salted or smoked so that it would keep longer.

Some cheese was produced in the West Country, Cheshire and Gloucestershire. In many towns cows were kept in stables close to houses and shops. It was possible to buy cows' milk from milkmaids, who milked the cows as and when required!

Very little food was imported. Sugar was grown in the West Indies and sent to Britain in sailing-ships. Most tea came from China. Only the richest citizens could afford to buy these goods.

(b) The Nineteenth Century

In the early part of the nineteenth century country people continued to enjoy a reasonable diet. Town-dwellers lived mainly on bread and potatoes. The potatoes were eaten along with cheap foods such as suet, bacon or herrings. Breakfast, tea and supper often consisted of weak tea and bread and lard.

Much of the food on sale in towns could be bad. The meat and fish on sale in markets had often gone off. The meat might have come from animals that had died of old age or disease or from calves that had been born prematurely. Townspeople were eating a diet low in food value, and many children grew up deformed and stunted.

In the second half of the nineteenth century the average diet improved a great deal. The new railway system brought fresh food direct from country areas to the towns. There were more imports in the form of rice, sugar and wheat, as well as new fruits, vegetable oil and cocoa. From the 1880s onwards, meat was sent from Australia and New Zealand in refrigerated ships.

In 1875 the Sale of Food and Drugs Act gave councils the power to have suspect food tested. Shopkeepers who sold contaminated food were taken to court. By the end of the century shopkeepers no longer dared to sell impure food, such as chalk mixed with flour.

(c) The Twentieth Century

By 1913 British farmers had come through 'The Great Depression' (see Section 3.11), mostly by turning from growing grain to growing fruit and vegetables and dairy farming. Most people had a better diet, which was a mixture of home-produced food and foreign food. However, the poorest people still lived on a poor diet.

During the two World Wars the government introduced food rationing. In the Second World War this meant that some families got more milk, eggs and meat than they had eaten before the war! People doing heavy work got more generous rations, and there were issues of milk, orange juice and cod liver oil for young children. A national system of school meals was started.

Since the 1950s there has been a revolution in our eating habits. Today families rely more and more on 'fast foods' or 'convenience foods', which are easy to prepare and cook. The use of freezers and microwave ovens has made it easier to store food for long periods of time and then cook it quickly. At the same time there has been more concern about 'E' numbers — which identify food additives used to give food a bright colour or a stronger flavour. There has also been a move back to 'organic' farming and food, because people are concerned about the long-term effects of chemicals and additives on the human body.

6.7 Working Conditions in Factories and Mines

(a) Factory Conditions (see also Section 4.19)

One hundred and fifty years ago working conditions in some textile factories were very harsh. The working week was very long, and factory workers had to work shifts of up to 12 hours a day. During 'brisk time', when trade was good, workers had to keep going for 16 hours a day. For working these long hours, spinners and weavers received fairly low wages. They were paid more money than were farm workers, but they had higher rents to pay and their food cost more. It was necessary for the whole family to go out to work in order for people to make a living.

Some textile factories were very dusty. In most rooms there were tiny pieces of cotton floating about. Sometimes the air was so thick with dust that workers could hardly see each other. The noise was terrible and could damage the workers' hearing. There were also very high temperatures to cope with. For ordinary spinning the temperature was 60 degrees Fahrenheit but fine spinning needed 70 degrees Fahrenheit. In some cotton mills women worked for 14 hours a day in temperatures over 80 degrees Fahrenheit.

Before 1833 there were no safety regulations in the mills, and employers did not always box off moving parts of machinery. The drive-belts were dangerous, especially if they had buckles on them. The belts rotated at high speeds, and there were many serious accidents.

On the other hand, some mill-owners such as Robert Owen and Benjamin Gott provided good working conditions for their employees. Owen made sure that his employees worked reasonable hours, and provided them with shops, schools and houses (see Section 5.4).

(b) Conditions in the Mines

In 1800 the growing demand for coal meant that there were many jobs for coal-miners. The work was dangerous, dirty and often poorly paid. As coal seams became exhausted, the miners had to dig deeper to find fresh supplies of coal. This created a number of problems (see Section 4.8). Some seams were only 18 inches high. In narrow passages there were no machines to pull tubs of coal along. Men, women and children tied themselves to their tubs and dragged the coal along like animals.

The men working at the coal-face were called 'hewers'. A miner became a hewer when he was 18 or 19 years old. The job was tough and tiring, although the hewer's hours of work were shorter than were those of other coal-miners.

Accidents in coal-mines were common. Few mine-owners bothered to take safety precautions. Most accidents were caused by pit collapse. An accident involving pit collapse could mean that miners were buried underground for days. During the nineteenth century the National Association of Miners put pressure on Parliament to improve pit safety and to introduce a fairer system of payment (see also Sections 4.7 and 4.8).

(c) Reforms in Factories and Mines

(i) *Factories*

Between 1802 and 1878 a number of men interested in social reform, such as Robert Owen, Richard Oastler and Lord Shaftesbury, persuaded Parliament to pass a series of Factory Acts. These led to improvements in working conditions in workshops, mills and factories (Table 6.6).

Table 6.6 The Factory Acts, 1802–1878

Year	Act	Importance
1802	Health and Morals of Apprentices Act	No apprentice in textile factories to work more than 12 hours a day. *This Act was not enforced*
1819	Factory Act	Robert Owen persuaded Parliament to pass an Act banning the employment of children under the age of 9. This Act was ineffective, as magistrates failed to enforce it
1833	Factory Act	• No child under the age of 9 to be employed in textile factories • Children aged 9–13 to work for no more than 48 hours a week • Children under the age of 13 to attend school for 12 hours a week • Four full-time inspectors of factories to be employed to make sure that the law was being obeyed
1844	Factory Act	Children under 13 to work no more than $6\frac{1}{2}$ hours per day. Women and children aged 13–18 to work no more than 12 hours a day
1847	Ten Hours Act	Women and children under 18 to work no more than 58 hours a week
1878	Factory and Workshops Act	Women to work no more than a 56 hour week in textile mills and 60 hours in other factories. Employment of children under 10 banned. There were laws to control safety, ventilation and meals

(ii) *Mines*

The most important Act affecting working conditions in the mines was the *Mines Act (1842)*:

- Women and girls, and boys under the age of 10, were not allowed to work underground.
- Boys under the age of 15 were not allowed to work machinery.
- Mines inspectors were appointed.

This Act was difficult to enforce. However, the inspectors attempted to ensure that the owners of coal-mines complied with the law.

SPECIMEN QUESTION AND GUIDANCE: WORKING CONDITIONS

Choose *two* of the following and describe their working conditions:

A policeman in 1830
A cotton-spinner in 1830
A coal-miner in 1840
A teacher or governess in 1840

Guidance

This is a difficult question. You need to know a great deal of factual detail here. Include information from TV programmes, films or videos if they help to answer the question. It's probably easier to score marks writing about the cotton-spinner and the coal-miner, as you can include information about working conditions and reforms in mills and mines. Avoid 'waffle' in your answers. Try to include as much worth-while information as possible. Note that you are not asked to write about working conditions from the point of view of the workers themselves.

SOURCE-BASED QUESTION: WORKING CONDITIONS

Extract 1

I believe that employing children in coal mines is perfectly consistent with good health. They earn good wages. Working on the night shift does no harm, the air and ventilation are the same at one period as at another. I have never heard of boys injuring themselves down pits from the nature of work, only by accidents. I do not think any change in the hours of work is necessary for children. I would not object to a law preventing children from working before ten years old but would rather leave it to the manager to accept or refuse them. Any such law would be unfair on parents with large families.

I do not think the means of education open to the boys is adequate, quite the reverse. Parents are anxious to send all their children to school but there is none. I do not think that working in the pit means that boys are incapable of having lessons after a day's work. Most coal mines could not carry on without the labours of young boys.
(Evidence of Henry Morton, Agent for the Countess of Durham's Collieries, to the Children's Employment Commission, 1842)

Extract 2

He is 16 and works as a putter [waggon-pusher]. A year ago the horse ran loose and knocked him down. He is lame now and will always be lame. The pit makes him sick. He has been bad in his health ever since he went down the pit. He was very healthy before. This is his sixth year. The sulphur rising up the shaft makes his head ache. When he gets home, he cannot eat nor sleep. Sometimes he eats his food down the pit.

Six months ago, a lad, John Huggins, was sick down the pit but the manager would not let him up and he died a month later. Three years ago, four boys were killed in the shaft. The rope broke when they were going down.

(Evidence of Nicholas Hudderson, a worker at Monkwearmouth Colliery, County Durham, to the Children's Employment Commission, 1842)

Extract 3

In the greatest of British coalfields, that of Northumberland and Durham, women were not employed underground. Children were employed on a variety of jobs. Often at six years of age they were set to open and shut the ventilating doors leading from the main shaft to the galleries. Older boys and girls hauled loaded waggons along underground tramways. On the surface small children were left in charge of pithead winding gear and there is more than one story of terrible accidents occurring because the child's attention wandered from the machinery, perhaps to chase a mouse across the floor.

(*British Economic and Social History 1700–1975*, C. P. Hill, 1978)

1. What was the cause of the 16-year-old boy's sickness in extract 2?
2. Would you agree that extracts 1 and 2 are more reliable than extract 3, because extracts 1 and 2 were written by people who actually saw conditions underground? Give reasons for your answer.
3. Write down *one* statement from extract 3 which can be supported by evidence from extracts 1 and 2.
4. Write down one thing about which the authors of extracts 1 and 2 disagree. How do you explain this difference?
5. Read the last sentence of extract 3. Is it true to say that mice caused accidents in coal-mines?
6. If you were to go down a modern coal-mine, you would be unlikely to find the bad conditions mentioned in extract 2. Why?
7. Does the information in extract 2 prove that John Huggins died as a result of working in a coal-mine? Give reasons for your answer.

6.8 Religion

(a) The Church of England

The Church of England (the Anglican Church) had a great deal of influence in the eighteenth century. For example, many posts in the army, the navy and the legal profession were open only to Anglicans. To become a student at Oxford or Cambridge, one had to be a member of the Church of England. Nearly all wealthy landowners, both aristocrats and gentry, were Anglicans. The village squire (see page 29) usually appointed the parson. Sometimes he appointed his own son! Many parsons spent more time hunting or fishing than they did preaching sermons or helping the poor.

Some wealthy members of the Church got themselves appointed to a number (or *plurality*) of parishes. They could not serve all their parishes properly, and they appointed curates on low salaries to take services. With the growth of the industrial towns and cities, the Church of England became more and more out of touch with the spiritual needs of the working-classes.

(b) Methodism

John Wesley (1703–1791) was a clergyman's son from North Lincolnshire. He trained as a Church of England priest at Oxford. In 1729 he founded a 'holy club', where a group of students prayed and studied according to a set *method*. The students became known as *Methodists*. Between 1738 and 1791 Wesley travelled the length and breadth of the country preaching sermons. He did not want to break away from the Church of England, but by 1784 very few clergymen would let him preach in their churches. So Wesley set up a separate Methodist Church, which ordained its own ministers. Methodist preachers often delivered their sermons in the open air. The message of Methodism was simple: stop drinking, gambling and swearing and lead a sober life, otherwise you will go to hell! Thousands of working-class people joined the Methodist Church. By 1815 there were half a million Methodists in Britain and America.

(c) Dissenters and Nonconformists

There were several religious groups, other than the Methodists, whose members disagreed with the teaching of the Church of England. The most important of these were the Quakers, Baptists and Unitarians. These groups became very influential in the eighteenth and nineteenth centuries. Many leading families in the Industrial Revolution, such as the Darbys (see Section 4.11) were Quakers. They set up Bible classes and schools, and handed out religious books to the poor. They were especially important in new industrial towns and villages and in mining areas.

(d) Hannah More (1745–1833)

Hannah More was a wealthy lady who decided to help the poor lead better lives. In 1789 she opened a school in Cheddar, a mining area in Somerset, where she provided classes for women and children. She believed that teaching people to read prayers and sing hymns would make them sober, obedient, respectful members of society. However, some people criticised her for giving the poor 'ideas above their station' in life.

6.9 Unemployment

Unemployment has always been a problem in Britain. In Tudor times bands of 'sturdy beggars' roamed the streets, looking for trouble. In the eighteenth and nineteenth centuries the Poor Law Authorities struggled to cope with the problem of how to look after the *able-bodied* poor (see Section 8.2). This problem continued well into the twentieth century. After 1920 Britain's 'old' industries (see Sections 4.6 and 4.17.) went into decline. The Wall Street Crash (see Section 10.10) led to thousands of workers losing their jobs. The statistics in Table 6.7 show the rising trend of unemployment in the period 1920–1985.

Government policies since 1980 have led to a high level of unemployment and bankruptcies. By 1985 unemployment was over three million, more than 13 per cent of the workforce. Today the government is still trying to find ways of reducing the unemployment figures. There are dozens of job-creation schemes, including YTS.

Table 6.7 Total numbers of registered
unemployed, 1920–1985 (thousands)

Year	Number	Year	Number
1920	1543	1955	232
1925	1226	1960	360
1930	1917	1965	329
1935	2036	1970	579
1940	963	1975	866
1945	137	1980	1668
1950	314	1985	3110

6.10 Immigration and Emigration

(a) Introduction

Britain has always been made up of many different races and nationalities. Between A.D. 500 and A.D. 1500 large numbers of Saxons, Vikings, Normans, Dutch, Jews and French came to settle here. By the eighteenth century there were about 20 000 black people living in Britain. At the same time large numbers of British people left the country to settle in British colonies. They emigrated to Canada, India, North America and the Far East. Over the past 200 years faster, cheaper methods of transport have speeded up these movements of population.

(b) The Nineteenth Century

During the early nineteenth century thousands of Irish workers emigrated to Britain. After the Great Famine of 1846, 100 000 Irish left their native country and settled in Scotland and Lancashire. Others emigrated to America.

In the 1880s many Jews were being persecuted in Russia and Eastern Europe. Thousands fled to Germany, Britain and the U.S.A. Of those who came to Britain, most settled in London, but there were also large numbers of them in Leeds and Lancashire.

(c) The Twentieth Century

Immigration and emigration declined during the early part of the twentieth century. During the 1930s many Jews fled from Nazi Germany to settle in France, Britain and the U.S.A. After the Second World War many people left Britain to start new lives in Australia, New Zealand, Canada, South Africa and Zimbabwe (formerly Southern Rhodesia). These countries were looking for skilled workers and offered Britons cheap passages out and jobs when they arrived. In the 1950s and early 1970s the shortage of skilled jobs in Britain led to thousands of British people leaving this country to search for work in Europe and the Middle East.

(d) Immigration

In June 1948 a group of 492 West Indians came to Britain in search of work. Larger numbers arrived here in the 1950s. By 1958 there were about 125 000 West Indians living and working in Britain. At the same time people from India and Pakistan came here to look for jobs. There were 55 000 Asian settlers in this country by 1958. These people came to Britain because there was high unemployment and widespread poverty in their own countries. The British government advertised in the West Indies for workers — there was a serious shortage of labour in many British service industries. Many West Indians got jobs on London Transport or in hotels, restaurants, hospitals and factories. They were often willing to work for less money than were white people. Unfortunately, many black people had to put up with racial abuse and discrimination. (Discrimination can mean that you are denied a job because of the colour of your skin, your race or your religious beliefs.) To combat racial discrimination, Parliament passed Race Relations Acts in 1965, 1968 and 1976. These were only partially successful.

By 1979 many young blacks were fed up with their poor job prospects, terrible social conditions, low wages and low status. There were serious riots in Southall, Greater London (1979), Bristol (1980) and Toxteth, Liverpool (1981). It is feared that there may be further unrest in other socially deprived inner-city areas over the next few years.

(e) Statistics

Table 6.8 shows emigration and immigration figures in the period 1900–1979.

Table 6.8 People leaving and coming into Britain, 1900–1979 (thousands)

Year	Emigrants	Immigrants
1900–1909	4404	2287
1910–1919	3526	2224
1920–1929	3960	2492
1930–1939	2273	2361
1940–1949	590	240
1950–1959	1327	676
1960–1969	1916	1243
1970–1979	2079	1440

SPECIMEN QUESTION AND GUIDANCE: EMIGRATION AND IMMIGRATION

Describe the major movements of population to and from this country in the period 1840–1980. You should explain how and why groups of people emigrated from and migrated to Britain. What effect have these population movements had on industry, trade and the social life of the nation?

Guidance

This is a fairly straightforward question, but you should note that you are asked to write about the *economic* and *social* effects of emigration and immigration in the second part of the question. Most important of all, you should avoid *bias* in your writing (being either strongly pro-immigration or anti-immigration).

GCSE ASSESSMENT OBJECTIVES

Primary and Secondary Sources

The national criteria for history state that GCSE candidates should be able to 'show the skills necessary to study a wide variety of historical evidence which should include both primary and secondary written sources' (Assessment Objective 4).

Primary Sources

Primary-source material provides a historian with information in its *original form*. It has not been changed by any other person.

Legal documents, old maps, parish records, photographs, diaries and letters are all examples of primary sources. They were written down or recorded at the time the events they describe actually occurred.

Secondary Sources

Secondary sources consist of accounts produced by historians, reporters, playwrights or TV producers. People producing secondary sources usually use primary evidence as their source of information. Secondary sources are nearly always produced some time *after* the events they describe have occurred.

Look at the list of sources below. Would you say they are *primary* or *secondary*?

- Shakespeare's play *Henry V*
- The diary of Samuel Pepys
- A portrait of Samuel Pepys
- A photograph of a suffragette
- William Wilberforce's model of a slave ship
- Joseph Arch's autobiography
- Hunter Davies's biography of George Stephenson
- An enclosure map
- A copy of *The Times* dated 21 March 1805
- A historical novel by Georgette Heyer
- A videotape of a school visit to Coalbrookdale
- A history textbook
- A letter from the Earl of Chesterfield to his son

The following quotations and pictures are taken from history books. Would you say that they are *primary* or *secondary* sources? Give reasons for your answers.

(i) 'Here I am between earth and sky, so help me God. I would sooner lose my life than go home as I am. Bread I want and bread I will have.'

(ii) 'A poor religious stocking-maker said "Let us be patient a little longer lads. Surely God will help us soon."

"Talk no more about Goddle Mighty!" was the sneering answer. "There isn't one. If there was one, he wouldn't let us suffer as we do." '

(iii) 'I drew 27 shillings and sixpence from the farmers and after I had given my wife 24 shillings and paid my union fourpence and my rent three shillings and a penny, I had a penny left. So I threw it across the field. I'd worked hard. A penny was what a child had. I wasn't having that. I would sooner have nothing.'

(iv) 'During the Industrial Revolution the towns grew in size and some places which had been little more than villages became large cities. All this happened without any proper controls, so that public health was a serious problem.'

(v) 'The houses are occupied from cellar to garret, filthy within and without . . .. But all this is nothing in comparison with the dwellings in the narrow courts and alleys between the streets. Heaps of garbage and ashes lie in all directions.'

(vi) 'You went down one step into the cellar in which a family of human beings lived. It was very dark inside. The window panes were broken and stuffed with rags. The smell was so foetid [strong] as almost to knock the men down. Quickly recovering themselves, they began to penetrate the thick darkness of the place, and to see three or four little children rolling on the damp brick floor through which the stagnant, filthy moisture of the street oozed up.'

(vii) Cruikshank's 'Oliver' drawing.

(viii) An engraving by G. Doré.

Now try to match up the authors or artists in (i) – (viii) with the names below:

- Friedrich Engels, a German writer (1847)
- George Cruikshank, an artist (1838)
- Elizabeth Gaskell, a novelist (1848)
- William Dawson of Upwell (1816)
- Thomas Cooper, a Chartist (autobiography, 1872)
- P.F. Speed, a historian (1977)
- Gustave Doré, an artist (1872)
- Len Thompson, a farm worker (1922)

WORK OUT SHORT-ANSWER QUESTIONS: SOCIAL CHANGE

1. What was a turnkey?
2. Which infectious disease killed thousands of prisoners in the eighteenth century?
3. Who was John Howard?
4. Which London prison did Elizabeth Fry visit in 1813?
5. Name the Home Secretary responsible for the 1823 Gaol Act.
6. What was penal servitude?
7. Who became chief magistrate for Westminster in 1748?
8. How many men were recruited into the Metropolitan Police in 1829?
9. How did the Municipal Corporations Act (1835) change the way in which towns and boroughs were run?
10. When was wireless radio first used to catch a criminal?
11. What is community policing?
12. What do the initials S.P.C.K. stand for?
13. How were charity schools financed?
14. Why did Robert Raikes set up a Sunday School in Gloucester in 1780?
15. What sort of children attended dame schools?
16. Who set up the first monitorial schools?
17. How did the monitorial system work?
18. When was the first Ragged School opened?
19. Name two important reformers who supported the Ragged Schools Union.
20. What sort of schools did the sons of rich landowners attend in the eighteenth century?
21. How did grammar schools get their name?
22. What subjects were taught in some of the better eighteenth-century academies?
23. How much money did the government hand out to the church schools in 1833?
24. What were two findings of the Newcastle Commission?
25. When were board schools first introduced?
26. What age range did elementary schools cater for?
27. At what age could you leave school in 1970?
28. How much did a 'back-to-back' house cost to build in 1820?
29. Who was responsible for the Public Health Report of 1838?
30. How did Edwin Chadwick collect the information he needed for the 1842 report?
31. Why did Chadwick have to publish the 1842 report under his own name?
32. What was the most important part of the average daily diet in 1750?
33. Why did the children of many nineteenth-century town-dwellers grow up deformed and stunted?
34. Why did the diet of some working people improve during the Second World War?
35. Why has there been a shift towards 'organic' farming over the past 20 years?
36. In a spinning-mill, what was 'brisk time'?
37. Name two factory employers of the nineteenth century who looked after their employees extremely well.
38. In a coal-mine, what was a 'hewer'?
39. Why were the first two Factory Acts difficult to enforce?
40. What was the maximum length of a working week for a female spinner in 1857?
41. How did the 1842 Mines Act help to improve safety in mines?

42. Name three Nonconformist groups which were active in the nineteenth century.
43. Why did Hannah More decide to set up Bible classes for working-class women and children?
44. What is 'inflation'?
45. How many black people were living and working in Britain in the eighteenth century?
46. Why did many people leave Ireland in 1846?
47. Why did many skilled workers leave Britain in the 1950s and 1970s?
48. When did Parliament pass three Race Relations Acts?
49. In which cities were there serious riots in 1979, 1980 and 1981?
50. Briefly explain *why* there were riots in these three cities.

7 Medicine

7.1 Introduction

During the Middle Ages the monasteries were almost the only places in Europe where sick people could be cared for. Between 1536 and 1540, however, King Henry VIII closed nearly all the monasteries in England.

By 1700 there was some improvement in health care. There were five hospitals in the country and St. Bartholomew's, St. Thomas's and St. Mary's in London. The eighteenth century saw a big increase in the number of hospitals. By 1800 there were over 50 hospitals in England. Table 7.1 shows some of the most important hospitals and when they were founded. These hospitals provided doctors with a form of medical training. Students could watch doctors and surgeons working with patients and could study different illnesses. They could watch operations taking place from galleries in operating theatres. However, most eighteenth-century hospitals were dirty, insanitary places, and many patients died of sepsis (blood poisoning) or other infections rather than their original illness!

Before 1850 hospital nurses were often poorly paid and qualified. Few educated people ever considered a career in nursing. Nurses were supposed to look after patients, provide them with food and wash clothes and bedding. They did not put on or take off dressings. This job was done by the surgeons themselves or 'dressers'. Nurses slept in the wards with the patients and cooked their own food. At night 'watchers' were hired to look after patients. 'Watchers' were even more unreliable than nurses, and some even came into hospital wards to sleep off the effects of drink.

Table 7.1 Hospitals in Britain, 1700–1900

Date	Hospital
1719	Westminster Hospital, London
1725	Guy's Hospital, London
1733	St. George's Hospital, London
1739	Foundling Hospital, London
1740	London Hospital, London
1745	Middlesex Hospital, London
1795	Retreat Mental Hospital, York
1814	London Chest Hospital, London
1828	Royal 'Free' Hospital, London
1851	Royal Cancer Hospital, London
1852	Children's Hospital, London

For many people, therefore, hospitals were places to be avoided. Better-off people never went into hospital but preferred to be looked after at home. Working people would only enter a hospital if they were desperate. As late as 1870 Florence Nightingale wrote: 'The first requirement of a hospital is that it should do the sick no harm'!

7.2 Disease

Terrible diseases swept through many British towns during the eighteenth and early nineteenth centuries. In the growing industrial towns, houses for factory workers were built as cheaply as possible, with no proper sewers or water supply. There was often only one pump to provide water for a whole row of houses. The streets were often unpaved and full of rotting filth. Refuse collection took place very rarely or not at all. These conditions were ideal for the spread of disease. Table 7.2 shows five of the worst killer diseases and their causes. These killer diseases led to a very high death-rate. By 1840 the average age of death in England and Wales was 29. One child in six died before it was one year old. Outbreaks of cholera in 1832 and 1848 killed thousands. In 1848 Parliament passed a *Public Health Act* (see Section 7.4) to provide towns with sewers, refuse collection, clean water and street lighting. These measures helped to improve public health in the nineteenth century.

7.3 Edward Jenner and Smallpox Vaccination

In the 1790s smallpox was a very common disease in Britain. Roughly 40 000 people died from smallpox each year. If you were lucky enough to survive the disease, you were often left covered in pock-marks, blind or insane. The first method of fighting the disease was through *inoculation* (giving a person a mild form of a disease to prevent a serious attack of the same disease). Lady Mary Wortley Montagu, wife of the British Ambassador to Turkey, introduced inoculation in 1721 after her return from the Middle East. However, inoculation often left people pock-marked or seriously ill.

Edward Jenner was a country doctor from Gloucestershire. He noticed that country people who had caught cowpox (a much milder disease than smallpox) never caught smallpox. Jenner realised that getting cowpox built up resistance to smallpox. In 1796 he took some fluid from cowpox sores and put it into two

Table 7.2 Killer diseases

Disease	Causes	Description
Cholera (see also Section 7.4)	Germs getting into drinking-water	Many epidemics in the nineteenth century. There were very serious outbreaks in 1831–1832, 1838, 1848–1849, 1854
Tuberculosis (T.B.)	Breathing in bacteria floating in the air or consuming infected meat or milk	Attacks the lungs and usually results in death. People who were badly fed and living in dirty, stuffy conditions were most at risk from T.B.
Typhoid	Germs getting into food or water	Like cholera, typhoid travelled along water supplies. Sewage used to seep into water and people would drink the polluted water
Smallpox	Contact with an infected person	Many epidemics in industrial towns. Later controlled by inoculation and vaccination (see Section 7.3)
Typhus	Carried by lice	Overcrowding, poverty and lack of hygiene led to several typhus epidemics in the nineteenth century

scratches on the arm of a healthy boy, James Phipps. The boy's arm became sore but soon got better. Six weeks later, Jenner scratched Phipps's arm and put in some smallpox germs. Phipps did not get smallpox. Jenner had shown that by *vaccinating* patients (giving them cowpox), doctors could control the spread of smallpox. But although Jenner had shown doctors a way of preventing smallpox, he had not been able to explain how the vaccine worked or what caused the disease.

7.4 Cholera

Cholera was the most dreaded disease of the nineteenth century. It did not kill greater numbers of people than did typhus or typhoid, but it struck suddenly, leaving people with little hope of recovery.

The disease started in India. In 1817 it began to spread westwards towards Europe. In 1831 it entered Britain at the port of Sunderland. During the next few months it spread through Britain's towns and cities, finally dying out in the summer of 1833. By then the disease had killed 22 000 people.

The germs that cause cholera are found in the excreta of patients suffering from the disease. Once these germs have spread through food and water supplies, they can be carried over a wide area. Dumping sewage into rivers and then using the water for drinking made it very easy for the disease to spread.

Table 7.3 Cholera epidemics, 1848–1866

Year	Deaths
1848	72 000
1853	20 000
1866	14 500

There were three further major cholera epidemics. Table 7.3 shows when they happened and the number of people who died in them. After the 1848 epidemic, Parliament passed a *Public Health Act*. There were two main parts to the Act:

1. *A Central Board of Health was set up* There were three commissioners: Lord Morpeth, Lord Shaftesbury and Edwin Chadwick. Dr Southwood Smith was the Board's Medical Inspector. The Board had the power to set up local boards of health in any area where the death-rate was 23 per 1000 or higher.
2. *The local Boards of Health*
   - The boards had the power to appoint a clerk, a treasurer, a surveyor and a Medical Officer of Health.
   - The boards had to make sure that all houses were built with drains and lavatories.
   - The local board could supply householders with water, if there was no water company in the area. If there was a water company, the board had to make sure that the company was doing its work properly.
   - If water companies could supply water for 2d. (1p) a week, the board could force householders to have it piped to their houses.
   - To pay for these improvements, the board had the right to charge a rate.

7.5 Surgery

In the eighteenth century techniques in surgery were very primitive. Surgeons were often barbers who did a bit of blood-letting or bone-setting in their spare time. They were often looked down on by the *physicians* (doctors), who had been trained in medical schools.

In 1750 there were three major problems facing surgeons:

1. *The problem of pain* Surgeons used drugs such as opium or hemp to make the patients drowsy or to dull the pain during an operation. But they had to work very fast to finish the operation before the patient started to come round. The absence of an effective painkiller made any progress in surgery difficult.
2. *The problem of infection* There was a strong possibility that during an operation a patient would die of shock. After the operation there was the danger of infection setting in. Thousands of patients died of gangrene (rotting limbs) or sepsis (blood poisoning). In 1800, 90 per cent of patient deaths in London were due to blood poisoning.
3. *The problem of bleeding* After an operation surgeons used to tie up blood vessels with silken thread. However, there was a huge risk of patients bleeding to death if the wound became infected and the blood vessels burst.

The two most important surgeons of the eighteenth century were William and John Hunter. In 1745 William Hunter (1718–1783) founded a medical school in Windmill Steet, London. Three years later he was joined by John Hunter, his brother. Together they carried out *dissections* (cutting up bodies of humans and animals) and collected dozens of specimens so that other people could learn about the way the human body worked. John Hunter (1728–1793) realised that the key to good surgery was a complete understanding of exactly what lay under the skin of the human body. He wanted to find out the shape and use of every human organ. Hunter dissected both human bodies and animals. By 1790 he claimed to have dissected over 500 different types of animal and 3000 human bodies.

In 1778 the Royal College of Surgeons was set up in Edinburgh. Between 1784 and 1800 similar training colleges were set up in Ireland and London. The training colleges insisted that all surgeons had to be properly trained and should obtain good qualifications. This training formed the basis of modern surgical practice.

7.6 Anaesthetics, Antiseptics and Obstetrics

(a) Anaesthetics

John and William Hunter had done a great deal to improve techniques in surgery, but it was not until the 1840s that the problem of people suffering pain during operations (see Section 7.5) was overcome. In modern operations patients are given *barbiturates* to make them sleepy and *anaesthetics* to keep them asleep! Anaesthetics therefore make a surgeon's job much easier.

In 1800 Humphry Davy found that breathing in laughing-gas (nitrous oxide) removed pain. Thirty years later his pupil, Michael Faraday, showed that *ether* produces similar results. Neither of these gases was suitable for long operations. The effects of laughing-gas wore off quickly; ether had a longer-lasting effect but it made the patient very sick. In 1847 James Simpson (1811–1870), the Professor of Midwifery at Edinburgh University, tried a dangerous experiment. With two of his friends he sniffed different chemicals to see which one would put them to sleep. After sniffing *chloroform* for a few minutes the three doctors ended up on the floor! Chloroform remained the chief method of dulling pain until the twentieth century. Surgeons could perform long, complicated operations without worrying about patients waking up.

(b) Antiseptics

The second problem, the danger of infection, was solved by Joseph Lister. In 1865 Lister, the Surgeon to Glasgow Royal Infirmary, read about the work of Louis Pasteur, a famous French scientist. Pasteur had put forward the theory that disease was spread by bacteria (germs). Lister believed the theory and tried to do something to prevent patients from dying of sepsis after an operation. Lister's first method of destroying germs was to apply a piece of gauze soaked in *carbolic acid* direct to a wound. This technique turned out to be successful, and by the end of 1865 Lister was insisting that doctors and surgeons should wash their hands regularly and that silk threads used for sewing up wounds should be soaked in carbolic acid. He later invented a pump for spraying a fine mist of

Table 7.4 Lister's record of amputations

Years	Total cases	Recovered	Died	Death-rate (%)
1864–1866	35	19	16	45.7
1867–1870	40	34	6	15.0

N.B.: The period 1864–1866 was the period when antiseptics were not in use.

carbolic acid into the air around the operation. The number of patients dying from sepsis after an operation dropped dramatically, as Table 7.4 shows.

Later research showed that germs floating about in the air were of minor importance and that sepsis was normally caused by *direct contact* with germs on a surgeon's hands, clothes or instruments. Hospital staff eventually gave up using Lister's spray and concentrated on keeping everything clean. This is known as the *aseptic* method of surgery. Today the risk of death in hospital from sepsis is practically non-existent.

(c) Obstetrics

In 1700 obstetrics (the science of childbirth) was a hit-or-miss affair. Thousands of mothers died in childbirth and many babies were stillborn. Queen Anne (1665–1714) had 17 children, yet none of them survived to reach the age of 5.

The man who did most for obstetrics in the eighteenth century was a Scotsman, William Smellie. In 1739 Smellie moved from Scotland to London. He began to train midwives in his own home. English doctors criticised some of Smellie's ideas, but he eventually convinced people that more could be done to help women during pregnancy and childbirth. In 1753 Smellie wrote a *Treatise on Midwifery*, in which he described the process of childbirth more accurately than ever before. Smellie produced valuable case studies on childbirth in 1754 and 1763, and laid down safety rules regarding the use of forceps. He did more than any other doctor to make childbirth easier for women.

7.7 Nursing

During the nineteenth century there were great improvements in the training of nurses. Until 1850 nursing was not a career for respectable women (see Section 7.1). The most serious complaint against nurses was that they were often drunk! Their heavy drinking was sometimes the result of appalling conditions of work. Nurses worked from 6 a.m. to 7 p.m. every day. They had no uniform, and had to buy and cook their own food. They paid no attention to cleanliness, either in themselves or in their patients, and so hospitals were full of infection. They were paid as little as £5 a year and received no training.

The person who did most to improve the training of nurses was Florence Nightingale (1820–1910). She realised that nursing was 'mostly done by those who were too old, too weak, too drunken, too dirty or too bad to do anything else', and she decided to try to improve the status of nurses. She trained as a nurse at a hospital in Germany.

In 1855 she read reports in *The Times* about the terrible conditions suffered by wounded and dying soldiers in the Crimea. The Secretary of War, Sidney Herbert, asked her to become 'Superintendent of the Female Nursing Establishment of the English Hospitals in Turkey'. When she reached the Crimea, she was shocked by the dirt and disorganisation in the army hospitals, and set about putting things right. The death-rate in the hospitals soon fell dramatically.

In 1856 Florence Nightingale returned to Britain. She raised money from people who had heard about her work in the Crimea. With this money she set up the Nightingale School for Nurses at St. Thomas's Hospital in 1860. Trainee nurses were very carefully chosen and put through a very tough course in practical nursing. They were given a uniform, provided with meals and kept in a special nurses' home, where a strict eye was kept on their behaviour. All 'probationers' (trainee nurses) had to agree to be:

- Sober
- Truthful
- Trustworthy
- Punctual
- Quiet
- Clean and neat

If a nurse failed in any one of these requirements, she lost her place on the course.

Between 1860 and 1910 the Nightingale School of Nurses produced 2000 highly trained, well-qualified nurses. The result of this high standard of training was that nursing became a respectable career for women.

7.8 The Public Health Movement

The 1848 Public Health Act (see Section 7.4) had gone some way towards improving the health of Britain's town-dwellers. But the Board had limited powers and existed for only five years. One member of the Board, Edwin Chadwick, was a strong-willed, impatient man who quarrelled with politicians, engineers and doctors. In 1854 opponents of the Public Health Act persuaded Parliament to close down the Public Health Board. Chadwick was given a grant of £1000 a year and pensioned off. However, a new Board of Health was set up

Table 7.5 Improvements in public health, 1855–1875

Date	Measure
1866	*Sanitary Act* Every town had to have sanitary inspectors with powers to order landlords to stop overcrowding and to remove health hazards from their properties
1869	*Public Health Commission* The Commission reported that new laws to deal with sanitation and water supply had to be passed by Parliament
1872–1875	*Public Health Acts*: • The whole country was to be given *Sanitary Authorities* • Medical officers and sanitary inspectors were to be appointed for each district • Local authorities had to lay sewers, drains and pavements, and provide lighting and street-cleaning services • Local authorities had to deal with infections, diseases and epidemics, and had to take measures to control the spread of disease
1875	*Artisans' Dwellings Act* Councils were permitted to take over and clear whole slum districts

in 1855. Its head was Dr John Simon. Over the next 20 years, John Simon extended the work of public health into many new fields, as Table 7.5 shows.

The Acts listed in Table 7.5 led to a lower death-rate in towns and cities. However, in 1884 a Royal Commission on working-class housing revealed that many town-dwellers still lived in slums. In 1890 an important Housing Act simplified and strengthened earlier laws. In 1909 the building of back-to-back houses was banned (see Section 8.8). Ten years later the government began to encourage local authorities to build *council houses*. By the middle of the twentieth century local councils were building a high proportion of all new houses. Today it is possible for council house tenants to buy houses they are living in from the council rather than paying rent.

SPECIMEN QUESTION AND MODEL ANSWER: PUBLIC HEALTH AND MEDICINE

    (i) Why was government action needed to cope with the problem of health and housing in nineteenth-century Britain?

   (ii) How successful were the laws passed to improve public health?

 (iii) How did medical discoveries help to improve the nation's health?

Model Answer

Industrial changes between 1780 and 1820 led to the rapid growth of many towns and cities. In 1780 the population of Birmingham, a centre of iron production, was 42 500. By 1801 it was 71 000. Large numbers of factory-workers lived in badly built houses. Thousands of back-to-back dwellings were damp, airless and poorly lit. There were inadequate supplies of fresh water and sewage disposal was primitive. Working people were often in poor health and many died at an early age. Half the children born to working-class parents died before the age of 5. Medical reformers such as Edwin Chadwick and Dr Southwood Smith investigated the living conditions of working-class people and produced reports to prove just how bad health services and sanitary conditions were. The cholera outbreaks of 1831 and 1848 frightened people so much that M.P.s put pressure on the government to take action.

The scale of the problem was so vast that it could only be solved by Parliament passing laws which gave statutory powers to local authorities. Some local authorities were unwilling or unable to take responsibility for public health. Eventually they were forced to. The Public Health Acts of 1848 and 1875 were the most important. The 1848 Act set up a general Board of Health to supervise local boards. The local boards of health appointed surveyors and medical officers, and employed people to provide sanitation, drainage and clean water. The Act of 1875 enabled local boards to appoint medical officers and sanitary inspectors. Sanitary authorities were set up for the whole country. Local authorities were instructed to maintain sewers, pavements, street-lighting, street-cleaning and fire-fighting services.

The local authorities were also given the power to seize contaminated food and then to destroy it. Before 1875 substances such as arsenic and lead could be added to food. The 1875 Act also suggested that local authorities could provide water, baths and wash-houses if they thought they were necessary. Skilled engineers such as Joseph Bazalgette, the Engineer of the Metropolitan Board of Works, provided towns and cities with well-built sewers and supplies of fresh water. The importance of these engineers has often been underestimated by historians.

The Public Health Acts helped to stop disease and infection from spreading through towns. The life expectancy of people living in towns increased as public health standards improved. However, when men volunteered to fight in the Boer War in 1897, army doctors found that 60 per cent of the recruits were medically unfit. It took many years to turn Victorian cities into reasonably clean, wholesome places. Even today, many of our inner-city areas contain dirty, dingy, substandard housing.

Medical discoveries made during the nineteenth century did much to improve the quality of life for many people and to reduce pain. The use of chloroform meant that surgeons could carry out long operations without worrying about whether their patients would wake up! Chloroform was first used by James Simpson (1811–1870) in 1847. In 1865 Joseph Lister (1827–1912) used a dilute solution of carbolic acid as an antiseptic in Glasgow Royal Infirmary. His *antiseptic* method of surgery led to a great reduction in the number of deaths resulting from sepsis [blood poisoning]. Surgery became safer and more effective. The work of Louis Pasteur (1822–1895) in isolating bacteria made it possible for people to be immunised against disease. Later in the century, doctors such as Robert Koch (1843–1910) discovered the microbes which cause such diseases as tuberculosis and cholera. It became easier to prevent the spread of infection and to cure sufferers. The nineteenth century was therefore a period of great progress in the research and treatment of infectious diseases.

7.9 Medical Training

In the nineteenth century Florence Nightingale dedicated her life to training nurses. *Doctors* were trained in either universities or medical schools. In the second half of the nineteenth century the training of doctors became better-organised. Parliament set up a *General Council of Medical Education and Registration* in 1858 which drew up a Medical Register of doctors and set examination papers for students in colleges and universities. Medical students had to pass frequent examinations in order to qualify as doctors. They had to work in hospitals and assist general practitioners (G.P.s). By 1914 many medical schools were training students for five years, and after 1922 this became standard practice. The General Council began to lay down higher standards for medical training. Students had to study anaesthetics, orthopaedics (children's diseases), pathology (the study of disease) and radiology (the study of X-rays). After passing their examinations, students had to spend a year in a hospital before starting their careers as doctors. There were four main branches of medicine open to them: general practice; hospital work; public and local health services; and research. Today most doctors go into *general practice*.

7.10 Hospitals

The improvements in medicine brought about by Florence Nightingale (see Section 7.7) and Joseph Lister (see Section 7.6) changed people's attitude towards hospitals. Going to hospital was no longer a death sentence. By 1900 most people believed that patients stood a better chance of recovery from an illness in hospital than at home.

The number of hospitals increased. In 1901 there were twice as many patients in *voluntary hospitals* as there had been in 1861. Some of the new hospitals specialised in ear, throat, eye or orthopaedic cases. In country areas panels of local doctors set up 'cottage hospitals', where they carried out simple operations on their own patients.

In 1946 a National Health Service Act was passed. All hospitals were taken over by Regional Hospital Boards under the Ministry of Health. England and Wales were divided into fourteen sections each under a Regional Hospital Board. County and county borough councils *had* to provide ambulances, midwives, home nurses and midwives for those in need. Finally, *health centres* were set up bringing together G.P.s, nurses and other medical services under one roof.

7.11 Bacteriology

Bacteriology is the study of germs which cause disease. Louis Pasteur (see Section 7.6) believed that germs caused human disease, but he had been unable to show that a particular germ caused a particular disease. In 1882 a German doctor, Robert Koch (1843–1910) identified the germs that cause sepsis, tuberculosis and cholera. Koch worked out methods by which germs which caused other diseases could be discovered, examined and kept alive in the laboratory. Many other German doctors followed Koch's lead, and between 1882 and 1900 the germs of 21 diseases were discovered.

7.12 Infectious Diseases

Today very few people in Britain die from infectious diseases. The conquest of many infectious diseases has resulted from the hard work of doctors and bacteriologists from many different countries.

In 1898 Ronald Ross, a doctor in the Indian Medical Service, discovered that the germs which cause malaria are found in the stomachs of a certain type of mosquito. When mosquitoes bite human beings, the germs pass into the bloodstream and develop there. This discovery helped to control the disease. Once the swampy breeding-grounds of mosquitoes had been drained or sprayed with chemicals such as DDT, the malaria germ had no means of reaching human beings.

Other doctors concentrated on treating a disease *after* the germs have taken hold on a patient. In some cases it was possible to give a patient *antibodies* until the body's natural immune system could cope with the disease. Antibodies are germs which can resist a disease.

For many years doctors and scientists worked at ways of fighting the harmful effects of viruses (tiny organisms) which cause infections such as influenza, colds, german measles and mumps. The main difficulty lay in the fact that most viruses are too small to be seen with an ordinary microscope. Since 1945, however, the *electron microscope* has been used to study viruses. This instrument will magnify up to 200 000 times! There are now vaccines available to prevent most virus infections. Table 7.6 shows the most important vaccines. Today doctors are desperately trying to develop a vaccine against another frightening infectious disease — AIDS (acquired immune deficiency syndrome).

Table 7.6 Vaccines

Date developed	Vaccine
1938	Vaccines against diphtheria and tetanus
1956	BCG vaccines against tuberculosis
1958	Whooping cough vaccine
1958	Salk vaccine against poliomyelitis

7.13 New Drugs

The most important medical discoveries of the twentieth century have been associated with new drugs. Giant chemical industries have begun to make new drugs on a large scale. Many of these drugs can now be bought from chemists' shops.

In 1928 a Scotsman, Alexander Fleming (1881–1955), discovered one of these drugs by accident. While growing bacteria (tiny organisms) on a dish, he noticed that some mould on the bacteria was killing off all the bacteria around it. He grew some more mould and found that it killed off many different bacteria. The mould turned out to be *Penicillium*. Fleming developed the antibiotic *penicillin* from the mould. This new drug was used to treat patients suffering from sepsis, pneumonia and meningitis. It was used during the Second World War to stop infection from wounds caused in battle.

Penicillin was the first in a long series of *antibiotic* drugs. Antibiotics are substances taken from other organisms which have the ability to kill other disease-causing organisms. In 1944 Professor S.A. Waksman discovered streptomycin, which was used to help cure T.B. patients. Chloramphenicol, developed in 1947, was used to treat typhoid and typhus. A year later aureomycin was being used to cure pneumonia.

Today doctors and scientists producing new drugs have two problems to face. They have to work out how to deal with germs which are already becoming resistant to antibiotics. They have also to find ways of preventing and curing diseases caused by viruses. It is unlikely that we will ever be able to rid the world of all disease. Nevertheless, doctors have been able to save the lives of millions of people who would otherwise have died in previous centuries. This represents a tremendous achievement for mankind.

SPECIMEN QUESTIONS: MEDICINE AND SURGERY

Look at the six questions on medicine, surgery and public health below. Decide which of the following categories they come under:

- Evidence.
- Short-answer.
- Multiple-choice.
- Essay-type.

Then see how many you can answer!

1. Which of the following led to a general decline in the death-rate between 1730 and 1850? Explain your choice in detail.
   Improvements in Medicine
   OR
   A Higher Standard of Living
2.

Source A

To find out whether the boy was free from smallpox . . . I inoculated him with smallpox matter. No disease followed. Several months later he was again introduced. Again, no disease followed.

Source B

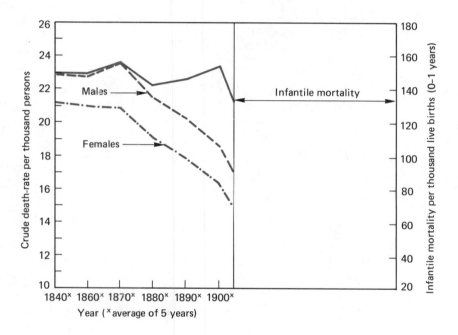

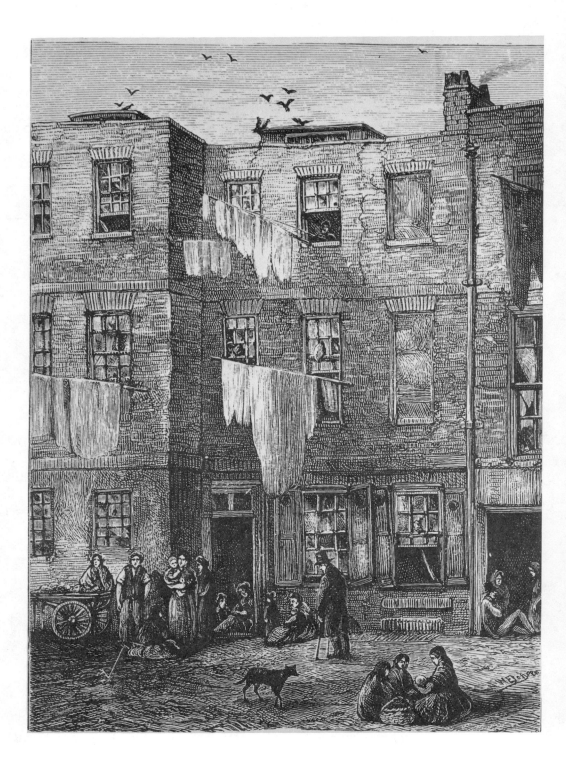

Wild Court, Seven Dials, London

A carbolic spray. The whole room would be sprayed with carbolic acid to prevent infection when operations were being carried out. The spray did work, but the acid hurt the surgeon's eyes, so surgeons eventually stopped using it

(i) What is meant by 'inoculation'? (source A)

(ii) What does source B tell us about the impact of advances in medicine and surgery and public health, 1840–1900?

(iii) Source C shows terrible slum conditions in the 1840s. Were conditions really as bad as this or has the artist made conditions look worse than they really were? Give reasons for your answer.

(iv) Who developed the piece of equipment shown in source D? Why was the introduction of this piece of equipment so important?

(v) Use *all* the sources *and your own knowledge of the topic* to write a short essay explaining why people's life expectancy improved dramatically during the nineteenth century

3. Which of the following diseases caused the greatest number of deaths in nineteenth-century industrial towns?

(i) polio

(ii) meningitis

(iii) smallpox

(iv) cholera

4. Name the doctor whose name is closely associated with the use of chloroform.

5. Write a sentence to explain the importance of Alexander Fleming's discovery of penicillin in 1928.

6. (i) Explain why there were major outbreaks of cholera in British cities in 1831, 1848, 1853 and 1866.

(ii) What was done to try to prevent outbreaks of the disease after 1840?

WORK OUT SHORT-ANSWER QUESTIONS: MEDICINE AND SURGERY

1. How were sick people looked after during the Middle Ages?
2. Name three important London hospitals which were caring for the sick by 1700.
3. When was Guy's Hospital founded?
4. What is sepsis?
5. In eighteenth-century hospitals, who were the 'watchers'?
6. Why did nurses in the early nineteenth century have such a poor reputation?
7. Where did middle-class patients go to receive treatment in 1800?
8. Why were eighteenth-century towns riddled with infectious diseases?
9. What disease do you associate with inflammation of the lungs?
10. When did the four main cholera outbreaks of the eighteenth century take place?
11. What was the death-rate in England and Wales in 1840?
12. How many people died from smallpox each year in the 1790s?
13. What is meant by 'inoculation'?
14. Who introduced inoculation into Britain in 1721?
15. How did Jenner discover that cowpox could be used to vaccinate against smallpox?
16. In which part of Britain did the first cholera outbreak occur?
17. When did the worst cholera epidemic take place?
18. Name the three commissioners on the first Central Board of Health.
19. How high did the death-rate have to be in any area before the Central Board of Health could take action?
20. What was a physician?
21. Name two drugs used to dull pain before the introduction of chloroform.
22. Where did William Hunter set up a medical school in 1745?
23. What are 'dissections'?
24. When was the Royal College of Surgeons set up?
25. What is the difference between barbiturates and anaesthetics?
26. Who put forward the theory that disease is spread by bacteria?
27. What was Joseph Lister's method of destroying germs?
28. When did Lister develop his antiseptic method?
29. Explain the difference between aseptic and antiseptic surgery.
30. Name the Queen of England whose 17 children all died in infancy.
31. Why was the work of William Smellie so important?
32. How much was a nurse's annual salary in 1800?
33. When was Florence Nightingale placed in charge of British hospitals in the Crimea?
34. How did nurses from St. Thomas's Hospital differ from those in other parts of the country in the 1850s?
35. What qualities did Florence Nightingale expect from her nurses?
36. Why was the Public Health Board closed down in 1854?
37. Who was the head of the new Board of Health set up in 1855?
38. What were the findings of the 1869 Public Health Commission?
39. Where were doctors trained in the early nineteenth century?
40. Explain what is meant by orthopaedics, pathology and radiology.
41. When was the National Health Service Act passed?
42. What was the importance of Robert Koch's work?
43. Where would you find the germs which cause malaria?
44. What are antibodies?
45. Who was Ronald Ross?
46. How has the electron microscope been used to fight disease?

47. AIDS is a terrifying disease of the 1980s. What do the individual letters in the abbreviation AIDS stand for?
48. How did Alexander Fleming discover penicillin?
49. What is an antibiotic?
50. When was streptomycin discovered and how was it used?

8 The Welfare State

8.1 Introduction

Looking after the poorer members of our society has always created problems. How can money be raised to help the poor? How can officials tell the difference between people who are genuinely poor and those who are just lazy? How do people feel if money collected for the poor is given to 'scroungers'?

Until 1750 most people lived or worked in the country. Families could get extra food or money from their own vegetable plots or from domestic industry (see Section 4.2). The industrial and agricultural changes of the eighteenth and nineteenth centuries, and the increase in population meant that many people lost their local jobs. Large numbers of people became unemployed or unemployable. At first, many paupers (poor people) were treated as 'spongers' or 'scroungers'. Middle-class people believed that paupers were poor because they were lazy, wicked, careless with money, or all three. By the early twentieth century, attitudes had changed. The Liberal governments of 1906–1914 started providing benefits for children, the sick, the injured, the unemployed and the old. By 1950 successive British governments had established a modern *Welfare State*. A Welfare State is a state which looks after the welfare of all its citizens 'from the cradle to the grave'.

8.2 The Elizabethan Poor Law

In the Middle Ages the old, the sick and the unemployed could get help from family, neighbours or the church. However, in 1538 King Henry VIII closed down the monasteries. The church was no longer able to help large numbers of poor people. Higher prices, wages and costs and higher levels of unemployment led to a growing number of poor and needy citizens. In 1601 Parliament passed a *Poor Law*. This remained the basis of poor relief until 1834. The terms of the Elizabethan Poor Law are set out below:

- In each district two 'overseers of the poor' collected a *poor-rate* from each household. The poor-rate was handed out to those most in need.
- Each parish was to build a *poorhouse* in which the poor and sick could live. The paupers in the poorhouse were given simple jobs to do, such as making cloth or rope. The money earned by the paupers was used to cover the cost of running the poorhouse. Looking after paupers in the poorhouse was known as *indoor relief*.
- In parishes where there were no poorhouses, the poor-rate was used to help people in their own homes. This system was known as *outdoor relief*.
- Orphan children were usually lodged with a local woman, who was paid about 2s. 6d. (12½p) a week for their upkeep. When the children were older, they were bound out by the parish as apprentices.

8.3 Gilbert's Act (1782)

By the 1780s the Elizabethan system of poor relief had begun to break down. Many agricultural labourers were experiencing great poverty, and the overseers of the poor (see Section 8.2) were often unable to help them. The government decided to provide more outdoor relief. A new Act was passed to help the poor, named after Gilbert, the man who steered the Act through Parliament.

The terms of the Act were:

- The overseers of the poor were no longer to be responsible for the paupers. Instead *Guardians of the Poor* were appointed to hand out poor relief.
- Many parishes had been too small to deal with large numbers of paupers. The Guardians of the Poor had the power to work with other parishes if they wished. They could form *poorhouse unions* in order to deal with the problem of poverty.
- Paupers were divided into two groups: the *able-bodied* (those who could work, and wanted to, but could not get a job) and the *infirm* (the old, the sick, cripples and children). The poorhouses were to be used only to house the infirm. The able-bodied were to be looked after in their own homes by means of outdoor relief.

8.4   The Speenhamland System

Poor harvests in the mid-1790s and sharp rises in food prices meant that many farm workers, particularly those in the South of England, were not earning enough to keep themselves and their families. In 1795 a group of magistrates and Guardians of the Poor met at Speenhamland, Berkshire. They decided 'that the present state of the poor does require further assistance than has been generally given them'. The magistrates worked out a system whereby a farm worker's weekly wage was made up to a certain level according to the price of bread and the size of his family. Table 8.1 shows how the amount of poor relief was calculated.

Table 8.1   The Speenhamland System

Cost of a loaf	Income for a man should be	Income for a single woman should be	Income for a man and wife should be	Income for a family with one child should be
1s. 0d.	3s. 0d.	2s. 0d.	4s. 6d.	6s. 0d.
1s. 1d.	3s. 3d.	2s. 1d.	4s. 10d.	6s. 5d.
1s. 2d.	3s. 6d.	2s. 2d.	5s. 2d.	6s. 10d.
1s. 3d.	3s. 9d.	2s. 3d.	5s. 6d.	7s. 3d.
1s. 4d.	4s. 0d.	2s. 4d.	5s. 10d.	7s. 8d.
1s. 5d.	4s. 0d.	2s. 5d.	5s. 11d.	7s. 10d.
1s. 6d.	4s. 3d.	2s. 6d.	6s. 3d.	8s. 3d.

Criticisms of the Speenhamland System were:

- Many people believed that the system encouraged farm workers to be idle. Their wages would be made up to a certain level whether they did any work or not!
- The cost of the poor-rates shot up. Most of the extra money had to be found by well-to-do farmers. Table 8.2 shows the cost of the poor-rate in the period 1795–1832.
- Some people argued that the system led to hasty marriages and large families. A farm worker received more money under the Speenhamland

Table 8.2 Poor rate per

Year	Cost (£)
1795	2 million
1803	4 million
1806	6 million
1832	7 million

System if he had a wife and children. This is hardly a valid argument, as the weekly allowance for a child was not enough for its keep.

- Some farmers may have deliberately paid their labourers low wages. The farmers knew that farm workers' wages would be made up to a higher level from the poor-rate.

Despite these criticisms, there is little doubt that the Speenhamland System prevented many farm workers and their families from starving. It worked well in the agricultural counties of the South, and was also used in certain parts of the Midlands and the North, although recent research has suggested that it was not very common there.

8.5 The Poor Law Amendment Act

While Britain was fighting wars against France (1793–1815), the poor-rate rose sharply. At the end of the war people hoped that things would improve, but there was a depression in industry and agriculture. Thousands of workers lost their jobs. The amount of money spent on poor relief reached a peak of £7 871 000 in 1818. In 1830 widespread riots and disturbances broke out among farm workers in the South. The worst riots took place in areas where the relief given to the poor was greatest. The government set up a Royal Commission to look into the workings of the Poor Law. The Royal Commission produced a report in 1834. Parliament passed an Act based on the Royal Commission's findings. The main terms of the Poor Law Amendment Act (1834) — a new system of poor relief — were

- Parishes were to join together to form *Poor Law Unions*. In each union Boards of Guardians were to take charge of poor relief and build *workhouses* to house the poor. The boards would pay officials to look after the poor. A Central Poor Law Commission was to be set up in London to inspect poor relief and to make sure that local officials were doing their work properly.
- Conditions in the workhouse were to be made as harsh and unpleasant as possible, so that 'scroungers' did not enter the workhouse just to obtain food and shelter. This was known as *the principle of less eligibility*.
- In workhouses families were to be split up: husbands and wives to have separate rooms, children to be separated from parents.
- Outdoor relief would be given only to the sick, the infirm and those paupers over 60 years of age.
- Outdoor relief for the able-bodied to be abolished. If a healthy person or his family wanted relief, they had to go into the workhouse to get it.

Several comments need to be made on the Act:

- The Act failed to tackle the root causes of poverty, such as illness, old age and lack of education. The idea remained that the poor were largely to blame for their poverty.
- The Act worked well in the agricultural areas of the South. In the North the idea of indoor relief had never been widely accepted. Factory workers hated the idea of workhouses with harsh discipline, poor food and separated families. There were riots in Yorkshire and Lancashire, and many workhouses were burnt down.
- The principle of less eligibility assumed that the able-bodied paupers who were willing to work could always find jobs. This was not so in times of economic depression, especially in the North.
- The Act was an administrative success. Within five years the system had been extended to 95 per cent of all parishes. There were fewer paupers applying for poor relief, because families refused to enter the workhouses. The cost of poor relief went down dramatically (Table 8.3).
- By the 1890s some of the powers of the Boards of Guardians had been taken over by county or county borough councils. By 1910 there were other forms of poor relief, such as insurance, pensions and Infants' Welfare Centres. The Act remained in force until 1929.

Table 8.3 Cost of poor relief, 1830–1840 (£1000)

Year	Poor-rates receipts	Spending on relief
1830	8111	6829
1831	8279	6799
1832	8623	7037
1833	8607	6791
1834	8338	6317
1835	7374	5526
1836	6355	4718
1837	5295	4045
1838	5186	4124
1839	5614	4407
1840	6015	4577

8.6 The Workhouse

Under the terms of the Poor Law Amendment Act (see Section 8.5), a Poor Law Commission was set up in 1834. Edwin Chadwick, a lawyer who was deeply interested in social reform, became Secretary to the Commission. The Commission instructed Boards of Guardians to stop the payment of outdoor relief to the able-bodied poor, to draw up plans for new workhouses and to introduce strict rules and regulations in them.

Rules in Southwell Workhouse, 1835

1. Men and women, even husbands and wives, to live apart.
2. No one to go out, except to leave the workhouse for good.

3. No one to have visitors.
4. No tobacco or beer to be allowed on the premises.
5. All able-bodied paupers to do some work.

When a pauper entered the workhouse, he was sent to a 'receiving ward' and examined by a doctor. He was washed and given workhouse clothes. He was then sent to a certain part of the building according to his class:

Class 1:   Men infirm through age or any other cause.
Class 2:   Able-bodied men above the age of 15 years.
Class 3:   Boys above the age of 7 years.
Class 4:   Women infirm through age or any other cause.
Class 5:   Able-bodied women and girls above the age of 15.
Class 6:   Girls above the age of 7.
Class 7:   Children under 7 years of age.

Every morning the paupers would get up at 5.45 a.m., wash and go to prayers. After this came breakfast, which was eaten in silence. During the morning the able-bodied men would be set to work at breaking stones or bones or oakum-picking (untwisting lengths of old rope). The women would do household jobs. The lunch break was usually from midday to 1 p.m. The paupers returned to work for five hours, had their supper from 6 to 7 p.m. and went to bed at 8 p.m. There was rarely a break from this routine.

The food given to the paupers was strictly controlled, so that their diet was more unpleasant than the food eaten by the poorest farm workers living outside the workhouse. Much of the food consisted of potato, bread or suet, but there would be meat twice a week and cheese for supper.

There were severe punishments for those who broke the rules or who failed to co-operate in some other way. For minor offences paupers had their food stopped. For more serious breaches of the regulations, the inmate could be sent to the refractory ward, a small cell where he or she would be expected to live on bread and water. If an inmate committed a very serious crime, he or she would be removed from the workhouse altogether and sent to a 'house of correction'.

Recent research has suggested that many workhouses were not as bad as people said they were. There were strict rules, tough workhouse masters, terrible meals and boring jobs to do in many workhouses, but there were also places where Boards of Guardians interpreted the rules and regulations in a more generous way. The main reason the poor objected to workhouse life was that, once in the workhouse, they lost their self-respect.

8.7   Booth and Rowntree

During the nineteenth century two important investigations into the lives of the poor were carried out. These investigations have provided historians and sociologists with some valuable source material.

One investigation was by Charles Booth, a wealthy shipowner. In *The Life and Labour of the People of London* Booth stated that over 30 per cent of Londoners lived in very poor conditions. Booth argued that low wages, sickness and unemployment were the root causes of poverty. He suggested that many poor people were poor through no fault of their own and that *society* had a duty to remove the causes of poverty.

Table 8.4 London in 1889

Class	Percentage of population
Middle and upper classes	17.8
Comfortable working classes (including servants)	51.5
The poor (18s. to 21s. weekly)	22.3
The very poor (under 18s. weekly)	8.4

The second important investigation was Seebohm Rowntree's *Poverty — A Study of Town Life*, a survey of York, published in 1901. Rowntree found that 43.4 per cent of the working classes in York were living in poverty. Ten per cent of the population lived in 'terrible poverty'. The other 17 per cent lived in 'secondary poverty', where the total family earnings were hardly enough to keep the family alive.

The two reports shocked many people. Booth and Rowntree had shown that laziness and drunkenness were *not* the main causes of poverty. The causes of poverty lay in social, economic and political conditions over which the poor had no control. However, the upper classes of Britain still believed that poverty would die out as the country became richer. By 1902 a number of Liberal and Labour M.P.s thought otherwise. They wanted to attack the causes of poverty and improve social conditions at the first opportunity. Their chance came in 1906.

8.8 Liberal Governments, 1906–1914

Between 1906 and 1914 the Liberals took the measures listed in Table 8.5 to provide relief for the needy.

8.9 The Welfare State in the Twentieth Century

In 1922 a serious depression hit trade and industry. Thousands of workers soon used up their unemployment insurance (see Table 8.5). They had little chance of finding other work. To save families from the workhouse, the government gave out *extended benefits*. These became known as 'the dole'. Soon so many people were out of work that the government decided to cut down on benefits by having a *means test*. This meant that any man who applied for the dole had to answer questions about his means (income). He had to give full details about his savings, earnings, and even part-time jobs done by his children, to a Public Assistance Committee. Table 8.6 shows other measures taken by governments to help the needy between 1925 and 1934.

During the Second World War (1939–1945) the government decided to change the National Insurance Scheme. Lloyd George's Act of 1911 had set up two schemes running side by side. Separate contributions for sickness and unemployment had to be made on different cards. In 1941 a committee under Sir William Beveridge was set up to take a fresh look at social security. A year later the Beveridge Report was published. It said that all insurance and pensions should be brought together under one scheme. The report also stated that everyone was entitled to the 'Five Freedoms' — freedom from want, disease, ignorance, squalor and idleness.

Table 8.5   The Liberal governments, 1906–1914

Year	Measure
1906	*Workmen's Compensation Act* Employers had to agree to pay compensation to employees who suffered injuries while at work
1906–1908	*Children's Acts* During this period Parliament passed laws to provide school meals, school medical services and Infants' Welfare Centres. Under an Act of 1908 no child under the age of 18 could enter a public house or buy cigarettes
1908	*Old age pensions* Everyone over 70 earning less than 10s. (50p) a week received a pension of 5s. (25p) a week. Old people no longer had to depend on help from friends or relatives, or enter the workhouse. To pay for the old age pensions, Lloyd George (Chancellor of the Exchequer) increased taxes on drink and tobacco, raised income tax and supertax and made rich families pay death duties
1909	*Town Planning Act* Local councils were given the power to buy and build council houses. There was a legal limit to the number of buildings which could be put up per acre. The building of 'back-to-back' houses was banned
1909	*Labour exchanges* Winston Churchill, the President of the Board of Trade, set up labour exchanges in 1909. Workers could get information about job vacancies at a local office. Later a national system of labour exchanges was built up which made it possible to pass news of vacancies around the country
1911	*National Insurance Act* This was probably the most important of all the Liberal reforms. Before the Act was passed, many workers insured themselves through Friendly Societies (see Section 5.1) but most preferred to 'take a chance'. Lloyd George's National Insurance Act was the first government scheme for insuring workers against sickness and unemployment. There were four parts to it:

1. Workers were to pay 4d., employers 3d. and the state 2d. into the scheme. If an insured person could not work because of sickness, he received 10s. (50p) a week *sickness benefit*.
2. The scheme applied to those workers earning less than £50 a year.
3. Under the scheme all workers were to join a doctor's 'panel'. The doctor looked after them when they were ill and received a sum of money for each patient.
4. In time of hardship workers in the building, engineering and ship-building industries could apply for unemployment insurance. They would receive 7s. (35p) a week for a maximum of 15 weeks.

In 1920 a second Insurance Act gave cover to *all* workers except farm labourers and domestic servants. Benefits were raised to 15s. (75p) a week for a maximum of 15 weeks in any one year.

Table 8.6

Act	Date	Importance
Contributory Pensions Act	1925	Old age pensions, widows' and orphans' pensions joined to insurance scheme
Local Government Act	1929	Poor Law changed. Boards of Guardians were replaced by Public Assistance Committees
Unemployment Act	1934	Men who had used up their insurance benefits were placed in the care of the Unemployment Assistance Board (U.A.B.). It paid out sums of money according to a means test

The Beveridge Report was described as 'social security from the cradle to the grave'. In 1945 a Labour government came to power. Many of Beveridge's ideas were put into practice. The four most important Acts were:

1. *Family Allowance Act (1945)* A weekly allowance of 5s. (25p) was paid for each child in the family (except the first). Free milk was handed out in schools.
2. *National Insurance Act (1946)* A comprehensive insurance scheme was set up to replace all existing schemes. Everyone was covered — workers, employers and the self-employed. Employers, employees and the state paid into a fund which was used for benefits in time of sickness, unemployment, retirement or death. A Ministry of Social Insurance was set up to administer these schemes.
3. *National Health Act (1947)* Everyone was to be entitled to free medicine. Medical services were reorganised. Doctors had to enrol patients on to panels and received annual payments for each patient on their books. The state took over most hospitals. Optical and dental services were also made free.
4. *National Assistance Act (1948)* The National Assistance Board had the power to increase the pensions and incomes of those in need. The Board also helped the blind, old people, vagrants and patients with T.B.

Today Britain's Welfare State remains one of the finest in the world. There have been some changes and cuts in services, but, all in all, the system is very thorough. The Welfare State is supported by the majority of the British people and most political parties. However, the cost of running it has steadily increased, as the statistics in Table 8.7 suggest.

Table 8.7 Cost of running the social services (£ million)

Date	Cost	Date	Cost
1909	2	1961	3 900
1914	21	1968	7 900
1939	260	1980	12 350
1950	1 500		

SOURCE-BASED QUESTION: THE WELFARE STATE

Evidence questions on the Welfare State are likely to be linked to GCSE assessment objectives 1 and 4:

Assessment Objective 1: To recall, evaluate and select knowledge . . . and to deploy it in a clear and coherent form.

Assessment Objective 4: To show the skills necessary to study a wide variety of historical evidence . . ..

You are therefore likely to get questions based on a *wide variety* of historical evidence. You will be asked to look at documentary evidence, statistics, pictures, graphs and possibly extracts from Acts of Parliament. The language in some of these sources may be difficult to understand.

Look at the five pieces of evidence below. All the sources relate to the period 1906–1914.

Source A

Liberal Party poster, 1911

THE DAWN OF HOPE.

Mr. LLOYD GEORGE'S National Health Insurance Bill provides for the insurance of the Worker in case of Sickness.

Support the Liberal Government
in their policy of
SOCIAL REFORM.

Liberal Party poster, 1911

Source C

National Insurance Act 1911
An Act to provide for insurance against loss of Health and for the Prevention and Cure of Sickness, for Insurance against Unemployment, and for purposes incidental thereto (16 December 1911)

Part 1
List of insured trades for the purposes of this Act relating to Unemployment Insurance
(1) Building: that is to say, the construction, alteration, repair, decoration or demolition of buildings . . ..
(2) Construction of works: that is to say, the construction, reconstruction or alteration of railroads, docks, harbours, canals, embankments, bridges, piers or other works of construction.

(3) Shipbuilding: that is to say, the construction, alteration, repair or decoration of ships, boats, or other craft by persons not being members of the ship's crew . ....
(4) Mechanical, including the manufacture of ordnance and firearms.
(5) Ironfounding, whether included under the foregoing headings or not.
(6) Construction of vehicles: that is to say, the construction, repair or decoration of vehicles.
(7) Sawmilling (including machine woodwork) carried on in connection with any other insured trade or of a kind commonly so carried on.

Source D

National income		
Year	*Total (£m)*	*Per head (£)*
1895	1447	36.9
1900	1750	42.5
1905	1776	41.3
1910	1984	44.2
1913	2183	47.0

Prices (1895 = 100)	
Year	*Total*
1895	100
1900	76
1905	86
1910	91
1913	103

Government expenditure as a percentage of national income	
Year	*Total*
1895	5.1
1900	5.1
1905	7.3
1910	8.4
1913	9.2

Main items of social security expenditure (£m)					
1900		*1910*		*1913*	
Poor relief	8.4	Poor relief	12.4	Poor relief	21.4
		Old Age Pensions	8.5	Old Age Pensions	10.8
		Housing	0.6	Housing	2.2
				Unemployment	3.9
				Health Insurance	5.1
Total in £m	8.4		21.5		43.4

The National Insurance Act was the most important piece of Liberal legislation, since it established the basis on which welfare payments were paid for thereafter . . .. It is curious that this Act is regarded as a piece of Socialist legislation. The whole purpose of the National Insurance Act was anti-Socialist. State insurance against sickness and unemployment was invented by Bismarck to take the sting out of Socialist agitation in Germany. Lloyd George tried the same thing in 1911. The National Insurance Act was also a confidence trick. Lloyd George publicised health insurance as a matter of a worker getting 'ninepence for fourpence'. The truth was that the worker paid for his benefits not only through his fourpence a week but also through taxation. In practice, healthy and employed workers were being asked to support sick and unemployed workers.

(Adapted from *Post-Victorian Britain*, L.C.B. Seaman, 1966)

1. Why, according to source E, was the National Insurance Act 'a confidence trick'?
2. Explain what the slogan 'ninepence for fourpence' (source E) means.
3. Which of the sources A–E is *not* a primary source? Give reasons for your answer.
4. Assume that the sick worker in source B is under 70 and has been ill for 28 weeks. What is the total amount of unemployment insurance he could have claimed during the period of his illness?
   [10s. = 50p].
5. Source C shows a list of trades protected by national insurance under the Act of 1911. Why do you think these particular trades were mentioned in the Act?
6. Which famous politician is sitting at the bedside of the worker in source B?
7. Why do you think posters A and B were printed in 1911?
8. Do the statistics in source D suggest that poverty had been stamped out by 1913? Give reasons for your answer.
9. According to source D, what was the percentage increase in the national income between 1895 and 1913?
10. Which of the sources A–E do you think would be most useful to a historian writing about the National Insurance Act? Give reasons for your answer.

WORK OUT SHORT-ANSWER QUESTIONS: THE WELFARE STATE

1. Explain what you understand by the term 'welfare state'.
2. What were (a) the poor rate? (b) the poorhouse? (c) indoor relief? (d) outdoor relief?
3. How did Gilbert's Act change the Elizabethan system of poor relief?
4. Why was the Speenhamland System introduced in 1795?
5. How was the amount of poor relief calculated under the Speenhamland System?
6. Why did some people criticise the Speenhamland System?
7. Why did an investigation into poor relief take place in 1832?
8. When did Parliament pass the Poor Law Amendment Act?
9. What was meant by 'the principle of less eligibility'?
10. What categories of pauper could receive outdoor relief after 1834?

11. Who became Secretary to the Poor Law Commission in 1834?
12. What happened to a pauper:
    (a) in the 'receiving ward'?
    (b) in the 'refractory ward' of a workhouse?
13. In which parts of the country was there greatest opposition to the Poor Law Amendment Act and why?
14. What sort of work would paupers have been expected to do in the workhouse?
15. Why was the quality of the food in a workhouse strictly controlled?
16. Who was Charles Booth and what was the title of the survey he published in 1889?
17. In which city did Seebohm Rowntree carry out an investigation into poverty?
18. How were children protected by the Liberal government's Children's Acts of 1906–1908?
19. How old did you have to be to qualify for an old age pension in 1908?
20. What sort of housing was banned under the terms of the Town Planning Act of 1909?
21. Name the politician who set up labour exchanges in 1909.
22. How much did workers have to pay into Lloyd George's National Insurance Scheme of 1911?
23. Name three industries which the National Insurance Act of 1911 applied to.
24. In the 1920s what were 'extended benefits'?
25. What was the importance of the Unemployment Act of 1934?
26. What were the 'five freedoms' mentioned by William Beveridge in his 1942 report?
27. What would the family allowances have been for a family of two adults and three children in 1945?
28. Which ministry was set up to administer the schemes laid down by the National Insurance Act in 1946?
29. Which groups of poor people benefited from the passing of the National Assistance Act of 1948?
30. By how much did the cost of running the Welfare State increase between 1909 and 1980?

9 Communications

Examination Guide

You are extremely likely to get questions on transport and communications in your GCSE examination. Most boards ask more questions on *railways* than on roads, canals, shipping or other forms of communication, and you therefore need to know Sections 9.12–9.20 in some detail.

The table shows you the transport and communications topics you need to revise for GCSE, according to which board's papers you are taking. As you can see, the Southern Examining Group and Midland Examining Group syllabuses require a detailed knowledge of developments in transport between 1750 and the present day. The Northern Examining Association and the London and East Anglian Group syllabuses contain fewer topics linked to transport and communications, but you will be expected to know a great deal about developments in roads, canals and railways.

| Topic | Board | | | |
	Northern Examining Association	Southern Examining Group	London and East Anglian Group	Midland Examining Group
Roads	✓	✓	✓	✓
Canals	✓	✓	✓	✓
Sailing ships		✓	✓	✓
Steamships		✓	✓	✓
Railways	✓	✓	✓	✓
Postal services	✓			✓
Telegraph and telephone		✓		✓
Bicycles	✓			✓
Public service vehicles	✓		✓	✓
Cars/motor industry	✓	✓	✓	✓
Aircraft		✓	✓	✓

The boards will be setting transport questions based on a wide variety of stimulus material. You can expect to see pictures, graphs, statistics and documentary material on your papers. The assessment objectives tested here will, in the main, be 1, 2 and 4 (see introductory chapter).

You will probably be asked to describe road-, canal- and railway-building methods, the various problems faced by engineers and the reasons for the decline of roads and canals *up to 1850*. After 1850 the questions are likely to be of a more general type, dealing with the *impact* of different forms of transport on society.

9.1 Introduction

By the eighteenth century there was an urgent need to improve ways of transporting people and goods. Merchants and farmers wanted to send their goods to new markets. Owners of mines, ironworks, potteries and breweries needed to send raw materials and finished goods from one part of the country to another. The people in the growing industrial towns needed food, clothing, household items and luxury goods, which had to be brought from other places.

The main improvements which occurred in methods of transport between 1700 and 1980 were as follows:

1700–1840: Improvements in river and road transport.
1760–1840: The development of a canal system.
1830–1910: The development of railways and steamships.
1920–1980: The development of motor and air transport.

9.2 Road Transport

When the Romans occupied Britain between A.D. 43 and A.D. 400, they built up a system of good military roads. After the Romans left, their roads fell into disrepair. By the Middle Ages, most roads in Britain were little better than muddy cart-tracks.

In 1555 Parliament passed a law called 'The Statute for Mending the Highways'. The law stated that village people had to work for 4–6 days a year on road-mending. The villagers received no money for doing the work. Each parish had to elect two surveyors each year to make sure that the work was done properly.

This system of 'statute labour' did not work at all well. The surveyors were unpaid and unskilled. Most people who helped with repairs did little more than tip stones into deep ruts. In summer the roads became dust-baths; in winter they were flooded, or churned up by cattle, sheep and horses. Road vehicles could only travel at very slow speeds, and sometimes villages and towns were cut off from one another for long periods each year.

9.3 The Turnpike Trusts

By 1750 it was obvious that statute labour (see above) would not provide the good roads the country needed. For this reason *turnpike trusts* became very common in the second half of the eighteenth century. Turnpike trusts consisted of groups of businessmen and landowners, who persuaded the government to pass private Acts of Parliament allowing them to take over and repair stretches of road. To pay for road-building and road-mending, the trusts were allowed to charge road-users a *toll*. Poles, pikes or gates were placed at both ends of a turnpike road, and toll-keepers were employed to collect the money.

Some turnpike trusts did a good job. Parts of Britain were provided with well-drained, well-surfaced roads. Skilled engineers such as Thomas Telford and John Macadam (see Section 9.4) were employed to make sure that the turnpike roads remained in good condition. Better roads made it easier and cheaper to transport such goods as pottery, coal, iron, wool and farm produce.

However, the turnpike system also had its disadvantages. Paying a toll at every gate made travel expensive. Certain trusts did not look after their roads properly, and travellers often found their routes impassable (difficult to travel along). There was no national system of turnpikes and some areas remained without good roads. Many people objected to paying for what had once been free, and there were violent anti-turnpike riots in some parts of the country.

9.4 Four Important Road-builders

The four outstanding road engineers of the eighteenth and nineteenth centuries were as follows.

(a) General George Wade (1673–1748)

Wade built 250 miles of military roads and 40 bridges in Scotland in the 1720s and 1730s. He gave his roads solid foundations, and he cambered (curved) the road surface so that water could run off into drainage ditches at either side. Wade used soldiers from Highland regiments as road-builders.

(b) John Metcalf (1717–1810)

'Blind Jack' Metcalf came from Knaresborough, in Yorkshire. Although blinded by smallpox at the age of 6, he later decided to become a road-builder. He built 180 miles of turnpike road in Yorkshire and Lancashire. When building a section of road over soft ground, he laid foundations of bundles of heather which helped to 'float' the road over the marsh. He placed jagged, broken stones on his road surfaces which eventually ground together under the weight of wheeled traffic. (See Figure 9.1.)

(c) John Loudon Macadam (1756–1836)

Macadam was a Scotsman from a wealthy family. As a young man he took up road-mending as a hobby. His roads were cheap to build and could be constructed quickly. Macadam believed that if the subsoil below the surface of the road was dry, then there was no need for expensive foundations. He thought that the surface of the road was of great importance, and covered his roads with hundreds of small, chipped stones which bound together under the weight of the traffic. Many turnpike trusts used Macadam's road-building methods. In 1815 he became Surveyor of the Bristol Roads and in 1827 he was appointed Surveyor General of the Highways of Great Britain. Parliament voted him a grant of £10 000 for his work.

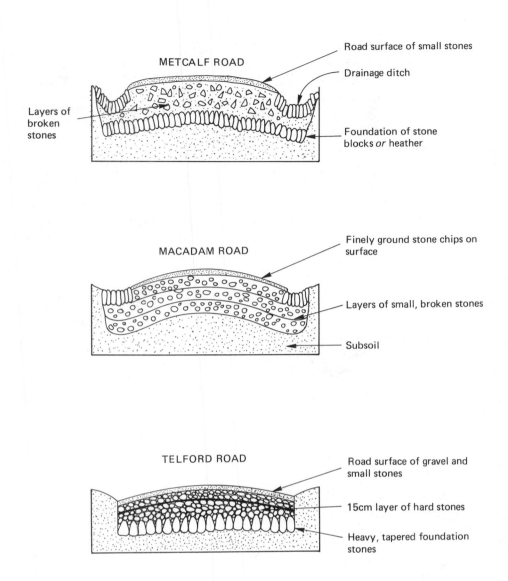

Figure 9.1 Cross-sections of Metcalf, Macadam and Telford roads

(d) Thomas Telford (1757–1834)

Telford was the son of a Scottish shepherd. In 1787 he became Surveyor of the Roads in Shropshire. By 1803 he was in charge of road- and bridge-building schemes in Scotland. Over the next 18 years he built 1000 miles of road, 1000 bridges and several canals.

His greatest achievement was the building of the London–Holyhead road (1815–1826). Telford believed that the best way of keeping a road hard and smooth was to have solid foundations, slight cambers and good drainage. The foundations of his roads therefore consisted of hand-laid blocks of stone. This meant that Telford's roads were long-lasting but expensive.

9.5 The Effects of Better Roads

Table 9.1 shows the effects of road-building on the British economy.

The coaching industry and the turnpike system made large profits until the 1830s. By 1840 many firms had gone out of business as a result of railway development.

Table 9.1 Effects of road-building

Development	Importance
Improvements in the design of road vehicles	Pack-horses became less common. Waggons, coaches and chaises became lighter and faster.
Mail coach routes established in 1784	Better communications between towns and villages, factories and shops, farms and markets. Fewer 'post-boys' (men who carried mail on horseback)
More coaches on the roads	The growth of a 'coaching industry', 1800–1830. New jobs for coach-builders, inn-keepers, drivers and grooms
A *faster* service	Less time and money wasted on sending goods from place to place
Lime, clay, coal and iron goods could be sent from place to place more easily	More raw materials for factory-owners, merchants and builders. Improved transport led to industrial growth
More food transported from farms and villages to towns	Cheaper, healthier, fresh food for town-dwellers

9.6 Roads, 1840–1980

The most important events in the history of road transport between 1840 and 1980 are as listed in Table 9.2.

9.7 Transport by Water

In the early eighteenth century rivers played an important part in Britain's transport system. Barges and boats carried timber, coal and farm produce from inland areas to the coast. However, sending goods by river had many disadvantages. Strong currents, bridges, sandbanks, fords and water-wheels could spell disaster for bargees and boatmen. There was also the problem that some growing centres of industry had no river links. By the 1760s factory owners and merchants were looking for new ways of sending goods from place to place. One solution to the problem of transporting bulky goods seemed to lie in the building of man-made waterways, or *canals*.

9.8 Canal-building, 1757–1820

The most important canals (see Figure 9.2) were as follows.

Table 9.2 Events in history of road transport

Date	Event
1835	*Highways Act* 'Statute labour' was abolished. Parliament gave parishes the power to raise money for road maintenance
1864	A parliamentary committee recommended the end of the turnpike system
1878	County authorities obliged to pay half the cost of main roads
1888	*County Councils Act* The larger local authorities were allowed to maintain roads, using government grants
1903	The government introduced a motor tax on cars, to help pay for road maintenance
1919	The new Ministry of Transport made plans for a nation-wide road system
1924	White lines painted on roads
1934	A 30 m.p.h. speed limit was introduced in built-up areas
1959	The first section of Britain's first motorway, the M1, was opened between London and Birmingham
1963	The *Buchanan Report* recommended that main roads should not run through the centres of busy towns
1967	*Breathalyser* introduced, to test alcohol levels in drivers
1971	900 miles of motorway completed throughout England and Wales

(a) The Sankey Brook Navigation, 1757

The 10-mile Sankey Navigation, built by Henry Berry, linked St. Helens to the River Mersey. The canal carried coal from the South Lancashire coalfield to Liverpool.

(b) The Manchester–Worsley Canal, 1759–1761

A 7-mile canal linking the Duke of Bridgewater's coal-mines to Manchester. The idea for the canal came from the Duke's estate manager, John Gilbert, who realised that flood water from the mines could be used to fill the canal. To reach Manchester the canal had to cross the River Irwell and two bogs. The canal was carried across the River Irwell on an aqueduct. In 1761 the canal was completed and the cost of the Duke's coal in Manchester was halved. By 1776 the canal had been extended to meet the River Mersey at Runcorn.

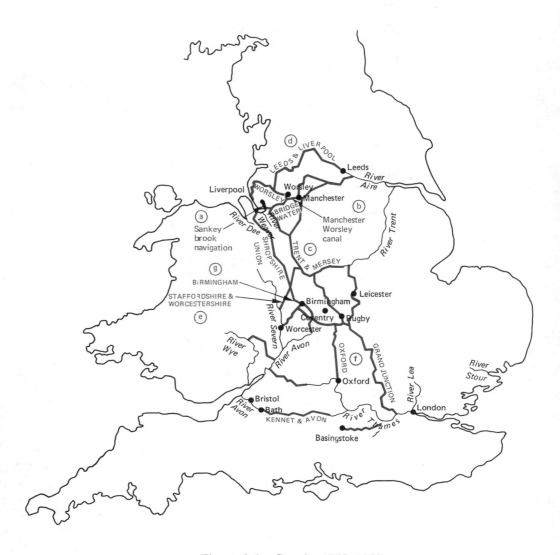

Figure 9.2 Canals, 1750–1850

(c) The Trent and Mersey Canal (sometimes known as the Grand Trunk Canal), 1766–1777

A 93-mile canal linking the Trent to the Mersey. James Brindley (1716–1772: see Section 9.9) built most of the canal, which supplied the Staffordshire Potteries with raw materials (china clay and flintstone) and took away fragile finished goods. Josiah Wedgwood, who provided most of the money for the canal, built his Etruria pottery works on its banks. Brindley's greatest engineering problem was the $1\frac{1}{2}$-mile Harecastle Tunnel, west of Stoke-on-Trent.

(d) The Leeds–Liverpool Canal, 1770–1816

The 127-mile-long canal over the Pennines took 46 years to complete! It linked the Yorkshire woollen industry to the port of Liverpool.

(e) The Staffordshire and Worcestershire Canal, 1766–1772

This waterway branched off the Grand Trunk to the River Severn at Stourport. It linked the Black Country to the ironworks of Shropshire.

(f) The Oxford Canal, 1778–1790

This canal linked the River Thames to the Trent and Mersey Canal. It took 12 years to complete, because the canal company kept running out of money!

(g) The Birmingham Canal, 1768–1772

The canal carried coal from pits along its line and goods from the Staffordshire and Worcestershire Canal to Birmingham. Iron and brass goods could be sent from Birmingham to Liverpool, Hull and Bristol. Birmingham became the largest single canal centre, the 'canal metropolis'.

9.9 Two Famous Canal Engineers

(a) James Brindley (1716–1772)

Brindley, the son of a Derbyshire farmer, received very little formal education. He became a millwright's apprentice and designed a new type of water-wheel. In 1752 he rebuilt a corn mill at Leek and installed a water-wheel at Gal Pit, near Manchester. The water-wheel was used for pumping water out of a flooded coal-mine. In 1755 Brindley was at work on corn mills at Wheelock and Trentham, and at Congleton he built a new silk mill.

In 1756 Brindley visited Birmingham and Wolverhampton to study Newcomen's steam engines (see Section 4.18). Two years later he built a windmill at Burslem for Josiah Wedgwood. By 1759 his natural flair for engineering was well known throughout Lancashire.

Francis Egerton, third Duke of Bridgewater, heard about Brindley's mechanical genius and employed him to build the Worsley Canal and the Bridgewater Canal (see Section 9.8). Brindley planned the Trent and Mersey Canal but died before the canal was completed. He also carried out surveys for the Bradford Canal, the Rochdale Canal, and the Leeds and Liverpool Canal.

(b) Thomas Telford (1757–1834)

Telford built harbours, bridges, lighthouses, docks and roads (see Section 9.4) in many parts of Britain. Between 1793 and 1805 he built the Ellesmere Canal, linking Shropshire to the coast of North Wales and Liverpool. In 1801 Telford started work on a coast-to-coast canal in northern Scotland. The Caledonian Canal took 20 years to build and cost £980 000.

Telford also helped to construct the Gotha Canal in Sweden.

9.10 The Effects of Canals

By the 1790s many canal companies were making large profits. Hundreds of people rushed to invest their money in canals. They hoped to obtain high dividends (money gained from investments). In 1793 and 1794 this craze for putting money into canals got out of hand. 'Canal mania' gripped the country. Investors from the East Midlands tried to buy shares in any canal company which came up for sale. The dividends people received varied a great deal. Some canal projects, such as the Southampton–Salisbury Canal Scheme and the Grand Western Canal, were never completed and the money invested in them was lost. On the other hand, the Loughborough Canal paid a dividend of 154 per cent in one year!

This massive investment in canals helped the British economy to expand. Businessmen and merchants could not find all the money needed to build canals, and so it was fortunate that members of the public were willing to risk their money. 'Canal mania' meant that canal-building could keep up with the demand from Britain's growing industries.

The other main effects of canal-building were as follows:

- Some investors made large sums of money from canal-building. They often put these profits into other transport schemes.
- Canals were a source of employment for navvies (labourers), craftsmen and engineers.
- It was easier to send agricultural produce (grain, vegetables, meat) to the growing industrial towns. People had a better diet.
- Canal towns grew up in some areas (e.g. Shardlow, Stourport).
- Some places which were well served by canals became centres of industry (e.g. South Lancashire, the West Midlands and Staffordshire).
- Canals meant supplies of cheaper coal, iron, lime, timber and clay for factory owners.

Canals provided the country with a useful transport network, but by the 1830s the entire system was in decline. Canals were unable to compete with railways (see Section 9.17). Canals were not suited to passenger transport or steam-powered barges.

SOURCE-BASED QUESTION: ROADS AND CANALS

Source A

Source B

1. Why do you think the toll-keeper in source A seems to be having problems?
2. Briefly describe the main benefits to the economy of the turnpike system.
3. Identify the feature marked X in source A and the feature marked Y in source B.
4. Are these primary or secondary sources? Give reasons for your answer.
5. If you had to travel from London to Oxford in 1800, would you prefer to travel by road or canal? Give reasons for your answer.
6. Why did roads and canals decline in importance in the 1840s?

9.11 Sailing Ships, 1800–1900

In 1800 British ships carried more goods than did the ships of any other country. However, there had been few changes in the design of British sailing ships for over 100 years. The typical eighteenth-century ship was built in the shipyards of North-east England or North America. She was shaped like a floating shoe-box, and carried few guns but a great spread of canvas, with topgallant sails.

By the 1840s British and American shipyards were building a new type of sailing ship, the *clipper*. Clipper ships had long, sharp bows, tall masts and billowing sails. Many of them sailed from British ports round the Cape of Good Hope to India, Australia and the East Indies. Their holds were crammed with such goods as tea, sugar, flour and wheat.

Clipper ships ruled the world's sea routes for 20 years. In the 1860s and 1870s the number of sailing ships carrying cargo began to decline. *Steamships*, with powerful engines and more cargo space, began to take trade away from sailing ships. In 1869 the Suez Canal was opened. Steamships could take a 'short cut' to the East but clippers could not use the canal, because of cross-winds.

9.12 Steamships

In the nineteenth century design of ships changed in two ways: in the form of *propulsion* they used (how they were driven through the water) and in the *materials* used to make them. In 1800 most ships relied upon wind power and were made of wood; by 1900 they were driven by steam and were made of iron. Table 9.3 shows the main developments in steam-powered ships between 1800 and 1850.

Bigger and faster steamships meant more passengers, freight and crew. Often steamships were overloaded and overcrowded. In 1870 Samuel Plimsoll, a Liberal M.P., began a campaign to improve conditions on ships. He pointed out that lives had been lost at sea, owing to carelessness on the part of shipowners who overloaded their ships in the hope of making large profits.

In 1876 Parliament passed a *Merchant Shipping Act*. This allowed the government to control conditions on ships and to prevent overloading by means of a 'Plimsoll line' along the side of the ship.

The development of steamships had a major impact on the British economy. The main effects of this form of transport were as follows:

- Travelling times across the Atlantic and to the East were cut dramatically. In 1850 it took 14 days to travel from Liverpool to New York. In 1900 the same voyage lasted 5 days.

Table 9.3 Developments in steam-powered ships

Ship	Date	Designer	Importance
Charlotte Dundas	1802	William Symington	The first British ship to be powered by a paddle-wheel
Savannah	1819	Francis Ficket	The first sailing ship fitted with an engine to cross the Atlantic
Aaron Manby	1822	Aaron Manby	The first iron ship to put to sea
Sirius	1838	D. Menzies	The first steamship to cross the Atlantic using steam power all the way
Archimedes	1838	F. Pettit-Smith	The first steamship to use screw propellers
Britannia	1840	Robert Napier	The first Cunard steamship to carry mail
Great Britain	1845	I. K. Brunel	The first iron ship to use screw propellers on the transatlantic run

- The price of sending goods by sea went down. The cost of sending grain across the Atlantic fell from 40p per quarter in 1863 to $7\frac{1}{2}$p per quarter in 1901. This led to lower food prices in Britain.
- Trade became easier because bulky goods (e.g. grain, coal, timber) could be sent cheaply by sea.
- New markets for factory-made goods were opened up to British merchants.
- The increase in ships, dock, warehouses and offices meant more jobs. Many people invested their money in shipping companies. Great shipyards grew up in North-east England, Clydeside and Barrow-in-Furness.

Since 1900 the British shipbuilding industry has been in decline. Many British ships were sunk during the First World War (1914–1918) and the world trade depression of the 1920s and 1930s resulted in the collapse of the industry in the North-east. After the Second World War (1939–1945) Britain was still the world's largest shipbuilding nation, but since the 1950s Germany, Sweden, Japan and the U.S.A. have overtaken us.

9.13 Railways, 1700–1812

(a) Introduction

Early railways or 'waggon-ways' consisted of horses pulling waggons along wooden rails. The waggon-ways linked inland coal-mines and quarries in Northumberland to the rivers Tyne and Wear. By 1767 cast-iron rails were being used at Coalbrookdale in Shropshire (see page 80) and nine years later the first *plate-rails* were produced in Sheffield. Plate-rails were L-shaped, and ordinary, smooth waggon-wheels could be used on them. A waggon-way with plate-rails was known as a 'plate-way' or 'tramway'. By 1809 *stationary* steam engines were being used to haul waggons along tramways.

(b) Early Railway Development

(i) *The Surrey Iron Railway*

In 1804 the first *public* railway was opened. Britain was at war with France and there was a need for a direct overland link between London and Portsmouth. Nineteen miles of tramway were built between Wandsworth and Croydon, but the line to Portsmouth was never completed. The Surrey Iron Railway was open to any members of the public who could provide trucks drawn by horses.

The railway was used to carry coal, manure, chalk, lime and sand. Few passengers travelled on it.

(ii) *Richard Trevithick (1771–1833)*

Trevithick, a Cornish mining engineer, developed a small-scale version of James Watt's steam engine (see Section 4.18). In 1801 he drove a high-pressure steam carriage along a road in Camborne, Cornwall. Three years later, in 1804, Trevithick built a locomotive for use on the Penydaren tramway in South Wales. In 1808 he put another locomotive, 'Catch-me-who-can', on display in London. After a few weeks Trevithick ran out of money. He dismantled 'Catch-me-who-can', and returned to building and designing *stationary* steam engines.

(iii) *Developments in Northumberland*

Trevithick's three locomotives had been largely unsuccessful, but it was not long before other engineers were copying his ideas. The first working locomotive was built by John Blenkinsop at an iron foundry near Leeds in 1812. A year later, in the North-east, William Hedley, an engineer at Wylam Colliery, near Newcastle, produced 'Puffing Billy', which could draw nine laden waggons at a speed of 5 m.p.h.

9.14 George Stephenson (1781–1848)

George Stephenson was an engineer at Killingsworth Colliery, Northumberland. In 1805 he saw a locomotive designed by Trevithick (see above) in Newcastle-on-Tyne. He realised that locomotives had many advantages over stationary steam engines for pulling coal waggons along sections of track. In 1814 he built a locomotive called 'Blücher' which pulled eight laden coal waggons for six miles along the Killingworth Colliery Waggon Way. Over the next six years Stephenson built sixteen more locomotives and many miles of track.

Stephenson is best remembered for three engineering achievements.

(a) Stockton and Darlington Railway, 1821–1825

Edward Pease, a wealthy Quaker businessman, decided that a railway link was needed between the river-port of Stockton and the coal-mines of south Durham. He appointed George Stephenson as engineer in charge of building the railway. Stephenson surveyed and constructed a route of 27 miles of track. He laid the rails 4 feet $8\frac{1}{2}$ inches apart, which has remained the standard gauge on British Rail right up to the present day. The new line was opened in September 1825, when 12 loaded waggons, a coach and 21 passenger cars were hauled along by Stephenson's locomotive 'Locomotion'.

(b) Liverpool and Manchester Railway, 1825–1830

The world's first complete railway for goods traffic and passengers was the Liverpool and Manchester Railway. A group of coal and cotton merchants decided to construct a railway line between the two cities, as the toll-charges on canals and roads were too high. In 1826 Parliament passed an Act giving the merchants permission to build the line. George Stephenson became chief engineer. He had to solve three major engineering problems:

1. *Chat Moss* was a huge, spongy bog twelve miles square. Stephenson floated the track on foundations of brushwood and heather over part of the marsh.
2. *The Sankey River*   Stephenson built a brick viaduct with a total span of 500 feet across the Sankey Valley.
2. *Olive Mount*   Near Liverpool a hill straddled the line of the railway. Stephenson had to dig a 2200-yard tunnel through the hill and then make a two-mile cutting through solid rock.

For many years the railway earned more money from carrying passengers than freight. In 1835 it began to carry livestock, and soon supplies of fresh fish and vegetables were being sent inland. In 1837 the railway company made a profit of £150 000. Soon businessmen all over the country began to promote other railway companies.

(c) The Rainhill Trials (1829)

In 1829 the directors of the Liverpool and Manchester Railway Company decided to launch a competition to see which design of locomotive would be best for the new line. There was to be a prize of £500. Three locomotives took part and one horse-powered machine (Table 9.4). The 'Rocket' was the clear winner. It reached a top speed of 29 m.p.h. and kept going for longest. The Stephensons won the prize.

Table 9.4   The Rainhill trials

Locomotive	Designer	Weight	Average speed
The 'Novelty'	Braithwaite and Ericsson	2 tons 15 cwt	20 m.p.h.
The 'Rocket'	Robert Stephenson	4 tons 3 cwt	$12\frac{1}{2}$ m.p.h.
The 'Cyclopede'	T. S. Brandreth	3 tons	5 m.p.h.
The 'Sanspareil'	Timothy Hackworth	4 tons 8 cwt	$12\frac{1}{2}$ m.p.h.

9.15   Robert Stephenson and I. K. Brunel

(a) Robert Stephenson (1803–1859)

Robert Stephenson helped his father, George, to build the Stockton and Darlington Railway (see Section 9.14) and designed the 'Rocket' locomotive. He worked on the Canterbury and Whitstable Railway and built an important line between London and Birmingham. He also designed tubular bridges at Conway and over the Menai Strait. In 1847 he was elected as Conservative M.P. for Whitby.

(b) Isambard Kingdom Brunel (1806–1859)

Brunel, the son of Sir Marc Brunel, was probably the greatest engineer of his age. At the age of 18 he helped his father dig part of a tunnel under the River Thames. He later drew up plans for a suspension bridge at Clifton, near Bristol.

In 1833 Brunel became chief engineer of the Great Western Railway (G.W.R.). He built one of the finest railway links in the country between London, Bristol, Exeter and Plymouth. He drove a two-mile tunnel through Box Hill and constructed a magnificent bridge over the River Tamar. He set the rails on the G.W.R. 7 feet apart, to help trains hold the track more firmly at high speed. He tried to get other companies to follow his example, but by 1840 60 per cent of Britain's railways had been built to Stephenson's 'narrow gauge' of 4 feet $8\frac{1}{2}$ inches. In 1846 Parliament decided that the standard gauge for the whole country should be 'narrow gauge', and by 1892 the G.W.R. had converted the last of its broad-gauge tracks to narrow gauge.

9.16 The 1844 Railways Act (the 'Cheap Trains Act')

The Act stated:

- Railway companies should provide third-class travel on all lines at a cost of no more than a penny (1d.) a mile.
- At least one train a day (the 'parliamentary train') had to run the length of the line, stopping at all stations.
- All passengers had to have a seated and covered ride.
- Trains should travel at a speed of not less than 12 m.p.h.
- Open carriages were to be abolished.

9.17 The Effects of Railways

In the 1840s people thought that by putting their money into railways they could make quick profits. A craze for railway building, 'railway mania', broke out and soon new lines were being built in places where they were not really needed. The most famous of the railway investors was George Hudson, the 'Railway King'. By 1848 he had bought control of a third of all the railways in Britain. In 1849 many of his companies went bankrupt and Hudson was taken to court. It turned out that many of his railway-building schemes had been a swindle and he was forced to resign in disgrace.

Other social and economic effects of railway-building in the nineteenth century were as follows.

(a) Economic Effects of Railways

- *Coal and iron* Railways needed large amounts of coal and iron. Mine-owners no longer had to rely on canals to transport raw materials.

- *Agriculture* Farmers could send perishable goods to distant towns. Tools and machines could be sent from factories to farms.
- *Jobs* There were more jobs for engineers, navvies, surveyors and railway staff. More people were able to travel in search of work.
- *Trade* More goods could be sent to and from the ports. Locomotives, steel goods, rails and machine-tools were sent to countries building their own railways.
- *Competition* Many canals and turnpike trusts went out of business. However, there was an increase in demand for road transport to and from railway stations and loading points.

(b) Social Effects of Railways

- Many towns and villages were much less isolated once a railway line had been built close by.
- Cities and suburbs grew in size. Working-class suburbs sprang up near city centres. Middle-class people moved out of town and travelled into work by train. Cheaper house-building materials became available.
- Coastal resorts such as Brighton, Torquay and Southend expanded. More people went on holiday.
- The postal service improved and newspapers could be sent from London to the provinces.
- Some railway towns grew up (e.g. Rugby, Crewe, Swindon).
- Police and troops could be sent to different parts of the country to deal with riots and disturbances.

9.18 Railways, 1846–1918

The main events in the development of the railway network were as listed in Table 9.5.

Table 9.5 Development of railway network

Date	Event
1854	A Railway and Canal Traffic Act stated that no railway or canal company should show favouritism towards one business or industry at the expense of another
1871–1873	*Regulations of Railways Acts* A Railway Commission was set up to decide upon amalgamations (railway companies joining up), the purchase of canals and the rates to be charged for goods traffic. Strict safety regulations were drawn up
1914–1918	During the First World War it was necessary to move large numbers of men and weapons, and the government took over the railway system. After the war, the government handed back control of the railways to private companies, together with £60 million in compensation. This sum was not enough to make good the money lost by the companies during the war

9.19 Tube Trains

In 1858 two railway promoters, Charles Pearson and J. H. Stevens, planned an underground railway line from Farringdon Street to King's Cross in London. Work began on the line in 1860. In some places it ran through open cuttings; in others the line burrowed deep underground. The grand opening of this new Metropolitan Railway took place in January 1863.

A second company, the Metropolitan District, started a similar service in 1868 with a line from South Kensington to Westminster. Between 1870 and 1900 the underground network was extended, and by the early twentieth century it was possible to travel to Richmond in Surrey and Hornchurch in Essex by underground. Many more people could travel in and out of the centre of the capital quickly and cheaply.

The early underground trains were pulled by steam locomotives. Conditions for passengers on these trains were smoky, grimy and uncomfortable. Few improvements were made to passenger comfort until the 1890s, when electrical power was used for the first time on underground trains. Travel by underground then became much cleaner.

The first electrified 'tube' railway was opened in 1890. It ran from the City of London under the River Thames to Stockwell. In 1933 a number of separate underground railways came under the general management of the London Passenger Transport Board. This was nationalised in 1948.

There are two other underground railways in Britain: there is a three-mile railway link between Liverpool and Birkenhead, and in Glasgow a circular underground railway stretches for seven miles under the city.

9.20 The Decline of Railways

In 1920 there were 120 railway companies in Britain. The *Railways Act* of 1921 stated that the companies should amalgamate to form four major companies by 1923. These were:

1. The London, Midland and Scottish Railway (L.M.S.).
2. The London and North East Railway (L.N.E.R.).
3. The Great Western Railway (G.W.R.).
4. The Southern Railway (S.R.).

A Railway Rates Tribunal was set up to fix rates and fares sufficient to provide each company with an adequate income.

By the 1930s the four railway companies were facing increasing competition from road transport. In 1937 the Railway Rates Tribunal allowed the companies a 5 per cent increase in charges. Two years later war broke out and the railways were once again taken over by the government. After the war the Labour government decided that the railway system should be *nationalised* (permanently brought under state control). The *1947 Transport Act* stated:

- A Transport Commission was to be set up to control railways, canals and road haulage.
- The railways were to be reorganised into six regions and the whole system was to be called *British Rail*.
- The Railway Rates Tribunal was to be replaced by a Transport Tribunal, which was to regulate fares and freight charges.

After nationalisation the railways continued to decline in importance. There was increasing competition from road transport, and by 1956 British Rail was making an annual loss of £120 million. A *Modernisation Plan* was drawn up, designed to make the railways pay their way. Non-profitable lines were to be closed, rolling stock and track were to be improved, and electric and diesel trains were to replace steam engines.

In 1961 Dr Richard Beeching became Chairman of British Transport. He published a 'Re-shaping Report' which contained many of the recommendations included in the Modernisation Plan. The 'Beeching Report' resulted in 2363 stations and 5000 route-miles of track being closed. By 1968 diesel trains had completely replaced steam locomotives and improvements had been made in freight services.

The *1968 Transport Act* made important changes to the structure of British Rail. A system of subsidies was introduced to support loss-making services. Since 1968 the railways have rarely made a profit, and it is now generally accepted that railways are a service rather than a business. Today British Rail is facing increasing competition from road-haulage firms and cut-price coach companies, which use the motorway system for transporting goods and people.

SPECIMEN QUESTIONS AND MODEL ANSWER: THE RAILWAYS

1. In what ways did the development of a railway system affect the lives of people living in the nineteenth century? How does this compare with the effects of cars, buses and lorries on the lives of people living in the twentieth century?
2. (a) What arguments were used *against* the building of railways in the 1830s and 1840s?
   (b) Describe the effects of railways on:
       (i) the growth of towns
       (ii) canals and turnpikes
       (iii) the expansion of industry
       (iv) leisure and recreation

(You will find a specimen answer to question 2 below.)

You may be asked to write about the life of a famous engineer *from the point of view of the engineer himself*. You should therefore know the biographical outlines of:

Thomas Telford (Roads and Canals)
John Macadam (Roads)
George Stephenson (Railways)
Isambard Brunel (Railways and Steamships)
James Brindley (Canals)

These seem to be the examiners' favourites!

Source-based Question

Source A

1700	Waggon-ways and tramways in use in Northumberland
1767	First iron rails made at Coalbrookdale
1804	First railway locomotive in use at Penydaren
1825	Important railway link opened in the North-east
1830	The first railway to carry passengers and goods opened in Lancashire
1835	Great Western Railway founded

Source B

The Pleasures of the Rail-Road.___ Cought in the Railway!

Source C

1830   I took a seat at Liverpool in that mail to London. One of our companions from Coventry was a person employed in surveying and taking levels of the line for the proposed railway from Birmingham to London. It will be a work of great magnitude and extent, and if carried into effect will make highways, horses and canals useless . . . .

1837   I set out on an excursion to Liverpool on the railway . . . . We left Birmingham at half-past eleven, and arrived at Liverpool precisely at four, without the smallest inconvenience; the trains stopped for five minutes at the different stations merely to deliver and take up passengers and parcels. The speed is so great it is hardly possible to gauge of the country you pass. The tunnel into Liverpool is a grand production of human effort. The railways from Manchester and Birmingham must contribute greatly to Liverpool's increasing wealth and commerce.

(William Dyott, *Diary 1781–1845*, ed. R. W. Jefferey)

Source D

When Colonel Sibthorpe stated his hatred of railways, he only expressed the feeling of the country gentry and many of the middle classes in the southern districts. Mr H. Berkeley, M.P. for Cheltenham, protested very strongly about the railways running through the heart of the hunting country. The critics of the railway continually harped on about the invasion of property, the intrusion of public roads into private domains, the noise and nuisance caused by locomotives and the danger of fire to nearby property. They said the lawlessness of navvies was a source of great terror to quiet villages, that the breed of horses would be destroyed, that country innkeepers would be ruined, posting towns depopulated, turnpike roads deserted and the institution of the English stagecoach destroyed for ever. They added that fox covers and game preserves would be interfered with, landowners and farmers reduced to beggary and labourers thrown out of jobs. Sanitary objections were also urged against railways and Sir Anthony Carlisle M.D. insisted that tunnels would expose healthy people to colds, catarrh and consumption.

(Life of George Stephenson, Samuel Smiles, 1857)

Use sources A–D *and your own knowledge of railways* to answer the questions below.

1. In which industry were waggon-ways and tramways used in 1700?
2. Who designed the Penydaren locomotive?
3. Between which two towns was an important railway line built in 1830?
4. When was source B first published?
5. According to source D, why were many landowners opposed to railways?
6. Source D mentions 'sanitary objections' to the early railways (line 14). What do you think these objections might have been?
7. Which source is biased against the early railways? Explain your choice.
8. Which of the four sources A–D is *not* a primary source?
9. Which source B–D is least reliable as a piece of historical evidence? Give reasons for your choice.
10. 'The railways brought the country more advantages than disadvantages between 1830 and 1860.'
    Using the sources and your own knowledge of the topic, explain whether you agree or disagree with this statement.

Essay Question 2: Specimen Answer

Plan

(a) Opposition to Railways

1. *Landowners* concerned about damage to the environment, fox-hunting, etc.
2. *Conservatism* (fear of change) and *ignorance* Letters, newspapers, speeches attacking railway development on the grounds that it was dangerous.
3. *Sabbatarians* (strict Christians) objected to people travelling on Sunday.
4. *Snobbery* There were some objections because people believed travel was harmful and that railways would encourage working-class mobility.

(b) Effects of Railways

1. *Growth of towns*   Some towns (e.g. Crewe, Swindon) grew rapidly. Bricks and building materials could be carried on railways.
2. *Canals and turnpikes*   Some canals bought up by railway companies; most turnpike trusts ruined.
3. *Industry*   Coal, iron, steel, timber needed for railway development, so these industries benefited. More exports.
4. *Leisure and recreation*   More holidays, outings, excursions. Growth of holiday industry. More newspapers and books.

Model Answer

(a) There was great opposition to railways in the 1830s and 1840s for a wide variety of reasons. In the first place, many landowners were against them. There were genuine fears that livestock would be injured and the countryside would be polluted. The Duke of Cleveland opposed railways because he believed they would ruin his fox-hunting. Many landowners forced the railway-builders to make costly detours or demanded huge sums of money in compensation for the inconvenience of having a railway line running across their estates.

Conservatism and ignorance were two further reasons why many people opposed railways. New ideas often meet with opposition. Doctors claimed that travellers would be suffocated in tunnels, driven mad by noise or blinded and deafened by high speeds. They thought that cinders would set fire to cornfields and that smoke would terrify farm animals.

Sabbatarians criticised the railways because they did not like the idea of people making long journeys on Sundays. In 1841 a poster in Newcastle proclaimed that passengers would be taken 'safely and swiftly to hell' if they travelled to Carlisle on a Sunday. There was also a great deal of snobbery directed towards railways. Neither Oxford nor Cambridge universities welcomed the new invention, and kept it safely distant from any colleges. The headmaster of Eton College strongly disapproved of railways and stopped the Great Western Railway from building a station at Slough, a mile away from his school. He believed that the railway might corrupt the morals of the boys in his charge.

There were also objections from people who lived in towns or villages close to railway lines. The 'navvies' who built the lines were tough, hard-working men who often got drunk and rowdy on pay-day. Fights were frequent and the local police often found it difficult to control them.

(b)

(i) The Growth of Towns

Some towns, such as Crewe and Swindon, became 'railway towns' and expanded very rapidly. Holiday towns such as Bournemouth and Blackpool began to cater for large numbers of tourists and trippers. Bricks, timber and other building materials could be transported quickly and cheaply to growing towns. Midland bricks and Welsh slate helped to produce the nineteenth-century suburbs we see today.

(ii) Canals and Turnpikes

Canal companies and turnpike trusts objected to railway development because they believed they would lose business. The Liverpool and Manchester Railway, for example, was built to compete with the Bridgewater Canal. The amount of traffic using turnpikes declined rapidly and many trusts were ruined overnight. In 1830 the Liverpool to Manchester turnpike was let out for £1700; by 1831 there were no takers at £800! However, cabs and carts continued to provide a useful 'taxi' service between people's homes and railway stations, and some new roads were built to link up the new lines. By 1850 long-distance coaches had become a thing of the past.

(iii) The Expansion of Industry

The building of railways made enormous demands on the metal and coal industries. Locomotives needed large amounts of coal for fuel, and iron was needed to build bridges and track. To satisfy these demands, new ironfields were developed in Middlesborough, Lincolnshire and Northamptonshire. By the 1860s rails were being made of Bessemer steel.

Railways created new businesses. They lowered the costs of industry and strengthened the position of British producers who wanted to sell goods abroad. Locomotives, steel, rails and machine-tools were exported to countries which wanted to build their own railways. Thomas Brassey (1805–1870), a British railway contractor, built railways in four continents.

(iv) Leisure and Recreation

More people could go on holiday to towns such as Bournemouth and Blackpool. There were daily excursions for working-class people to seaside towns such as Southend and Worthing. A new 'holiday industry' grew up in coastal resorts. Postal services improved, and there were more books, pamphlets and newspapers available. People could travel to see relatives and friends more easily. For the population as a whole, railways represented a new possibility of movement.

9.21 Postal Services

Between 1650 and 1850 improvements in land transport led to a dramatic improvement in the speed and reliability of the country's postal services.

A government-run postal service had been started in 1637. Mail was carried by post-boys (usually men!) on horseback, and charges were made, according to the distance travelled and the weight of the package. The person who received the package or letter had to pay for it. By 1750 there was a thrice-weekly service operating between the larger towns but it was slow and unreliable. Highwaymen were a constant threat to the early postal service.

In 1784 John Palmer, a Bath theatre-owner, suggested that the Post Office should go into competition with post-boys and private stagecoach companies. Palmer became Comptroller General of the Post Office, and introduced mail coaches which ran to a strict timetable on the London to Bristol route. The coaches carried passengers as well as mail, and there were armed guards to deter highwaymen. To allow for greater speeds the mail coaches did not have to pay tolls at turnpikes. By 1795, 400 towns enjoyed the benefits of a regular mail service.

In 1801 Parliament decided to introduce a tax on letters. Members of the public started to find ways of sending letters privately and thus avoiding the tax. Fewer and fewer people used the official postal service. By the 1830s less than a quarter of British mail was being carried by the Post Office!

In 1836 Rowland Hill, a teacher, published a booklet called *Post Office Reform: Its Importance and Practicability*. He argued that a single pre-paid fee of a penny should be charged on all letters, regardless of how far the letter was being sent. He believed that this scheme would greatly increase the volume of mail and the service would make large profits. The *penny post* was introduced in 1840, and within ten years there were five times as many letters being posted. Stamps such as the 'penny black' were issued so that payment could be made quickly and in advance. The railways began to carry mail in 1838, and the first travelling sorting office ran on the London to Birmingham line in 1840. By 1911 mail was being carried by aeroplane.

Today the Post Office provides postal, Giro (banking) and data-processing services. It provides daily deliveries to 23 million households. In 1984 a national network of 83 high-speed sorting offices was opened. The G.P.O. hopes to introduce a wide range of other services in the 1980s and 1990s.

9.22   The Telegraph and the Telephone

On the early railways signalmen used a system of flags and lanterns for passing messages to engine-drivers and guards. However, this method of signalling was not totally reliable and human error led to many accidents and derailments.

In 1837 two British scientists, William Cooke and Charles Wheatstone, invented a *needle telegraph*. The telegraph took the form of magnetic needles which were deflected by sending an electric current through a coil of wire. Such deflections could be used to send messages in code. The first telegraph wires were set up between Euston railway station and Camden Town station, about a mile away. At about the same time, Samuel Morse (1791–1872), an American, invented a system whereby an electric current caused a pencil to mark a line on a strip of paper. Long and short bursts of current produced dots and dashes on the paper. This form of telegraphy became known as *morse code*.

By 1859 a single-needle electric telegraph was in use on British railways. A year later a submarine cable was laid across the English Channel so that messages could be sent from London to Paris. A second cable was laid across the Atlantic in 1866. In 1869 Parliament granted the Post Office a monopoly on all inland telegraph business.

An invention of equal importance was the *telephone*. In 1875 a Scottish-born American, Alexander Graham Bell, discovered that vibrations caused by sound could be sent from one place to another by using electric currents. No special knowledge was required to use a telephone, and so its effects on trade, industry and social life were much greater than those of the telegraph. By the 1880s there were many private telephone companies, but the Post Office had taken over all the main trunk lines by 1892 and all the telephone exchanges (except Hull) by 1912.

Today Britain has the world's third-largest telecommunications system. There are over 23 million phones in the country, 72 000 telex connections and 50 000 data transmission terminals. In 1986 the telecommunications system was de-nationalised and members of the public were able to buy shares in this highly profitable organisation.

9.23 The Bicycle

Bicycles first appeared on Britain's roads in about 1820. They were known as 'hobby horses' or 'dandy horses' and were modelled on a French design. In 1839 Kirkpatrick Macmillan, a Scottish blacksmith, produced a machine which was driven by two treadles. Over the next thirty years attempts were made to design bicycles which could be pedalled along by using leg action. A French company built and sold 'velocipedes'. These were bicycles with pedals attached to the front wheels. In England these machines became known as 'boneshakers'!

By the 1870s the city of Coventry had become the centre of Britain's bicycle industry. Bicycle manufacturers were soon selling large numbers of 'penny-farthing' bicycles, which had a front wheel four feet in diameter and a much smaller back wheel. In the 1880s Starley's 'safety bicycle' appeared. It had a chain-driven back wheel and direct steering.

Cycling became a popular pastime for many people in the 1890s. Dunlop inflatable tyres cost only a few pounds and made cycling smoother and safer. Working-class people found that they could use their bicycles for getting to work, visiting friends or going on holiday. Since 1900 many improvements have taken place in frame construction, speed gears and safety equipment.

9.24 Motor Cycles

The first motor cycles appeared in 1885. Bicycle companies began to add a small power unit to the cycles they sold. The cost of running a 'motor cycle' was quite low and they soon became popular with young men.

By 1907 there were more than 34 000 motor cycles on the roads. In the same year the first T.T. (Tourist Trophy) races were held on the Isle of Man. The number of motor cycles in use increased enormously between 1907 and 1930, but during the depression of the 1930s the number of motor cycle owners decreased. Since 1945, however, the motor cycle has once again grown in popularity, and today many young people are prepared to put much time, money and energy into owning a 'bike'.

9.25 Public Service Vehicles

The first person to run a horse-drawn bus service in Britain was George Shillibeer. In 1829 he began a service from Paddington to the Bank of England, a distance of five miles. The bus carried 22 passengers, who each paid one shilling (5p) for the trip.

By 1850 the General Omnibus Company was running double-decker coaches in London. Anyone who wished to travel on one simply hailed the driver. Bus stops did not exist!

The first trams appeared on the streets of Birkenhead, in 1860. Rails were laid out along the roads, and horses drew the tramcars along the trackway. A few steam-powered trams were tested out but they were not very successful.

The invention of the internal combustion engine in 1883 (see Section 9.26) had an important effect on the construction and design of public service vehicles. Between 1900 and 1914 motor buses began to replace horse-drawn vehicles on the streets of London. The 'B' class bus became a common sight in 1910 and by the outbreak of the First World War (1914) there were 2500 of these in operation. At the same time electrically powered trams became popular in some cities. These vehicles were fast and reliable, and could carry many passengers.

After the First World War, many more motor buses and coaches appeared on Britain's roads. There were larger double-decker buses which ran on pneumatic tyres rather than solid ones. More people could travel to towns, to coastal resorts or to the countryside. Some firms ran long-distance coach services in competition with the railways.

In 1930 Britain's road passenger transport system was reorganised. A *Road Traffic Act* empowered traffic commissioners to issue licences to companies in their areas. This system of licensing local bus companies is still in use today.

Since 1945 there have been more and more buses on Britain's roads. Diesel-engined buses have replaced trams and trolleybuses, and today bus companies operate long-distance services on Britain's expanding motorway network.

9.26 Early Cars

In the early nineteenth century engineers had found that steam engines were unsuitable for driving road vehicles, because of their size and weight. In the second half of the century scientists tried to develop a smaller, lighter engine. Table 9.6 shows the development of the *internal combustion engine* between 1859 and 1909.

Table 9.6 Developments in the internal combustion engine

Date	Event
1859	Etienne Lenoir produced a gas engine
1862	Lenoir mounted one of his engines on a small 'horseless carriage', which he drove at 3 m.p.h. from his factory to Vincennes in France
1868	Siegfried Markus, an Austrian, fixed a four-stroke engine to a road cart. The machine worked reasonably well and was put on display at the Vienna Exhibition in 1873
1876	Nikolaus Otto, a German, developed a four-stroke gas engine similar to the engine used on a modern car
1883	Gottlieb Daimler, a manager at Otto's factory, built an engine which burnt petrol rather than gas
1885	Daimler fitted a petrol engine to a wooden cycle and thus invented the motorbike
1885	Another German, Karl Benz, built a motor cycle which ran at 8 m.p.h.
1888	Benz started to sell petrol-driven cars
1896	Fred Lanchester built the first British four-wheeled car
1906	Henry Royce and Charles Rolls founded the famous company of Rolls-Royce
1909	Henry Ford of Detroit, U.S.A., used mass-production methods to produce a reliable family car for about £115

In Britain there was a great deal of opposition to the new form of transport. Early motor cars were noisy. They frightened horses and people, and were not very reliable. The *Red Flag Act* of 1865 had stated that 'horseless carriages' (steam-driven traction engines) should not travel faster than 4 m.p.h. on country roads and 2 m.p.h. in towns. A man with a red flag was supposed to walk along in front of them. This law made it difficult to sell cars in Britain and held back the mass-production of automobiles. Motorists started a campaign to repeat the Red Flag Act. In 1896 Parliament passed a Locomotives on Highways Act which scrapped the rule about the red flag and put the speed limit up to 14 m.p.h. Motorists were so pleased that they drove in 33 vehicles from London to Brighton to celebrate. Only 13 cars completed the journey! A London to Brighton rally is still held today.

9.27 The Motor Industry

The first British cars were made by bicycle manufacturers, although by 1911 Henry Ford's mass-produced American cars were being sold in Britain. Ford's production methods were later used by William Morris, a bicycle manufacturer from Oxford. The *Morris Cowley* was the first British car to be mass-produced. It cost £190! Even £190 was too expensive for many people, and in 1922 Henry Austin designed the Austin 7, an economical little car which cost only £165. The motor industry expanded into a number of small firms, such as Lawson's Daimler Motor Company in Coventry. By 1920 there were 90 firms producing cars in Britain. Their number had fallen to 33 by 1938, yet production increased dramatically, as the figures in Table 9.7 suggest.

Table 9.7 Motor vehicles in use, 1904–1938

Date	Cars (private)	Total (all vehicles)
1904	8 465	8 465
1910	53 196	143 177
1914	132 110	388 860
1918	77 707	229 428
1921	242 500	845 709
1929	980 886	2 181 831
1932	1 127 681	2 227 099
1938	1 944 394	3 084 896

During the depression of the 1930s, the motor industry was one of the few industries to expand. Britain became a producer and exporter of cars, lorries and tractors. The industry brought great prosperity to towns which had no industrial tradition, such as Luton and Oxford. By the late 1930s about 1.5 million people had jobs in making, running and servicing motor vehicles. In contrast to other industries, there was a low rate of unemployment. The industry created a demand for a wide range of other products, such as machine-tools, aluminium, steel, glass, rubber and petrol. The other effects of the expansion of the motor industry were as follows.

(a) Economic and Social Effects of the Motor Industry

(i) *Economic Effects*

- There was an improvement in the distribution of goods. Door-to-door delivery of many goods was possible. More bread, meat and vegetables were sent by lorry or van rather than by railway.

- Factories no longer had to be close to railways. Many new or light industries (e.g. chemicals, electrical, vehicle production) grew up in the South-east.
- Ribbon development (houses and factories spreading outwards from towns along main roads) took place. Railways had encouraged the development of factories around a central point. Motor vehicles made possible the building of factories along main roads.
- The growth of the motorway system in the 1960s and 1970s.

(ii) *Social Effects*

- More people travelled more widely and more often. Trips to the seaside and countryside became common. Country people visited the towns; town-dwellers visited the country.
- People tended to live farther away from their place of work. Suburbs grew up around towns.
- An increase in the number of people killed on the roads (see below).
- More sport, entertainment, recreational facilities. People were able to travel to watch their favourite football or cricket teams. People found it easier to visit pubs, theatres and cinemas.

One terrible effect of the growth of motor traffic during this period was the increase in the number of road accidents. Between 1920 and 1935 the government took a number of steps to improve road safety (Table 9.8).

Table 9.8 Government measures to improve road safety, 1920–1935

Date	Event
1920	Ministry of Transport set up. Roads were classified, A, B or C, according to their importance
1920s	Tarmac laid down on many road surfaces
1924	White lines painted on roads
1930	A Road Traffic Act stated that people had to be physically fit to receive a driving licence
1933	Traffic lights introduced
1934	Compulsory driving tests and 30 m.p.h. speed limits in towns introduced
1935	Leslie Hore Belisha, the Minister of Transport, introduced zebra crossings for pedestrians

(b) Later History of the Motor Industry

After the Second World War (1939–1945) car production became Britain's fastest-growing industry. The number of cars, lorries and vans on the road increased from 2 million in 1946 to 20 million in 1973. In the late 1970s, however, there was a slump in world trade and British firms found it hard to compete with German and Japanese car-producers. In 1965 British factories supplied the U.K. with 95 per cent of all cars sold in the U.K. By 1980 one in eight of all cars sold in Britain was Japanese.

To make the car industry more efficient, a big new company was formed in 1968. Austin-Morris joined up with Leyland, a company producing trucks and buses. In 1975 the government took over the company and *British Leyland* became 95 per cent state-owned. Today BL cars and lorries are exported to many parts of the world.

The increase in traffic was not matched by an improvement in our roads Little was done to improve the road network in Britain until after the Second World War. In 1959 the first motorway, the M1, was opened between London and Birmingham. Since then many more motorways have been built and local roads have been greatly improved. By 1978, 1300 miles of motorway were open to road-users.

SOURCE-BASED QUESTION: ROAD TRANSPORT, 1880–1980

Figure 9.3 (page 214) shows street scenes photographed at different times over the past 100 years.

1. Write down the correct chronological (date) sequence of photographs A, B and C.
2. When do you think each photograph was taken?
3. How many different forms of transport can you see in the three photographs?
4. How reliable are these three pieces of historical evidence?
5. Use the photographs and your own knowledge of the topic to describe some of the problems created by increased road traffic between 1880 and 1980.
6. What measures have governments over the past 100 years taken to reduce the number of road accidents? How successful have these measures been?

9.28 Early Aircraft

During the nineteenth century many inventors tried to build machines which would fly. Hiram Maxim's flying machine (1894) weighed three tons and was powered by two huge steam engines. It skimmed through the air for a few feet and then came down to earth with a thud! In 1903, however, the Wright brothers, two American bicycle-makers, fitted a twelve horse-power engine and two propellers to a wooden glider. This machine took to the air for only twelve seconds but the short flight proved that powered flight in a fixed-wing aircraft was possible. In 1909 Louis Bleriot flew across the English Channel and in the same year J. T .C. Moore-Brabazon became the first person to fly an aircraft in Britain. In 1910 Louis Paulhan, a Frenchman, won the £10 000 prize offered by the *Daily Mail* to the first man to fly from London to Manchester.

Many people believed that travelling by air was dangerous. Few were willing to invest their money in aviation, and for many years aircraft companies made very little profit. Lorries and ships provided a much safer, cheaper way of sending people and goods from place to place. Aeroplanes could carry fewer goods and people but they could offer a *faster* service. For these reasons air transport became popular only with the very well-off between 1910 and 1940.

9.29 The Aircraft Industry, 1914–1980

During the First World War (1914–1918) great advances were made in aircraft design. By 1919 there had been so many improvements in safety and comfort

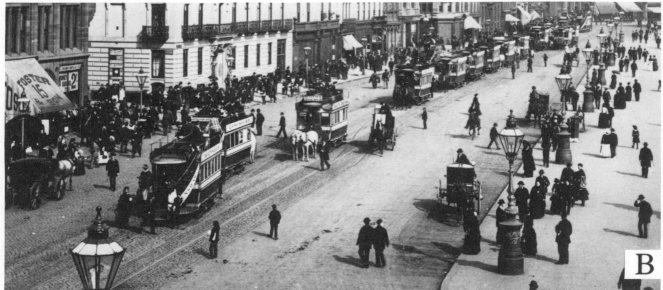

Figure 9.3 Road transport

that regular flights from one country to another became a practical possibility. Two R.A.F. officers, John Alcock and Arthur Whitten-Brown, proved that transatlantic flights were possible when they flew a converted Vickers Vimy bomber from Newfoundland to Ireland.

By the middle of the 1930s there were 20 companies running 76 air services in Britain. Table 9.9 shows the main developments in civil aviation between 1923 and 1940.

Early aircraft companies found it difficult to make large profits. The government set up a committee to look into the problems facing small aircraft companies. The committee produced a report which stated that a better service would be provided if small companies joined together. In October 1935 several small companies joined up to form British Airways. Five years later the government bought out both Imperial Airways (see Table 9.9) and British Airways, and formed the British Overseas Airways Corporation (B.O.A.C.).

During the Second World War (1939–1945) aircraft construction became Britain's largest industry. A new Ministry of Aircraft Production built a number of famous bombers such as the Wellington and the Lancaster and fighters such as the Hurricane and the Spitfire. In 1941 the first British jet aircraft, the E28, designed by Frank Whittle, took to the air. By 1945 jet aircraft were being used in combat by both the Germans and the Allies.

Table 9.9 Developments in civil aviation

Date	Event
1923	Croydon Airport in Surrey handling 30 cross-Channel flights a day
1927	An American, Charles Lindbergh, flew from New York to Paris in a monoplane
1924	The British government formed Imperial Airways from four private companies. Flights began to India, South Africa and Canada
1930	Amy Johnson flew from Britain to Australia in a Gipsy Moth
1939	Transatlantic Air Service started

After 1945, the aircraft industry prospered. The government set up B.E.A. (British and European Airways) to carry passengers to different parts of Britain and Europe. By 1949 all British routes were controlled by B.O.A.C. and B.E.A. These two corporations were joined together to form British Airways in 1972.

Since 1950 airports have been built all over the country. Some, such as Gatwick, Heathrow and Prestwick, are large and can accept heavy intercontinental flights. Others, such as Exeter, Cardiff and Gloucester, are smaller and cater for local flights.

The design of airliners has changed a great deal over the past 40 years. After the war piston-engined aircraft such as the Vickers Viscount were in use. In the 1950s jet aircraft such as the De Havilland Comet went into service with B.O.A.C. In 1954 two dreadful disasters occurred when Comets broke up in mid-air. By the time the Comet's technical faults had been ironed out, Britain's lead in jet aircraft had gone. By the 1970s huge American 'jumbo jets' were flying across the Atlantic. These aeroplanes carry 400–500 people. Today jumbo jets are in service with many of the world's airlines.

From the mid-1960s, Britain and France worked together on a new supersonic airliner, *Concorde*. This dart-shaped aircraft proved to be very expensive to develop. Its heavy operating costs made it unattractive to aircraft companies, and advance orders for the aircraft were cancelled before the first prototypes (test models) were built. But in terms of speed and technical achievement,

Concorde has been a success. Many businessmen and rich holidaymakers take advantage of the fast *Concorde* service between London and New York.

Below are listed the ways in which the development of aircraft between 1914 and 1980 affected people's lives:

- New airports have been built (e.g. Heathrow, Gatwick, Prestwick).
- Thousands of people go on 'package' holidays to places such as Majorca and Ibiza.
- Local flying clubs have become popular in many areas.
- There has been damage to the environment, resulting from new airports, noise and pollution.
- There have been a number of deaths from air crashes but far fewer people have died in aircraft than in motor vehicles.

9.30 The Press

John Palmer's mail coaches (see Section 9.21) also delivered newspapers. The first daily newspaper in Britain was the single-sheet *Daily Courant* (1702). Its publisher was a woman called Elizabeth Mallet. It cost one penny ($\frac{1}{2}$p) and was printed on a sheet of paper measuring eight inches by fourteen inches. The *Daily Courant* contained mainly foreign news copied from newsletters and journals published in France.

Later in the eighteenth century other newspapers went on sale. They had two or three pages and contained advertisements, gossip, letters and political articles. In 1785 John Walter published the *Daily Universal Register*, the forerunner of *The Times*. It cost $2\frac{1}{2}$d. (1p) and consisted of a four-page sheet. There were no headlines or pictures to introduce news stories. In the 1840s *The Times* became a very influential force in politics under its editor John Delane. When the paper published reports of the terrible conditions endured by troops in the Crimea, there was a public outcry and the government was forced to resign.

During the nineteenth century various taxes on newspapers were abolished. The price of newspapers fell and their circulations went up. As educational standards improved, more people started to read newspapers and magazines. One result of the spread of elementary education was the growth of the 'popular press'. Alfred Harmsworth (1865–1922) started printing a weekly paper called *Answers* in 1888. In 1896 he launched a national newspaper, the *Daily Mail*, and eight years later the *Daily Mirror*. Harmsworth became one of the first 'press barons' and was later given the title Lord Northcliffe. In 1900 Arthur Pearson founded another popular paper, the *Daily Express*, which was later bought by the Canadian businessman Lord Beaverbrook.

The popular press was successful because papers used eye-catching headlines and photographs. Journalists wrote about subjects which they knew would interest their readers and used a 'chatty' style which people found lively and entertaining.

(a) Effects of the Popular Press

- People were better informed about current affairs than ever before.
- People were able to find out about important events shortly after those events had happened.
- Magazines spread a whole range of knowledge and literature across the country.
- People became more interested in politics. Newspapers influenced the public by the way in which they reported the news.

- Some 'press lords' or 'press barons' became powerful national figures. They could influence politicians and the public by putting across their own ideas in newspaper editorials.

(b) Newspapers Today

Many newspapers have developed political bias. They often support the politics of one political party. The *Daily Telegraph*, for example, supports the Conservatives, while the *Daily Mirror* supports the Labour Party. Thus, the people who read a certain newspaper tend to be influenced by its political opinions.

Table 9.10 shows the readership of British newspapers in 1985. Three groups of newspapers — the *Daily Mirror*, Associated Newspapers and Beaverbrook Newspapers — owned two-thirds of the circulation of daily newspapers. These groups also had control of local papers.

Table 9.10 Readership of British national newspapers, 1985 (millions)

Daily papers		Sunday papers	
Mirror	9.3	News of the World	13.0
Express	5.0	Mirror	10.0
Sun	11.7	People	8.9
Mail	4.9	Express	6.7
Telegraph	2.9	Times	4.1
Guardian	1.5	Observer	2.4
Times	1.4	Mail	4.9
Financial Times	0.7	Telegraph	2.4

9.31 Shipping in the Twentieth Century

During the First World War (1914–1918) Britain had to make good use of her merchant navy. When the war started, everyone believed that the fighting would be over within a few months. Unfortunately, the Germans had developed a new and deadly type of submarine, the U-boat. These submarines were able to sink large numbers of merchant ships carrying grain and meat to Britain. There were also great sea battles between German and British warships. The most important of these was the Battle of Jutland (1916), when two giant fleets met each other in close combat. Jutland was the last major sea battle to be fought at close quarters by two opposing fleets.

In 1918 Britain still had one of the largest fleets of merchant ships in the world. Over the next 20 years the balance of the world's merchant shipping changed, as Table 9.11 suggests.

By the 1930s the British shipbuilding industry had begun to feel the full effects of the world slump in trade. Shipping depends on trade, and when trade suffers, shipbuilders, shipowners and merchant seamen are badly affected. There was high unemployment in the shipyards of the Tyne and Clyde. So many workers lost their jobs in Jarrow, County Durham, a great shipbuilding centre, that it became known as 'the town that died'.

In the late 1930s there was a slight recovery in the shipbuilding industry. There were some technical improvements in the type of engines used on merchant ships, with oil engines and petrol engines replacing steam power. By 1939 half

Table 9.11 Merchant shipping tonnage of the UK, 1918–1938

Date	UK fleet (million net tons)	UK share of world tonnage (%)
1918	12.35	35.23
1923	14.20	37.54
1928	14.78	35.88
1933	12.64	30.45
1938	10.53	28.70

the world's ships had oil-driven engines. Many others used steam turbines to generate the electrical power needed to drive a vessel through the water.

Some shipping companies amalgamated (joined together) in the hope of reducing their costs and making larger profits. These companies built some fine ships, such as the Cunard Company's *Queen Mary* and *Queen Elizabeth* liners. The *Queen Elizabeth* was the biggest passenger ship of all time, with berths for 2300 passengers.

During the Second World War (1939–1945) the Royal Navy and the merchant navy played a vital part in keeping the sea lanes open to Allied shipping. Losses of merchant ships were high. Five hundred were sunk in the Atlantic Ocean and a total of 18 million tons of shipping was destroyed as a result of enemy action. Britain's merchant navy never really recovered from the effects of the Second World War. There was increasing competition from airline companies, which provided a faster, more efficient service. Today few businessmen consider making a four-day crossing of the Atlantic by sea when they can fly to America on *Concorde* (see Section 9.29) in a few hours.

There has also been strong competition from foreign shipping companies. German, Dutch and Japanese shipbuilders have produced ships more quickly and cheaply than their British counterparts. A number of British firms have gone bankrupt. Japanese 'supertankers' of over 100 000 tons now carry oil to many different parts of the world. It remains to be seen whether British shipbuilding companies will be able to compete successfully with foreign firms over the next few decades.

9.32 Wireless and Television

(a) Wireless

Long before the invention of the telephone (see Section 9.22) scientists had been working on ways of sending signals *without* using wires. A British physicist, James Clerk Maxwell (1831–1879), proved the existence of electromagnetic waves and showed that they followed the same natural laws as light. In 1896 Guglielmo Marconi (1874–1937), an Italian inventor, arrived in England to carry out experiments in wireless communication. In 1899 he sent a signal from London to a colleague on the French coast. Two years later he astonished the world when he succeeded in transmitting the morse letter 'S' across the Atlantic from St. John's, Newfoundland, to Poldhu in Cornwall.

Marconi set up his own company and soon wireless communication was possible between coastal stations and ships at sea. During the First World War (1914–1918) both German and British ground forces used wireless communications. Later, ground-to-air communication became possible.

The spoken word was transmitted by wireless and radio during the 1920s, and many 'radio hams' built their own transmitters and made private broadcasts. In 1922 a group of radio manufacturers set up the British Broadcasting Company (BBC), and within a few years thousands of people were listening to talks, plays and music programmes on the 'wireless'. In 1926 the government set up the British Broadcasting Corporation, an independent body with its own Royal Charter. The new corporation was financed by licence fees paid by listeners. By the outbreak of the Second World War (1939), most homes had a radio set. During the war the radio became very important as a means of relaying important information to the public.

(b) Television

No single person invented the television. Before 1920 many scientists had tried to find a way of sending 'live' pictures over a distance. In 1922 a Scotsman, John Logie Baird (1888–1946), began working on a method of transmitting pictures using electromagnetic waves. In 1924 Baird managed to obtain an image of objects in outline on a screen. A year later (1925), in a laboratory in London, he transmitted an image of the human face. In January 1926 Baird demonstrated the first working television system to the Royal Institution of Great Britain. Unfortunately, Baird used a system which depended on a mechanical device, the Nipkow Disk. This device was often unreliable. When the BBC started television broadcasts from Alexandra Palace in 1936, they used a VHF system, which produced better results.

By 1939 there were 80 000 television sets in use in the London area. BBC television was closed down shortly after the outbreak of war. TV equipment was needed for radar (Radio Detection and Ranging), which enabled enemy aircraft to be detected at a distance. A television service restarted in 1946, and the BBC remained based at Alexandra Palace until 1954.

Table 9.12 shows the main developments in mass communication between 1954 and 1983.

Table 9.12 Developments in mass communication

Date	Development
1954	Independent TV authorised by Parliament — the new service to be paid for from *advertising*
1955	The first commercial TV broadcasts (ITV)
1956	The first video tape-recorders in use
1960	The first transistorised TV sets on sale
1962	The *Pilkington Committee* recommended:
	• There should be improvements in the design of TV sets
	• A 625 line system was preferable to 405 lines
	• Colour TV should be introduced as soon as possible
	Telstar (a communications satellite) launched
1964	BBC2 started transmission
1967	Colour transmission on BBC2
1969	Colour transmission on all three channels
1982	Channel 4, financed by commercial TV companies, launched
1983	Breakfast television on BBC and ITV

WORK OUT SHORT-ANSWER QUESTIONS: COMMUNICATIONS

1. For how many days a year were villagers required to work on road repair in 1750?
2. What were turnpike trusts?
3. Why did turnpike riots occur in some parts of Britain?
4. Which engineer do you associate with the London to Holyhead road?
5. What sort of jobs grew out of the coaching industry between 1800 and 1830?
6. When was 'statute labour' abolished?
7. Name the first motorway to be opened in Britain.
8. What did the Buchanan Report recommend in 1963?
9. What was carried on the Sankey Canal between St. Helens and the River Mersey?
10. Name the Lancashire estate manager who hit upon the idea of using flood-water to fill a canal.
11. When was the Bridgewater Canal completed?
12. Which canal ran across the Pennines?
13. What was 'canal mania'?
14. Name one town which grew up as a result of canal development.
15. What were 'clipper' ships?
16. Why did the opening of the Suez Canal in 1869 make it difficult for clipper ships to compete with steamships?
17. Which steamship was the first to cross the Atlantic using steam power all the way?
18. What is the 'Plimsoll line' on a ship?
19. In which parts of the country could you have seen 'waggon-ways' in 1700?
20. Name the country's first *public* railway (1804).
21. Who designed 'Catch-me-who-can'?
22. When was the Stockton and Darlington line constructed?
23. Name the three natural obstacles along the route of the Liverpool and Manchester railway.
24. Why were the Rainhill trials held in 1829?
25. How far apart did Brunel set the rails on the Great Western Railway?
26. What was the 'parliamentary train'?
27. Who was the 'Railway King'?
28. How did the development of railways affect other forms of transport in the 1830s and 1840s?
29. Name three coastal resorts which grew up as a result of railway expansion.
30. Name the four major railway companies formed in 1923.
31. When were the railways nationalised?
32. Which controversial report resulted in the closing down of many unprofitable railway lines in the 1960s?
33. Who set up a postal service between London and Bristol in 1784?
34. Why were very few letters carried by the Post Office by the 1830s?
35. Who invented the 'needle telegraph'?
36. What was a 'hobby horse'?
37. When did Henry Royce and Charles Rolls set up their famous car company?
38. Why did 33 motorists drive from London to Brighton on 14 November 1896?
39. Name the first British car to be mass-produced.
40. Who was the first man to fly across the English Channel in a monoplane?
41. What was the importance of John Alcock and Arthur Whitten-Brown's long-distance flight in 1919?
42. What do the initials B.O.A.C. and B.E.A. stand for?
43. Name the first daily newspaper in Britain.

44. Who was the editor of *The Times* in the 1840s?
45. Who launched the *Daily Mail* in 1896 and the *Daily Mirror* in 1904?
46. Which shipbuilding centre in County Durham became known as 'the town that died'?
47. What is a 'supertanker'?
48. Who transmitted a radio signal across the Atlantic in 1901?
49. What do the letters RADAR stand for?
50. When did BBC2 first go on the air?

10 Trade and the Economy

Examination Guide

This is an important topic, but it is not popular with students and some examiners. However, it appears in some form or other on the four main syllabuses, sometimes as part of the core, sometimes as an optional topic. It is essential, therefore, that you know something about Britain's development as a trading nation. Below is a brief guide showing what each board requires.

(a) Northern Examining Association

'Trade' forms part of Theme 1 (Industrialisation), a compulsory theme.

(b) Midland Examining Group

You need to know about the 'Effects of development in industry on economic life of Britain, e.g. trade and exports' as part of the core topic 'Industry'. Topics F and G on Agriculture and Industry since 1850, which are optional, refer to 'The effects of membership of the European Community'.

(c) London and East Anglian Group

This syllabus contains optional topics on 'Trade and Economic Ideas, 1760–1980'.

(d) Southern Examining Group

Theme 1, Agriculture and Industry, which is compulsory, contains reference to 'foreign competition' and the 'influence of the European Community'. Optional topic 2, 'The Corn Law and its Repeal', has a section on 'the importance of free trade'.

The questions you will get on Trade and the Economy will fall into two categories — short-answer questions like the ones at the end of this chapter or fairly straightforward essay-type questions like the examples on page 224.

10.1 Introduction

The eighteenth century saw a great increase in Britain's national wealth. By 1800 people were earning higher wages, had more money to spend and wanted to buy a wider range of goods.

Historians disagree as to what sparked off the growth of the economy, and what were the most important reasons for its continuing growth. However, one likely reason for the improvement in the economy was the growth and expansion of British trade.

10.2 British Trade in 1700

When trade is at stake it is your last retrenchment. You must defend it or perish.

(The Earl of Chatham, 1739)

In 1700 most British trade was with the East Indies (India and China), the West Indies, North America and Europe. Parliament had passed two Navigation Acts in 1651 and 1660 which stated that only British ships could trade between Britain and her colonies. Goods coming from a foreign country had to be sent either in British ships or in that country's own ships. Thus, a Dutch ship could not trade between Britain and France.

The government placed high tariffs (taxes) on foreign goods coming into British ports. The government also forced British colonies to provide Britain with raw materials such as cotton, iron and timber, and to buy manufactured goods from Britain such as guns, coaches and clocks. The colonies were not allowed to make things that British merchants wanted to sell. The American colonies, for example, were allowed to send us pig-iron but not to make wrought-iron!

This system of regulated trade was known as *mercantilism*. As trade increased and tariffs went up, merchants tried to break the government's trading rules. The Isle of Man, Romney Marsh, Devon and Cornwall became famous areas for smuggling. Adam Smith (see Section 10.3) remarked that smugglers were Britain's top salesmen to France and France's top salesmen to England! The only way to stop widespread smuggling was to reduce tariffs. With lower taxes on imports, smuggling would not be worth while. This became one of the strongest arguments against mercantilism later in the eighteenth century.

10.3 Adam Smith and Free Trade

In 1776 Adam Smith (1723–1790), a Professor at Glasgow University, wrote a book called *The Wealth of Nations*. In it he argued that government restrictions and tariffs hampered the growth of trade and industry. He believed that merchants should be left to organise trade and run businesses without government interference. This policy became known as *laissez-faire* ('let it alone').

Adam Smith's ideas caught on. They influenced politicians such as William Pitt (1759–1806), Britain's Prime Minister from 1783 to 1801 and from 1804 to 1806. Pitt believed in free trade and signed a trading agreement with France in 1786. Under the terms of the *Eden Treaty*, Britain reduced the tax on French wines coming into Britain and France lowered tariffs on British textiles and hardware. In the 1820s the movement towards free trade grew stronger. British merchants felt confident that they could compete successfully with foreign traders. Merchants in the cotton, iron and pottery industries started a campaign against tariffs and restrictions.There was opposition to free trade from men who controlled the older industries such as silk and paper and from wealthy landowners, who wanted to keep the price of British grain as high as possible. Despite this opposition, William Huskisson, the President of the Board of Trade, removed the duties on many imported goods between 1823 and 1827.

By 1839 a group of Lancashire merchants in favour of free trade had formed the Anti-Corn Law League (see Section 3.9). Robert Peel, the Conservative Prime Minister, and William Gladstone, the President of the Board of Trade, agreed to abolish tariffs on most goods. Between 1842 and 1845 their budgets removed tariffs from all exports and most imports. Foreign trade increased dramatically. To make up the loss of government income, Peel introduced *income tax* in 1842 at 3p in the pound. By 1860 Britain had become a 'free trade' country.

SPECIMEN QUESTION: FREE TRADE

(i) What do you understand by the phrase 'free trade'?
(ii) Write down *two* arguments against free trade and *two* arguments in favour of free trade.
(iii) Describe the part played by *two* of the following in the development of free trade:

Adam Smith	John Bright
William Pitt the Younger	William Gladstone
Richard Cobden	Robert Peel

10.4 The Slave Trade

One of the most profitable forms of trade in the eighteenth century was the slave trade. The pattern of trade was basically triangular (Figure 10.1). Ships would

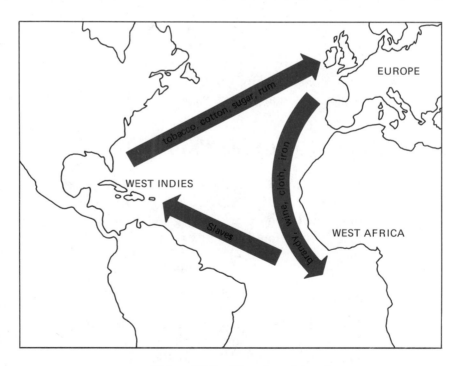

Figure 10.1 The slave triangle

leave Liverpool or Bristol loaded up with cloth, guns and alcohol, and sail to West Africa. These manufactured goods were exchanged for black Africans who had been captured by slave-traders or enemy tribes. The English sea captains would ferry the slaves across the Atlantic to the West Indies or North America. On board the slave ships the conditions were appalling. Hundreds of slaves were cramped together below decks like sardines in a tin. As many as a quarter of them died on the voyage. In the West Indies the surviving slaves were sold off at auctions. The ships were then loaded with rum, sugar, tobacco and cotton, and set off back to Britain.

In the second half of the eighteenth century William Wilberforce (1759–1833), a wealthy Hull merchant, started a campaign to abolish slavery. However, the slavers had many powerful friends in Parliament and it was years before anything was done to stop it. Eventually Wilberforce persuaded M.P.s to ban British ships from taking part in the slave trade in 1807. In 1833 slavery itself was abolished throughout the British Empire.

SPECIMEN QUESTION: THE SLAVE TRADE

    (i) In the eighteenth century, what was the 'slave triangle'?
   (ii) How did Wilberforce and Clarkson manage to persuade people that the slave trade was wrong?
  (iii) Why was there such a long delay between the abolition of the *slave trade* and the abolition of *slavery*?

10.5   Banking

During the seventeenth century goldsmiths were often willing to look after people's money and valuable possessions in return for a small charge. The goldsmiths later found that they could make more of a profit by lending out the money they were looking after and charging *interest* for the loan. People began to write notes to goldsmiths asking them to pay out cash from their deposits (the money the goldsmiths were looking after). These notes were the first *cheques*. Goldsmiths began to write notes 'promising to pay' people certain sums of money when the notes were handed back to them. These 'promises to pay' were Britain's first *bank-notes*.

In 1694 King William III needed money to pay for a war against France. A group of London merchants loaned the King £1.2 million in return for a Royal Charter allowing them to set up the Bank of England. The bank received deposits, made loans and issued bank-notes. It remained a privately owned bank until it was nationalised in 1946.

In the second half of the eighteenth century British trade and industry expanded rapidly. Merchants and factory-owners set up dozens of small private banks. By 1805 there were 60 of them in London and 800 in other parts of the country. Many of these banks issued their own bank-notes, which proved useful at a time when there was a serious shortage of coins. However, some bankers were unable to run their business affairs properly and many banks went out of business between 1793 and 1830. The failure of these banks led to a government investigation into banking in 1824. A report which followed the investigation stated that many small banks had too few reserves (the gold needed to back up cheques and bank-notes) and had loaned out too much money. Between 1824 and 1946 the government took the steps listed in Table 10.1 to regulate banks.

Table 10.1 The government and banking

Year	Act	Importance
1826	Bank Act	Merchants allowed to set up privately owned banks, provided that their banks were 65 miles from London
1833	Bank Act	Commercial banks allowed to open in London but not to issue bank-notes
1844	Bank Charter Act	• All bank-notes were to be issued in future by the Bank of England. Banks which already issued notes were to be allowed to carry on doing so • All bank-notes were to be backed by gold bullion
1946	Nationalisation Act	The Bank of England to be taken into public ownership. The bank was to be controlled by governors, who were responsible to the government of the day

10.6 Taxation

(a) Taxation in the Eighteenth and Nineteenth Centuries

In 1750 most taxes were *indirect*. They consisted of customs duties on imports and exports. People had to pay taxes on goods such as tea, wine, spirits and tobacco. There were also *excise duties* (taxes on goods produced in Britain). These had to be paid on goods such as beer, candles, soap and leather. The taxes were indirect in the sense that if you didn't buy the goods, you didn't pay the tax.

A few *direct* taxes existed. These fell mainly on the rich and were paid directly to the tax-collector. There were direct taxes on land, windows, carriages, racehorses, hats, servants and gold plate.

In 1798 England was at war with France. William Pitt, the Prime Minister, introduced *income tax* to help pay for the war. The tax was paid on all incomes over £60 a year. By 1815 income tax was producing £15 million, one-third of the government's total income. In 1815 the war came to an end, and a year later income tax was abolished. To raise more money, the government had to increase indirect taxes on all goods, including food. The poorest members of society became even worse off. During the 1820s trade improved, and William Huskisson, who was in favour of free trade (see Section 10.3), began to reduce import duties. However, indirect taxes remained at a high level.

In 1842 Prime Minister Robert Peel reduced or abolished many customs duties. He hoped that lower indirect taxation would increase the flow of trade and make the country more wealthy. To make up the lost revenue (government income), he reintroduced income tax at a rate of 3p in the pound. Peel originally planned to phase out income tax within three years, but his free trade policies were so successful that he decided to keep income tax and reduce customs duties even more.

William Gladstone, Chancellor of the Exchequer in the 1850s, continued Peel's free trade policy. Like Peel, he planned to abolish income tax but the Crimean War prevented him from doing so. However, by 1874 income tax had reached its lowest-ever figure, 1p in the pound!

(b) The People's Budget

During the last 40 years of the nineteenth century the government had to find more money to pay for the increasing costs of the expanding social services. In 1909 David Lloyd George, the Chancellor of the Exchequer, had to find an extra £15 million to pay for old age pensions and new battleships. He introduced a 'People's Budget' into the House of Commons. The measures proposed by Lloyd George were as follows:

- Death duties were greatly increased.
- Supertax was introduced on incomes over £5000 at a rate of 2p in the pound.
- Income tax was raised from 5p to 7p in the pound.
- Stamp duties and liquor licences were made more expensive.
- Petrol and motor vehicles were taxed for the first time.
- Taxes on spirits and tobacco were increased.
- There was a 20 per cent tax on increases in the value of land.

For the first time taxation was being used to take from those who owned wealth to give to those in need. By 1914 government spending had risen to £200 million.

(c) Taxation, 1914–1980

The First World War led to a massive increase in spending. Income Tax went up to 25p in the pound. Supertax and death duties were also increased.

Between 1918 and 1939 income tax remained at 25p in the pound, to pay for health, education, social services and unemployment pay.

During the Second World War the rate of taxation was very high. Income tax went up to 50p in the pound and there were higher indirect taxes on beer and tobacco. There was also a new *purchase tax* on consumer goods.

Since 1945 governments have used taxation as a way of fighting inflation (money losing its value). Income tax now brings in about half the government's revenue. After the war purchase tax was phased out but *value added tax* (VAT) was introduced in 1973 on many goods. Today (1988) the standard rate of income tax is 25p in the pound, while VAT is charged at 15 per cent.

10.7 The National Debt

The National Debt is the difference between what the nation spends and what the nation earns. During peacetime, governments can normally achieve a balance between spending and earning, but in wartime this has not always been possible. In 1694 the government ran up wartime debts of £1.2 million. Today the National Debt stands at £97 300 million.

Two Prime Ministers, Robert Walpole and William Pitt the Younger, tried to pay off some of the debt. They set up 'sinking funds' which were to be used to pay the money back. Both schemes ran into trouble when the country went to war. In the nineteenth century several Chancellors of the Exchequer managed to reduce the size of the debt, as the figures in Table 10.2 suggest.

Table 10.2   The National Debt (£ million)

1694	1.2	1850	793.5
1700	4.7	1900	568.7
1750	78.0	1950	26 000.8
1800	411.4	1980	97 300.3

Today few people worry about the size of the national debt and it is unlikely that it will ever be paid off. Governments since the Second World War have concentrated on meeting the interest payments on the debt rather than attempting to pay off the debt itself.

10.8   Chamberlain and Tariff Reform

By 1870 both Germany and the U.S.A. were challenging Britain's industrial superiority. Germany had placed tariffs on British goods, while Britain, a 'free trade' country (see Section 10.3), allowed German goods into Britain without payment of import taxes. In 1881 a group of British businessmen set up the *Fair Trade League*. They wanted Parliament to place tariffs on goods from those countries which taxed British goods. This idea was unpopular with many politicians. Most M.P.s still believed in free trade.

In 1890 the U.S.A. started to tax imported foreign goods. France imposed tariffs on British goods in 1892. British *protectionists* (people who wanted to see tariffs reintroduced) set up a *Tariff Reform League*. Their leader was Joseph Chamberlain (1836–1914), the Colonial Secretary. Chamberlain believed that Britain should return to a system of protected trade. He wanted to see lower tariffs placed on goods from the British Empire. This idea became known as *Imperial Preference*. But few people supported the Tariff Reform League. The election of 1906 resulted in a sweeping victory for the Liberals, the party of free trade. Britain remained a free trade country until 1932.

10.9   The Effects of War on the Economy (see also Section 4.2)

(a) The First World War

The war required vast amounts of money. The government borrowed some from private citizens in the form of war bonds, the first national savings certificates. Some of the money for the war came from simply printing more bank-notes! This later led to inflation, but at a time of full employment and high wages most people's standard of living did not change very much.

One result of the war was that the U.S.A. became one of the strongest trading nations in the world. Britain loaned huge sums of money to France and Belgium but she also had to borrow heavily from the U.S.A. High rates of interest had to be paid on the loan. For four years Britain was cut off from many of her old markets. Britain never recaptured the commercial markets she lost during the First World War.

(b) The Second World War

The effects of the Second World War on the economy were similar to those of the First World War, although the government moved the economy onto a wartime footing much more quickly. Unemployment fell, as a result of men going into the forces or finding jobs in wartime industries.

Many of the long-term effects of the war were disastrous for Britain. Our position as a trading nation was seriously weakened, for the following reasons:

1. Income from overseas trade fell from £248 million in 1938 to £120 million in 1946, owing to the sale of British businesses abroad and an increase in foreign competition.
2. Thirty per cent of Britain's merchant fleet was destroyed in the war. Britain lost income and trade from the decline in her shipping services.
3. There were sharp increases in the price of food and raw materials. The pound sterling bought fewer goods abroad.
4. After the war it was necessary to find the money to pay for troops stationed in occupied countries.
5. In 1945 the world became divided into Communist and non-Communist countries. This affected trade, because it created commercial as well as political divisions between nations.
6. The damage done to British factories by bombs and missiles was considerable. It took British industry ten years to recover from the effects of German bombing.

10.10   The 1931 Depression

The depression began in America. In 1929 there was a sudden fall in the value of shares on Wall Street (the New York Stock Exchange). Thousands of investors tried to sell shares in a market where there were few buyers. The 'Wall Street Crash' began a world-wide slump in trade, which badly affected Britain.

Between 1929 and 1931 British exports halved in value, while unemployment rose to three million. The government tried to reduce the impact of the depression by introducing the following measures.

(a) Wage Cuts

- There were cuts in salary for government-paid workers such as judges (10 per cent) and teachers (15 per cent).
- Insurance benefits were cut by 10 per cent and paid out for a shorter time.
- The dole (unemployment benefits) was cut by 10 per cent.

(b) The Means Test

The amount of financial help an unemployed man received depended on his family's total income, including pensions and savings. Many of the unemployed failed the means test because another member of the family was working or because they owned goods which could be turned into cash. The means test saved the government millions of pounds, but only at the cost of great bitterness and discontent.

(c) Industry

Shipyards and steelworks which could no longer pay their way were closed down (see Section 4.21). Other industries were modernised. Some plants were modernised, while in the South and Midlands there was a rapid expansion in new industries, particularly motor cars and electrical goods (see Section 4.26).

(d) Imports

Parliament passed an Import Duties Act to protect British producers against foreign competition. There was a 20 per cent duty on foreign factory-made items and a 33 per cent duty on luxury items.

The depression created great misery among the poor and unemployed. There were many demonstrations, meetings and 'hunger marches'. In 1936, 200 men from Jarrow in County Durham marched 300 miles to London to present a petition to the Prime Minister. The unemployment rate in Jarrow, a former shipbuilding town, was over 70 per cent.

SOURCE-BASED QUESTION: TRADE AND THE ECONOMY

Source A

He who wants to study every form of ship . . . can have no better field than these watery acres that give welcome to every flag. We thread our way round the busy basins, through bales and bundles and grass-bags, over skins and rags, and antlers, ores and dye-woods to the quay — and the great river where fleets are for ever moored. The four thousand feet of river frontage of the St. Katherine's Docks, only lead east, to where the London Docks take up the striking story of human skill and courage. At Limehouse the activity in the coal trade was the striking feature. The rows of black ships, the dusty workmen and quays, are in striking contrast to the brightness of the scenes where the huge Australian emigrant clippers lie, and where our corn and wine are landed.
(From *London — A Pilgrimage*, by Gustave Doré and Blanchard Jerrold, 1872)

Source B

In 1840 there were entered for home consumption in the United Kingdom 4,445,000 cwt cotton, 48,421,000 lbs wool and 1,896,000 lbs flax and hemp. In 1870 the consumption was 9,836,000 cwt cotton, 171,000 lbs wool and 5,300,000 lbs flax, hemp and jute. Ever since 1840 the increase in the consumption of foreign articles of food has been very large. The consumption of butter has increased from 1.05 lbs to 4.15 lbs per head; of cheese from 0.95 lbs to 3.67 lbs per head; of corn from 42.47 lbs to 124.30 lbs per head; of tea from 1.22 lbs to 3.81 lbs per head; of sugar from 15.2 lbs to 41.93 lbs per head. What crime was it by law to hinder the people from getting what will sustain life?
(*History of British Commerce*, L. Levi, 1872)

Source C

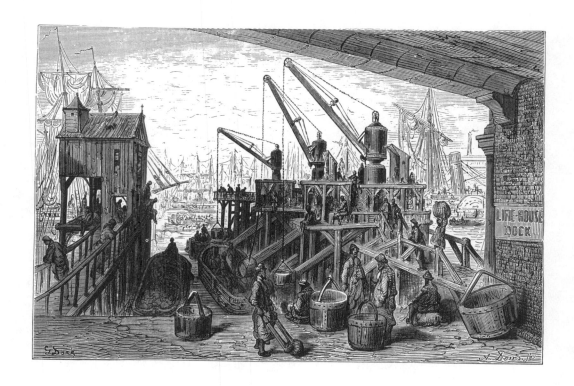

Source D

1. The London dock shown in source D is mentioned in source A. What is its name?
2. How were raw materials transported to the dockside in source D?
3. What was a 'clipper'? (Source A)
4. What evidence is there in source C to suggest that steam-powered vessels were used along the River Thames in 1872?
5. According to source B, what was the average percentage increase in the consumption of butter, cheese, corn and tea per head between 1840 and 1872?
6. Explain what is meant by the last sentence in source B.
7. Describe some of the main changes that have taken place in London docks such as C and D between 1872 and 1980.
8. How did the expansion of the port of London help the growth of the British economy in the nineteenth century?

10.11 The Changing Pattern of Britain's Trade

In the 1950s Britain exported more manufactured goods than she imported, to pay for imported food and raw materials. However, in the next 30 years, the pattern changed so that by the mid-1980s imports of factory-made goods exceeded exports. The statistics in Table 10.3 show this trend quite clearly.

Table 10.3 Imports (% of all sales)

Goods	1978	1984
Cars	35	51
All goods	26	34

Sales of manufactured goods, exports and 'invisible exports' (money earned abroad from banking, insurance and commercial services) have all declined. However, sales of British oil and gas to other countries have increased sharply. By 1984 our oil exports were worth four times as much as our car exports.

10.12 The Common Market (see also Section 3.16)

Over the past 30 years Britain's role as a trading nation has changed because of the Common Market. In 1951 France, Germany, Italy, Belgium and the Netherlands set up the European Coal and Steel Community. Coal, iron and steel could be bought and sold within these countries without any trade restrictions.

The community turned out to be a success. In 1958 the six members of the ECSC set up the European Economic Community (EEC) or *Common Market*. Members of the EEC were to work towards free trade between themselves. They agreed to apply the same tariffs on all trade with non-members. They also agreed to work towards common policies on nuclear power, social welfare, tax, agriculture and transport.

In 1961 and 1967 Britain applied to join the EEC, but Charles de Gaulle, President of France, felt that Britain had too many commitments to Commonwealth countries and the U.S.A. He rejected Britain's application to join the community. In 1970 a third attempt was made to join the EEC. This was successful, and in 1973 Britain became a member of the community. The effects of Britain's membership of the EEC are as follows:

1. Britain joined the EEC too late to improve her trading prospects. The community had been in existence for 16 years and the six original members had shaped the community in a way which suited them.
2. Britain had a different trading pattern from those of other countries, and this worked to our disadvantage. We lost our close economic ties with the Commonwealth.
3. Britain had to pay huge sums of money towards the total EEC budget.
4. Most EEC countries have more efficient industries than does Britain. Free trade between EEC members has opened up Britain to foreign manufacturers and British industry has had to struggle to compete.
5. The Common Agricultural Policy (CAP) has kept food prices high, even though there have been massive food surpluses (e.g. butter and beef 'mountains').

SPECIMEN QUESTIONS AND MODEL ANSWER: THE COMMON MARKET

(a) The Common Market

(i) Why was the EEC set up in 1958?
(ii) Describe the events leading up to Britain joining the EEC in 1973.
(iii) How has membership of the EEC affected Britain?

(b) The Common Market

'Have you been out to vote in the referendum, John?'
'Yes, dad. I've voted "NO". I think we should get out of the Common Market while the going's good.'
'That's the trouble with you young people today. You've no sense of vision. I remember Winston Churchill and his dream of a United States of Europe.'
'You've got it wrong, dad. The Common Market is just a rich man's club. You see . . ..'

Carry on with the discussion.

(c) The Economy

Describe the main changes that have taken place in the British economy over the past 40 years. In your answer you could mention:
(i) the effects of the Second World War
(ii) the Common Market
(iii) the effects of inflation
(iv) high unemployment since 1979.

In the next section there is a model answer to (b) above.

Model Answer: The Common Market

'You've got it wrong, Dad. The Common Market is just a rich man's club. It's a way of helping people in business to make bigger profits by reducing tariffs between European countries.'

'You forget that lower tariffs will mean cheaper goods, John.'

'In theory, yes. But cheaper imports will ruin British industry. Look what foreign cars have done to the British motor industry. What's happened to British-made motor cycles? In practice, membership of the EEC will mean *higher* food prices. Belgium, France, West Germany, Italy and the Netherlands will want us to raise our prices to bring them in line with theirs. And you know how much food costs when you go abroad!'

'Look, John, you know how inefficient some British farmers are. Membership of the EEC will help them a lot. With the Common Agricultural Policy they'll be much better off *and* they'll be producing more food.'

'You're talking rubbish, Dad. British farmers are some of the most efficient in Europe. The effect of the CAP will be that food prices will go up and certain items will be produced in too great a quantity. Farmers won't have to worry about foreign competition. They'll be able to produce as much butter or beef as they like. They'll get a fixed price for their produce whatever happens. Worse still, Dad, we'll get bigger and bigger food mountains and wine lakes. All the surplus food will be sold off to the Eastern Bloc or just dumped in the sea. This seems criminal when a few thousand miles away there are people starving.'

'But, John, you must remember that in some parts of Europe farming methods are old-fashioned and inefficient. Many farms are too small for modern machinery. The aim of the CAP is to increase the size of European farms. The commissioners will be handing out sums of money to uneconomic farmers to persuade them to give up small farms.'

'Dad, it's only in Belgium, the Netherlands and Italy that you see a lot of these tiny farms. The British taxpayer will be subsidising foreign farmers!'

'Why are you so inward-looking, John? I'd have thought you'd like the idea of a united Europe. You're in favour of peace aren't you? Since the EEC was set up in 1957, there have been no major wars in Europe.'

'But there have been some dreadful acts of terrorism and violence. We need stronger links with the Commonwealth and the Third World countries, not with Europe. The future of the world lies with the developing nations.'

'The Commonwealth? You're beginning to sound like an imperialist, John. With all your talk of tariffs and the Empire you seem to have a lot in common with the protectionists.'

'You remember the 1930s, Dad. We had to bring back tariffs then to protect British industry.'

'Was the European Free Trade Association in favour of tariffs? When Britain joined EFTA with Austria, Denmark, Norway, Sweden and Switzerland in 1959, there wasn't much talk of tariffs then.'

'That was 1959. Be realistic, Dad, we live in a changing world and have to be adaptable. I'm convinced that staying in the EEC will weaken Britain's ties with the U.S.A. and the Commonwealth. It will harm our trade with Scandinavia. We'll have higher food prices and unemployment and less efficient farming. We'll be governed from Brussels or Strasbourg rather than from Westminster. And British industry will be destroyed by harmful competition.'

'Well, John, you're entitled to your own views on this but I sincerely believe that our future lies with Europe. EFTA was never a success and geographically we're closer to Europe than the Commonwealth. Staying in the EEC will give us a wider market for industrial goods and cheaper food imports. We'll have more jobs in farming and industry. Workers will be able to travel freely from one European country to another in search of employment. We'll all have a higher standard of living and there'll be less likelihood of war breaking out in Europe. Finally, don't forget that in this referendum it looks as if over 65 per cent of the voters are going to vote 'YES' to staying in.'

'I can see that we're not going to agree about this, Dad. People may vote to stay in this time but when the next referendum is held, the result will be very different.'

'We'll see, John, we'll see.'

This is quite a difficult essay to plan and write, but it is certainly more interesting than the traditional '*Describe . . .*' or '*Explain . . .*' questions you used to see on CSE and some GCE papers. You need to strike a balance between a relaxed, conversational style and enough factual detail to earn you high marks. In this essay you are really being asked to produce two detailed arguments for and against Britain's continued membership of the EEC. You will earn most of your marks for *content* rather than *style*, so do make sure there are plenty of relevant facts in the conversation. If you can strike the right balance between the two, you should be able to score high marks on this type of question.

GCSE ASSESSMENT OBJECTIVES

Facts, Opinions and Judgements

The GCSE assessment objective 4.2 states that candidates should be able to 'distinguish between fact, opinion and judgement'.

Facts

It is a *fact* that Britain joined the Common Market in 1973. How could you prove that this fact is correct? Make a list of the different ways that you could check that the fact is correct.

To state a fact involves no opinion or judgement. Sometimes people get their facts wrong. If someone told you that Britain joined the Common Market in 1974 or 1975, you would know that they'd made an *incorrect statement of fact*. A lot of people believe that certain incorrect facts are true. Here are a few examples from history:

(i) Columbus discovered America in 1492.
   Incorrect fact: Columbus reached the West Indies in 1492.
(ii) King Harold II was killed when a Norman arrow struck him in the eye.
   Incorrect fact: Harold was probably struck down by a Norman knight.
(iii) Charles Lindbergh was the first person to fly across the Atlantic.
   Incorrect fact: John Alcock and Arthur Whitten-Brown, two RAF officers, flew across the Atlantic in 1919.
(iv) Big Ben is a famous clock situated outside the Houses of Parliament in London.
   Incorrect fact: Big Ben is neither a clock nor a tower, but the *bell* which strikes the hour.

The moral is that well-known *facts* should be treated with some caution!

Opinions

Opinions are a little more difficult to detect. An opinion is someone's own point of view. Opinions are sometimes woven very cunningly into a series of facts, so be careful! A newspaper editorial, for example, may contain a number of facts but the main substance of the editorial is nearly always *opinion*.

Historians normally voice an opinion after a great deal of thought and study. They weigh up all the evidence that they have in front of them in the form of primary and secondary sources, maps, documents, statistics and pictures, and then make an informed statement which is based on all the evidence. Not everyone may agree with the statement — it is, after all, an *opinion*, somebody's own ideas. Opinions about historical issues often change as new evidence comes to light. You are more likely to come across opinions in secondary sources than in primary sources.

I opened a well-known history book at random and copied down the following statements. Would you say they are facts or opinions?

    (i) The Harecastle Tunnel was Brindley's masterpiece.
   (ii) Seven million slaves were shipped across the Atlantic during the eighteenth century.
  (iii) As industrial production rose, the importance of the slave trade declined and this may be a reason for its abolition.
  (iv) In 1801 there were 697 353 families engaged in farming.
   (v) The railways created a vast fund of employment.
  (vi) The Speenhamland System had many disadvantages.

(*Economic and Social History of England 1770–1977*, R. B. Jones, 1979)

Judgements

A judgement is more difficult to define. Often historians try to weigh up the good and bad points about a person or an event from history. They describe things people have done in the past and then try to assess their historical importance. Here is one description of William Wilberforce:

The man mainly responsible for the abolition of slavery was William Wilberforce, a fashionable young man . . . who devoted his large fortune and abilities to the cause of abolition. In 1807 he secured the passing of a measure which banned the slave trade. In Wilberforce's hands the Anti-Slave League became one of the best pressure groups of any age. It stands as a great tribute to the humanitarian spirit of nineteenth-century Britain . . .. But it comes as something of a surprise to discover that Wilberforce himself, anxious to free slaves 3000 miles away, was indifferent to the frightful conditions of the workers and child-labourers in the county of Yorkshire which he represented in Parliament.

(*Economic and Social History of England 1770–1977*, R. B. Jones, 1979)

A *judgement* of Wilberforce can be found in the last sentence. Is it fair? Can you find one *fact* and one *opinion* in the passage?

WORK OUT SHORT-ANSWER QUESTIONS: TRADE AND THE ECONOMY

1. Why were two Navigation Acts passed by Parliament in 1651 and 1660?
2. What is a tariff?
3. What do you understand by the word 'mercantilism'?
4. Which parts of Britain were famous for smuggling in 1750?
5. Who was Adam Smith?
6. What is *laissez-faire*?
7. Name two politicians who were influenced by Adam Smith's ideas.
8. What were the terms of the Eden Treaty (1786)?
9. Who formed the Anti-Corn Law League?
10. In what year did Britain become a 'free trade' country?
11. What was the 'slave triangle'?
12. Name the Hull merchant who organised a campaign against the slave trade.
13. How many years passed between the abolition of the slave trade and the abolition of slavery?
14. Which group of craftsmen acted as bankers in the seventeenth century?
15. Why did King William III need money in 1694?
16. When was the Bank of England nationalised?
17. Why was a government inquiry into banking held in 1824?
18. What is an indirect tax?
19. On what sort of goods did people have to pay excise duties in 1750?
20. Who introduced income tax in 1798?
21. How did the government obtain revenue after income tax was abolished in 1816?
22. Name the Prime Minister who phased out customs duties in the 1840s.
23. How much in the pound was income tax in 1874?
24. What was 'The People's Budget' (1909)?
25. What is the current rate of VAT?
26. Explain what is meant by the term 'National Debt'.
27. Who set up the Tariff Reform League in 1903?
28. What was the 'Wall Street Crash' (1929)?
29. Why was the means test introduced?
30. When did Britain enter the Common Market?

11 The Role of Women

Examination Guide

This topic is likely to appear more frequently in GCSE examinations than on previous CSE or GCE papers. Many teachers are interested in the concept of feminism, and the issue of women's rights is always in the news. There has been a tendency in the past for male historians to write too much about the role of men in history. To redress the balance, you can expect to see plenty of questions on suffragists, suffragettes and feminists in the future.

When writing about the role of women in history, do try to avoid *sexism* (strong anti-male or anti-female bias) in your writing. Try to be fair and put both sides of a case. You will never lose marks for trying to be *objective* in what you say!

The only board that does not specifically mention the role of women in its syllabus is the Northern Examining Association. However, the topic will probably appear on the NEA syllabuses sooner or later!

(a) Short-answer Questions

Questions will test recall and understanding — for example:

(a) Which job was most widely available to women in 1850?

lawyer   domestic servant   novelist   teacher

(b) Which of the following women is best known for prison reform?

Florence Nightingale   Hannah More   Grace Darling
Elizabeth Fry

(c) The woman who set up the Women's Social and Political Union was

Emmeline Pankhurst   Emily Davison   Millicent Fawcett
Charlotte Despard

(d) Amy Johnson was a famous

astronaut   aeronaut   nurse   doctor

(e) The first woman M.P. to take her seat in the House of Commons was

Nancy Astor   Ellen Wilkinson   Edith Summerskill
Florence Horsburgh

(f) In 1975 women won the right to

> take part in active service in Northern Ireland
> receive equal pay for equal work
> take three months' maternity leave
> enter any profession they liked

(b) Essay Questions

Essay questions will fall into three categories:

(i) *Descriptive Essays*

1. Compare the day-to-day life of a girl from a working-class home and a girl from an upper-class background in 1800.
2. Write about three of the following. You should show what part each played in the emancipation of women and say why future generations will regard them as important:

Elizabeth Fry	Marie Stopes
Florence Nightingale	Germaine Greer
George Eliot	Margaret Thatcher

3. Describe the aims and methods of the suffragettes. How successful were the suffragettes in achieving these aims?
   Why did the suffragettes receive so little support from the trade unions and the Labour Party?
4. How did women try to achieve greater equality and more freedom between 1850 and 1950? You should mention

   education
   property
   children
   jobs
   the right to vote

(ii) *Empathetic Essays*

1. 'Grandfather — can you remember the days when women weren't allowed to vote?'
   'Of course I can. I was a young chap in London in 1912 working on the buses and I remember the women's campaign very clearly.'
   'What happened? Why did women campaign so fiercely for the right to vote?'
   'Well, up until that time some women felt they'd been treated very badly. For example, . . .'

   Carry on with the discussion.
2. It is 1930 and you are a woman who has worked in domestic service for most of your life. You have been asked to describe your life and work over the previous 50 years. Write an account of your life, describing all the changes you have seen in that time.
3. Imagine you are *either* a woman working in a coal-mine in Northumberland in 1840 *or* a woman working in a cotton mill in South Lancashire in 1830. Describe a typical day in your working life. You should mention hours of

work, rates of pay, working conditions, your fellow-workers and your home life.

(iii) *Source-based Questions*

You can find a worked example of a source-based question on pages 245–247.

(c) The National Criteria — Assessment Objective 1

All candidates will be expected to *recall*, *evaluate* and *select* knowledge relevant to the context and to *deploy it in a clear and coherent form*.

(From *The National Criteria — History*)

- *Recall* involves remembering enough historical facts to answer the questions which test *memory*.
- *Evaluate* and *select* means choosing from these facts those bits which will enable you to answer a question.
- *Deploy . . . in a clear and coherent form* means using the facts to write an answer which is well argued and clearly thought out.

The best way of learning how to satisfy these objectives is to practise answering questions, memorising information and selecting specific material from long wordy passages as often as possible. If you have a poor memory, you will find the examination very difficult. There are many different techniques which you can use to help you to remember information. One of the worst ways of revising is sitting staring blankly at a book for hours. Make up mnemonics, rhymes and lists to help you learn the basic facts. Better still, get someone to test you or try setting yourself your own questions.

At the end of this chapter you will find 20 short-answer questions on the *Role of Women*. See how many you can answer. Then set yourself another 20 questions on this chapter.

11.1 Introduction

This chapter deals with the changing role of women in society in the period 1750–1980. In 1750 women had very few legal rights. They were unable to vote and could claim little protection under the law. Changes affecting women's rights came very slowly. However, the employment of women in factories in the early nineteenth century gave them a new status as wage-earners. This was the first step towards social, economic and political equality with men. By 1928 women had the vote on the same terms as men, and by 1980 all women enjoyed greater protection under law both at home and in the workplace.

11.2 Women in Factories and Mines

(a) Factory Work

In 1750 most women's work was carried out in or close to the home. Between 1780 and 1850 the Industrial Revolution (see Chapter 4) changed the pattern of people's working lives. Women were greatly affected by these changes. Many of them spent less time working in the home. By the 1840s thousands of women were working in industry. Table 11.1 shows some of the jobs they did.

The first female factory workers came from agriculture, from domestic service and from the unskilled trades. In the 1830s a typical female factory worker was the wife or daughter of a handloom weaver who had given up housework and entered a factory. In 1835, out of a total of 288 700 people working in textile factories, 46 per cent were women and 15 per cent were children.

The main drawbacks of factory life for women were long hours, low rates of pay and dangerous working conditions. In the second half of the nineteenth century various reformers worked hard to improve factory conditions (see Chapter 6). However, factory work also had its advantages. it was better paid than other jobs open to women. It also gave working-class women the chance to be more independent of their fathers and husbands.

Table 11.1   Occupations of women in 1841

Job	Over the age of 20	Under the age of 20
Cotton	65 839	49 586
Boot- and shoe-makers	8 611	1 953
Dressmakers	70 518	18 561
Factory workers	4 338	4 449
Glovemakers	4 249	1 600
Hosiery	5 934	2 371
Lace-making	14 394	5 651
Pottery	3 843	3 253
Domestic servants	447 606	264 887
Spinners	3 458	1 906
Weavers	17 728	8 583

(Source: *Women Workers and the Industrial Revolution*, Ivy Pinchbeck, 1930)

(b) The Mines

In coal-mines many women began work as *trappers*, opening and closing air-doors underground. Older women would do jobs such as *hurrying* or *putting*. They had to carry coal from the coal-face to the mine shaft along underground passages.

In the larger pits women would push 'corves' (waggons) along rails. In smaller pits the 'girdle and chain' method of drawing coal was used. The hurrier would buckle a broad leather belt around her waist. A chain was attached to her belt, passed between her legs and hooked onto a sledge. Once the sledge had been filled with coal, the hurrier would drag the load along the gallery to the shaft. In 1842 a government official described women hurriers as 'black, soaking wet and more than half-naked, crawling on their hands and knees, dragging their heavy loads behind them'. In 1842 Parliament passed a Mines Act banning the employment of women underground (see Section 6.7).

11.3 Domestic Service

In the nineteenth century there were few labour-saving devices in people's homes. The well-to-do therefore employed servants to do their housework. This kind of work is called domestic service.

More women and girls worked in domestic service than in any other kind of job. By 1841 there were over 700 000 domestic servants in Britain (see Table 11.1). The work was tiring and monotonous. Housemaids had to carry coal, clean carpets, scrub floors, make beds and polish brasswork. Their working day usually lasted about twelve hours. Domestic servants earned very low wages. As late as 1900, many housemaids earned only 12½p a week, much less than a factory girl. Housemaids also had very little personal freedom. Their employees laid down strict rules about what they could and couldn't do in their spare time! However, many girls put up with these conditions because they believed that their work was more 'respectable' than factory work. They received regular meals and a uniform, and the skills they learned at work came in handy later on when they set up homes of their own.

11.4 Middle-class Ladies

In the nineteenth century a *lady* was the wife or daughter of a gentleman. She did not go out to work for a living and spent most of her time at home. She would spend her day doing needlework, organising the household, visiting friends and chatting to neighbours. Household jobs such as cooking, cleaning and looking after children were passed over to domestic servants.

Many ladies enjoyed this life of luxury and ease. Others decided that they wanted to lead more interesting and challenging lives. One lady, Elizabeth Garrett, decided that she wanted to be a doctor. Florence Nightingale (see Section 7.7) left home to become a nurse. Their parents were horrified! Other groups of middle-class ladies such as the Female Political Union campaigned for all women over the age of 21 to be given the vote. Most *suffragettes* (see Section 11.8) came from middle-class or upper-middle-class backgrounds.

11.5 Nursing (see also Section 7.7)

Florence Nightingale's work in the Crimea changed people's attitudes to nursing. At St. Thomas's Hospital School young ladies paid £30 a year to train to be sisters and matrons. The Nightingale system of caring for the sick spread from the voluntary hospitals to the Poor Law Infirmaries. William Rathbone, a Liverpool businessman, paid for 24 Nightingale nurses to work in the city's Poor Law Infirmary. The first matron of the infirmary, Agnes Jones, set up a training school for nurses who wanted to work with the poor. After their training, nurses left the Liverpool school to take charge of other Poor Law Infirmaries. The 1860s saw the start of a great expansion in the number of hospitals and careers for nurses. Many middle-class ladies became nurses and doctors during this period.

11.6 Women's Education (see also Chapter 6)

In the 1850s the daughters of the middle-classes rarely went to school. They stayed at home, where governesses taught them reading, writing, dancing and music. The girls learned social skills which later helped them to find husbands and run homes. In the nineteenth century, steps were taken to put the education of wealthy young ladies on a more equal footing with those of boys. Table 11.2 shows the most important developments between 1847 and 1920.

Table 11.2 Women's education, 1847–1920

Year	Event
1847	King's College, London, started 'Lectures for Ladies' to train women who wanted to become governesses
1850	Frances Buss founded the North London Collegiate School for Girls. Her pupils studied the same subjects as boys at public schools
1858	Dorothea Beale became headmistress of Cheltenham Ladies College, the first public school for girls
1863	Girls of 16 were allowed to sit the Cambridge Local Examination. This had to be passed before a student could enter university
1864	A Royal Commission was set up to look into girls' education. The commission found that there was a low standard of education in some schools
1870	Forster's Education Act (see also Section 6.4) made elementary education compulsory for boys and girls in some areas
1872	The Girls' Public Day School Trust was founded. The trust collected money, which was used to start grammar schools for girls
1874	Newnham College, Cambridge, was founded. This was the first college for women students
1878	Lady Margaret Hall and Somerville Colleges opened at Oxford
1920	Oxford University decided to award women degree diplomas

11.7 Women and the Law

In 1830 women from all ranks of society had few political, legal or social rights. A married woman could not own property, could not keep her weekly earnings for herself and could not leave her husband without his consent. She was not always allowed to keep her children if her husband died. Women were not allowed to vote in elections or become M.P.s, and many jobs were not open to them.

In the 1860s and 1870s a new movement sprang up which campaigned for a fairer deal for women. It was called *feminism*.

Supporters of women's legal rights won some remarkable successes in the nineteenth century, as Table 11.3 shows.

11.8 Votes for Women

By the end of the nineteenth century many middle-class women desperately wanted the vote, because they believed that women M.P.s would campaign for women's social and economic rights in Parliament. The Chartists (see Section 5.5) had campaigned for manhood suffrage (votes for all men) and had achieved some degree of success. By 1900 most men had the vote.

Women's Suffrage Associations had been set up in the 1850s. Between 1860 and 1900 Parliament discussed female suffrage (votes for women) many times but on each occasion the idea of giving women the vote was rejected. People who

Table 11.3 Women and the law, 1838–1925

Year	Act	Importance
1838	Infants Custody Act	Until this time a husband could take his children away from his wife and refuse to let her see them. The Act gave a wife a legal right to see her children
1857	Matrimonial Causes Act	• A man or woman could get a divorce in a court of law rather than by Act of Parliament • A wife deserted by her husband could keep any money she earned
1870	Married Women's Property Act (1)	Married women could keep their earnings while still living with their husbands
1882	Married Women's Property Act (2)	A wife had the right to own property and give it to whom she wished
1886	Guardianship of Infants Act	A mother became the legal parent of her children if their father died
1886	Married Women's Act	This forced a husband who deserted his wife to pay money towards her keep
1925	Guardianship of Infants Act	In a divorce case the court could decide which parents should keep the children

supported the campaign to give more men and women the vote became known as *suffragists*. In 1903 Mrs Emmeline Pankhurst set up the Women's Social and Political Union (W.S.P.U.). The members of the union became known as *suffragettes* (women campaigning for the vote). The W.S.P.U. started a campaign to put pressure on leading politicians. Women heckled Liberal M.P.s at meetings, organised petitions and chained themselves to the railings outside the homes of government ministers. In 1912 Christabel Pankhurst organised an even more violent campaign. W.S.P.U. members smashed shop windows, set fire to houses and slashed pictures in the National Gallery. Emily Davison, a militant suffragette, threw herself under the King's horse in the Derby. She died four days later.

The government struck back. Suffragettes who broke the law were put into prison. Many women prisoners went on hunger strike. The government allowed prison governors to feed suffragettes by force. One woman had liquid food pumped into her lung by mistake and nearly died. In 1913 the government decided to stop force-feeding the suffragettes. Instead they released the starving women from prison and then rearrested them as soon as they were fit. This Prisoners' Temporary Release Act reminded people of a cat playing with a mouse so it was nicknamed 'The Cat and Mouse Act'.

By the outbreak of war in 1914, women were no nearer getting the vote. Emmeline Pankhurst called off the campaign of violence and told the suffragettes to help the government win the war against Germany. Large numbers of women were employed in war work (see Section 11.9). Immediately after the war the government gave the vote to all women over the age of 30 who were householders or wives of householders. In 1928 the voting age for women was lowered to 21, the same age as for men.

SPECIMEN QUESTION AND MODEL ANSWER: SUFFRAGETTES

Look at the sources and questions below. The questions ask you

   (i) to remember some facts about the suffragettes.
  (ii) to work out answers using these facts.
 (iii) to select certain facts.
 (iv) to use the facts and other information to write a clear, well-informed answer.

Source A

A Memorable Derby

The Derby will long remain memorable in the annals [records] of the Turf . . . the desperate act of a woman who rushed from the rails onto the course, as the horses swept around Tattenham Corner will impress the crowd more than the disqualification of the winner. She did not interfere with the race but she nearly killed a jockey as well as herself and she brought down a valuable horse. She seems to have run right in front of Anmer which Jones was riding for the King. It was impossible to avoid her. She was ridden down, the horse turned a complete somersault and fell upon the rider. That the horse was the King's was doubtless an accident. It would need miraculous skill to single out any particular animal as they passed a particular point. Some of the spectators close to the woman supposed that she was under the impression that the horses had all gone by and that she was merely attempting to cross the course. The evidence, however, is strong that her action was in the supposed interest of the Suffragist movement.

(*The Times*, Thursday, 5 June 1913)

Source B

The Sacrifice of a Human Life

She went to the races at Epsom and breaking through the barriers which separated the crowds from the race course, rushed in the path of the King's horse, which was leading all the others. The horse fell, throwing his jockey and crushing her in such a shocking fashion that she was carried from the course in a dying condition.

(*My Own Story*, Emmeline Pankhurst)

Source C

SUFFRAGETTE·BRINGS·DOWN THE KING'S HORSE AT THE DERBY
ROYAL JOCKEY and WOMAN INJURED. THRILLING INCIDENTS at EPSOM

MISS EMILY WILDING DAVISON, THE SUFFRAGETTE WHO BROUGHT DOWN HORSE AND JOCKEY.

H. JONES, WITH FACE NEARLY BLACK WITH BRUISES AND LIMPING PAINFULLY.

THE KING'S HORSE ARMER AND HIS JOCKEY H. JONES.

PLAN OF THE COURSE, SHOWING THE HALF-CURVE AT TATTENHAM CORNER WHERE MISS DAVISON ENDEAVOURED TO STOP THE KING'S HORSE.

H. JONES, THE INJURED JOCKEY BEING TAKEN BY THE POLICE OR AN AMBULANCE.

REMARKABLE SNAPSHOT OF THE INCIDENT AT TATTENHAM CORNER SHOWING THE WOMAN FALLING AND HORSE AND JOCKEY ON THE GROUND.

Terrible Injuries to Woman who Attempted to Stop the Famous Race at Epsom.

Miss Emily Wilding Davison, the suffragette who was injured on Wednesday when she flung herself in front of the King's horse during the race for the Derby, and now lies at Epsom Cottage Hospital, was yesterday afternoon reported to be sinking.

In the morning it was stated that she was much weaker, and later it was admitted that her condition was extremely grave, heart weakness having shown itself.

The woman's relatives have been summoned, and a serious operation has been performed, without, however, giving much hope of her recovery.

A detective is now stationed at the hospital, and it is understood that the police will institute proceedings when the patient is better.

It was at the famous bend on the Epsom Racecourse at Tattenham Corner that Miss Emily Wilding Davison made her mad dash. Here there are double rails to keep back the press of people who congregate to see the final effort up the home straight. Hundreds

The Jockey's Injuries.

Miss Davison's Record.

RICH FOR HALF AN HOUR:

THE ACCIDENT ON A FILM.

M.P. WHO WAS NOT AT THE RACES.

Use the sources *and your own knowledge of the topic* to answer the questions below.

1. Name the suffragette who threw herself under the King's horse.
2. Where was the Derby held in 1913?
3. Which sentence in source A suggests that the suffragette was not killed instantly?
4. Source A mentions 'the Suffragist movement'. Explain the difference between 'suffragists' and 'suffragettes'.
5. Why do you think that some people have said that source B is less reliable than source A?
6. Write down one *opinion* contained in source A.
7. What part did the author of source B play in the struggle for women's rights?
8. Would you say that the death of the suffragette helped or hindered the suffragette cause?
9. Write a letter to *The Times* attacking the tone of source A and justifying the dead woman's actions.

Model Answer

1. Emily Wilding Davison.
2. Epsom.
3. 'She did not interfere with the race but she nearly killed a jockey as well as herself and she brought down a valuable horse.'
4. 'Suffragists' were men or women who believed in giving more people the right to vote. 'Suffragettes' were women who campaigned for female suffrage [i.e. giving more *women* the vote].
5. Mrs Pankhurst's account (B) may be more biased than source A. Mrs Pankhurst was a founder member of the W.S.P.U. and had fought hard for women's rights for many years. It would be difficult for her to write objectively about Emily Davison's death. She may also have tried to win converts to the suffragette cause by depicting Miss Davison as a martyr.

   The Times's article is likely to be less biased. It was probably written by a reporter or editor who had firsthand reports of the incident. Most reporting in *The Times* is fairly objective. However, the report was clearly written by a man hostile to the suffragists' cause.
6. 'The desperate act of a woman who rushed from the rails onto the course . . . will impress the crowd more than the disqualification of the winner.'
7. *Emmeline Pankhurst* (1858–1928) Feminist leader — joint founder and leader of the Women's Franchise League (1898) and W.S.P.U. (1903). Negotiated with Prime Minister in 1906 on behalf of suffragettes and feminists. When talks broke down, she led a violent campaign against the Liberal government. She took part in arson attacks and hunger strikes while imprisoned. She encouraged women to join armed forces and to work in industry, 1914–1918.
8. Many people were shocked by Emily Davison's death, but the suffragettes probably gained few supporters from the incident. There had been a series of violent acts leading up to Emily Davison's death and these had attracted a great deal of public hostility. Churches had been burned down, shop-windows smashed and golfing greens torn up.

On the other hand, the death of a suffragette made it clear that feminists were willing to die for their cause if necessary. The incident was widely reported in papers all over the world and made more people aware of the campaign for women's rights. Emily Davison had been harshly treated in prison and this came to light in her obituaries. Her funeral was a great public occasion and attracted widespread publicity.

10. Dear Sir,

I have just read your article 'A Memorable Day' published on June 5 in your paper. I strongly object to the tone of the article and wish to state why. Your reporter describes the sacrifice as a 'desperate act' in the 'supposed interest of the suffragette cause'. I would describe it as a heroic act designed to bring public attention to a thoroughly deserving cause.

Your reporter seems more concerned about the horse's state of health than the sad condition of Miss Davison.

Women have laboured under the yoke of their husbands and fathers for too long in this country. Until 1882 women could not own property and until 1870 they were not allowed to keep their weekly earnings for themselves. Until 1886 we were not always able to remain the legal parent of our children if our husband died.

There are still certain jobs which we are barred from entering. There are very few women doctors, solicitors and barristers. We have been led to believe that we are fit for less responsible jobs such as governesses, domestic servants, nannies and shop-workers.

Even in factories women put up with poor conditions for low rates of pay. Most of the workers in the sweated trades are women. They work extremely long hours for terrible wages.

Above all, we are not allowed to vote in parliamentary elections or become M.P.s. We are therefore denied the chance to improve social conditions for women through the parliamentary process. Very few M.P.s have spoken up for the women's cause in Parliament. Is it any wonder that women have resorted to acts of violence and supreme self-sacrifice? The suffragettes tried to change the hostile attitude of male politicians through peaceful means — through meetings, petitions and demonstrations — and they all failed. The noble act of Emily Davison was a last resort. Your sneering references to the tragic events of 5 June do your newspaper little credit. The verdict of history will be very different.

Yours faithfully,

Miss Florence Dugdale, M.A.

11.9 Women at War

(a) First World War

When war broke out in August 1914, the suffragettes called off their campaign of violence (see Section 11.8). By 1916 it was clear that the war against Germany was going to be a long one. All fit men aged between 18 and 41 were called up unless they were doing jobs essential for the war.

All over Britain women stepped into the places of the men who had gone away to war. They did clerical and 'service' jobs such as nursing, catering and cleaning. They worked in munitions factories, making shells and bullets for soldiers on the Western Front. They also worked as porters, bus-conductors, road-sweepers, postwomen and farm labourers. They often worked in bad conditions but they received higher rates of pay than before the war. Table 11.4 shows the main industries which employed women in the period 1914–1918.

Table 11.4   Women at work, 1914–1918 (thousands)

Industry	Women employed, 1914	Women employed, 1918
Government	2	225
Transport	18	117
Metal	170	594
Chemical	40	104
Food and drink	196	235
Timber	44	79

Women were also needed in the armed forces. They took over the non-fighting jobs so that more men could be released for combat. There were two women's sections in the forces, the Women's Auxiliary Army Corps (W.A.A.C.) and the Women's Royal Naval Service (W.R.N.S.). A Women's Land Army was also set up to fill in the gaps left by male farm workers who had joined up.

In 1918 *most* women over the age of 30 were given the right to vote (see Section 11.8).

(b) Second World War

During the Second World War women were again called upon to do the jobs of men who had been called up into the army. As in the First World War, they became a vital part of the workforce. For the first time all unmarried women between the ages of 20 and 30 were drafted into the armed forces or factories. Eight hundred thousand women were sent to do jobs in local government, transport and fishing. Other girls worked in the Women's Land Army. By 1943 there were 90 000 of them working on Britain's farms.

Women who chose to join the armed forces did not take part in the fighting. By 1945 there were half a million women in the W.R.N.S., the Women's Auxiliary Air Force (W.A.A.F.) and the Auxiliary Territorial Service (A.T.S.). There were also many women in the Home Guard.

The Second World War brought more women into work outside the home than ever before. However, the government did not treat women workers as the equals of men. Women got less pay for the jobs men had done. After the war, women found themselves excluded from many jobs when the men returned from the war. However, after 1945 there was a need for increased industrial production and so large numbers of women continued to work in industry.

11.10   Women and Employment

In 1919 many women had to give up their wartime jobs to men coming out of the forces. However, there were new jobs for women in the electrical, chemical and light engineering industries. More women took on 'white collar' jobs such as office work,banking, teaching or nursing. It became more acceptable for women to stay on at work after they got married, but some employers did not allow this. There was still a great deal of prejudice (bias) against women. Some working men still believed that 'a woman's place was in the home'. Others argued that women should not take men's jobs. In the depressed regions of the old coalfields there were very few jobs for men and almost none for women.

After the Second World War there were shortages of many goods. The government rationed food, clothes and furniture. To help provide more of these items, large numbers of women were asked to stay on at work in factories, workshops and mills. Many women stayed at work because they wanted their families to have their share of the better food, clothing and entertainment the extra money would help to buy. Other women carried on working outside the home because they felt the need to lead lives independent of family and home. Between 1951 and 1976 the number of women going out to work increased by 3.3 million. Most women did one of four types of job:

1. *Secretarial work*   Women took on jobs as clerks, typists, receptionists, etc.
2. *Services*   There were jobs in classrooms, nurseries, old people's homes and hospitals.
3. *Shops*   Women took the place of men who moved from shops and service work to higher-paid posts in other industries.
4. *Light industry*   In the South-east there were jobs in light industry making consumer goods and household appliances.

11.11   Sex Discrimination

In the 1950s women were still treated as second-class employees in many jobs. They were paid at lower rates than men and they often had worse working conditions. Women teachers were one of the first groups to win the battle for equal pay. Between 1955 and 1961 women teachers' pay increased in stages to match men's. However, some unions argued that higher pay for women would mean lower pay for men! Employers said that paying women higher wages would make some firms bankrupt. Nevertheless, Parliament passed a series of Acts between 1970 and 1975 designed to give women greater equality in the workplace (Table 11.5).

Table 11.5   Anti-discrimination Acts

Year	Act	Importance
1970	Equal Pay Act	Employers had to pay women the same wages as men if they were doing similar jobs
1975	Sex Discrimination Act	It became illegal to discriminate between men and women (or married and unmarried people) in job recruitment, promotion or training
1975	Equal Opportunities Act	Employers could no longer label jobs for either men or women only. The Act set up an Equal Opportunities Commission to investigate cases of sex discrimination

Nowadays women at work expect to be treated in the same way as men. Yet many people feel that the laws of the 1970s do not go far enough. Employers have found ways of paying women lower wages than men. The Equal Opportunities Commission has turned out to be a rather weak organisation which has done little to campaign on behalf of women or to speak out against discrimination. In 1978 the Commission produced a report which showed that there was still a wide gap between men's earnings and women's earnings.

11.12 The Women's Movement

By 1918 the women's movement had made great progress in education, health, work opportunities, political power and legal rights. This progress continued after 1918.

(a) Women's Health

Childbirth became less dangerous and family sizes became smaller. In 1921 Marie Stopes (1880–1958) opened the first birth-control clinic in North London, and in 1930 she set up the National Birth-Control Council. By 1939 the Council had more than 60 clinics and had changed its name to the Family Planning Association. The widespread use of birth-control methods reduced family size and led to less physical strain on mothers.

(b) Work Opportunities

See Section 11.11.

(c) Political Power and Legal Rights

In the 1960s and 1970s there was a revival in the type of feminism favoured by the suffragettes (see Section 11.8). Some feminists wanted equal rights for women in all walks of life: work, marriage, morals and leisure. Gradually the idea of 'Women's Liberation' developed. During the 1960s American feminists argued that women were enslaved through low pay, third-rate jobs and the negative attitude of men. Feminists wanted women to join a crusade for a free, equal, just society. Some men and women made fun of feminist ideas but their influence soon spread to other countries, including Britain. In 1969 Germaine Greer (b.1939) wrote about the growth of the women's movement in a book called *The Female Eunuch*.

There were also changes in attitudes to sex. Feminists argued that Victorian attitudes to sex were unfair to women. They believed that women should have the right to choose what kind of lives they led and that men should take a greater share of the responsibilities which came with sex, home and family life. Today these arguments still rumble on.

SOURCE-BASED QUESTION: THE ROLE OF WOMEN

In 1980 the government announced that 96 American cruise missiles were to be sited at the U.S. base at Greenham Common, Berkshire. In August 1981, 40

251

women set out on a protest march from Wales to Greenham Common. When they got there, they decided to stay near the base and try to prevent the arrival of the missiles.

Source A

We are ordinary women who feel that nothing is more important in our lives than preventing nuclear disaster. We choose non-violence because we believe that we cannot fight violence with violence, that we must use other methods of solving our differences if we are to survive.

There are no leaders at the women's peace camp, no formal organisation. The camp at Greenham is a focus for us. Some women live there all the time, some visit for a day and then take back their ideas to their own areas and encourage other women to act. We feel we must take responsibility for what the government is doing, supposedly in our name.

(Statement issued by the campaigners, September 1981)

Source B

The women staged symbolic 'die-ins'. They climbed over the camp fence and danced on the silos built to house the missiles. They got arrested, fined, evicted and stoned. They painted peace symbols on U.S. war planes. They cut the wire of the fence. The Ministry of Defence warned that they risked being shot. On 17 November 1983 the missiles arrived. The women formed a blockade; 117 were arrested.

On 11 December 50 000 women encircled the base and pulled part of the fencing down. There were hundreds of arrests, mainly for 'breach of the peace'. The women's reply was that it is a breach of the peace to have these weapons on the Common.

(*A Woman's Place*, Diana Souhami, 1986)

Source C

Source D

253

1. (i) What were the women at Greenham Common protesting about?
   (ii) What offence were many of them charged with?
   (iii) How many women encircled the base in 1983?
2. In which piece of evidence is there reference made to the scene depicted in source D?
3. Can you detect any bias in sources A–D?
4. Is there any evidence in sources A–D to suggest that the police were too rough with some of the demonstrators?
5. How does the Greenham Common protest compare with the activities of the suffragettes between 1912 and 1913?

11.13 The Role of Women Today

Today women have more independence and freedom than ever before. Many men are beginning to accept that women have been unfairly treated in the past. Some sociologists have argued that there is increasing equality in the family and that men and women regard each other as equals. Feminists reply that many men retain traditional attitudes to morals, marriage and family life. They say that the family is a trap for women. Women give up their work, their social lives and their financial independence in return for the roles of housewife and mother.

The rising status of women in society and their refusal to accept their traditional roles has led to a very high divorce rate. For the women who feel they are 'trapped' in the home there is a ray of hope. The increasing use of labour-saving devices in many homes has helped to liberate thousands of married and single women from the grind of household chores. With smaller families, labour-saving gadgets and fast food, some women find it possible to go out to work *and* run a home.

WORK OUT SHORT-ANSWER QUESTIONS: THE ROLE OF WOMEN

1. When did women gain the vote on the same terms as men?
2. How did the Industrial Revolution affect women's lives?
3. In which occupation were most women employed in 1841?
4. In coal-mines, what were 'hurriers' and 'putters'?
5. When was the Mines Act passed by Parliament?
6. Write down three advantages of working in domestic service rather than in a factory.
7. Who was Elizabeth Garrett?
8. Name the businessman who paid for properly qualified nurses to work with the poor in Liverpool.
9. Who were Miss Buss and Miss Beale?
10. What is 'feminism'?
11. How did the Married Women's Property Act help women?
12. What was the difference between a 'suffragist' and a 'suffragette'?
13. How did the 'Cat and Mouse Act' earn its nickname?
14. Why did Mrs Pankhurst call off the suffragettes' campaign of violence in August 1914?
15. What sort of jobs did women do during the First World War?
16. What do the initials W.A.A.F., W.R.N.S., W.A.A.C. and A.T.S. stand for?

17. Which group of women won the battle for equal pay with men between 1955 and 1961?
18. Name the organisation which investigates cases of sexual discrimination.
19. Who was Marie Stopes?
20. Name the woman who wrote a book called *The Female Eunuch* in 1969.

12 Coursework and Revision Techniques

12.1 Coursework

At least 20 per cent of the final mark for your GCSE History examination will consist of coursework. The number of pieces of coursework and the number of marks awarded for coursework vary from board to board. For LEAG, NEA and MEG syllabuses, coursework is worth 30 per cent of the final mark. For SEG, the coursework is worth 20 per cent.

Table 12.1 shows the different skills and concepts tested in the coursework.

You should put a lot of effort into your coursework. It could make a great deal of difference to your final grade. The coursework is a chance for you to show the examiners what you *know, understand and can do*.

Table 12.1

Board	HI	E	Co	C	Em
LEAG	✓	✓	✓		✓
MEG	✓	✓	✓	✓	
NEA	✓	✓	✓		✓
SEG		✓			✓

KEY:
- *HI* Historical investigation
- *E*   Evidence
- *Co* Concepts
- *C*   Context
- *Em* Empathy

(a) Activity 1

Consult your syllabus and/or your teacher to find out the answers to the following questions about your coursework:

1. What percentage of the marks for the examination is the coursework worth?
2. How many pieces of coursework do you have to hand in?
3. What are the deadlines for the coursework?

4. How long should the pieces of coursework be?
5. Do you have to do the coursework at home or in class?
6. How does the coursework have to be presented?
7. Do the pieces of coursework have to be presented in writing or can you hand in tapes, photographs, videos, models, etc.?
8. What assessment objectives are being tested in the coursework?
9. How will the coursework be marked (i.e. how many marks will be awarded for each assessment objective)?

Choosing a Coursework Topic

Each board has its own approach to coursework. Some boards allow you a completely free choice, while others ask you to choose a topic from a list. Make sure you read through any regulations or advice issued by your board. If in doubt, ask your teacher or write to your examining board. There is a list of the addresses of the examining boards on pages xi–xiii.

When you choose and plan a piece of coursework, ask your teacher what he/she thinks of your choice. Think about the three questions in Activity 2, below.

(b) Activity 2

1. Can you think of a topic which interests you and which will give you a chance to show the examiner your enthusiasm for and interest in the subject?
2. Once you have chosen a topic, write down ten questions associated with the topic.

   For example, if your chosen topic is *The Poor, 1760–1860*, you might ask:

   How were poor people treated in 1760?
   Why was the Speenhamland System introduced in 1795?
   Why did the problem of poverty increase during the wars with France, 1793–1815? etc.

3. The title for your coursework assignment could take the form of one of these questions — for example:

   Why did the first Industrial Revolution take place in Britain?
   Did the early industrial changes do more harm than good?
   Were the suffragettes right to adopt violent tactics after 1912?
   Why did Britain join the Common Market in 1973?
   Why did Britain abandon free trade in 1932?

   Can you think *why* the best pieces of GCSE coursework will be those in which candidates set themselves a specific question? Write down *three* questions you might set out to answer about each of the topics below:

   The Chartists
   Medicine and surgery
   Women's rights

(c) Activity 3: Sources of Information

Make a list of all the sources of information you might use to write a GCSE coursework assignment (include your teacher!). Which of these sources are primary and which are secondary?

As you write the coursework, keep a list of all the sources you have used. If you are using a particular book, make a note of the title, date of publication, author, publisher and page numbers. Write down whether the book contains mainly primary or secondary material.

Writing the Coursework

How do you actually write the coursework? Follow the simple steps below.

1. Make *detailed* notes on all your sources. These could be in a rough book, A4 paper or scrap paper. These notes will be your *first draft*.
2. Read through your notes. Make any changes, corrections or additions in a different-colour pen.
3. Using your notes as a guide, write out a *second draft* in your own words. Check spellings, punctuation, grammar, etc.
4. Finally, copy out your work *in your best writing*. You should make it quite clear to the examiners if you are quoting directly from a textbook. If you like, box in or colour in the quoted information. *Never copy directly from the textbook*. Some boards may disqualify candidates for this. The NEA regulations state:

Candidates must understand that to present material copied from books or other sources without acknowledgement, will be regarded as deliberate deception . . .. If the boards are satisfied that an offence has been committed, the candidate will be liable to disqualification.

So you *must* acknowledge the amount of help you have received from parents, teachers and other people. Honesty is the best policy here.

(d) Presenting Coursework

Your *introduction* should state what you are setting out to do and how you intend to do it. Your *conclusion* should sum up the main points and pinpoint any difficulties you came across when writing the assignment.

Do present your coursework neatly. Pay attention to spelling, grammar and punctuation. Good presentation is an important skill in itself.

Your teacher or examination syllabus will give you guidance on how to set out your assignments. Most boards will require the following information:

Subject title (Social and Economic History)
Title of assignment
Your name
Your school
Your examination number
The number of your examination centre
How long you spent on the assignment
The sources you used

In addition, your teacher will have to fill in a special form evaluating the coursework, like the one below.

SOUTHERN EXAMINING GROUP   *COURSEWORK ASSESSMENT*
GCSE   *SHEET*
HISTORY

Centre Number _____   Centre Name _____   Syllabus _____

Candidate Number _____   Candidate Name _____

ASSESSMENT OBJECTIVE	BRIEF TITLE	MARKS MAXIMUM	SCHOOL	MODERATOR/ GROUP
3 EMPATHETIC		10		
4 SOURCE-BASED		10		

THE FOLLOWING DECLARATION MUST BE SIGNED BY THE TEACHER REPONSIBLE FOR THE ASSESSMENT ASSIGNMENTS

I certify that to the best of my knowledge the above work has been produced by the candidate's own genuine efforts and that the marks awarded represent the level internally standardised at this centre.

Signature of Teacher/Examiner ....

(From the SEG History Syllabus, 1988 Examination)

(e) Activity 4

Which titles listed below do you think would be best for a GCSE coursework assignment? Which would show the examiners what you *know, understand and can do*? Choose the *four* most suitable titles. Give reasons for your choice.

The History of Science
The History of the Wool Industry in Yorkshire
The Internal Combustion Engine
The 1984 Miners' Strike
Lace-making in Honiton, 1700–1800
The History of Transport
Pop Music Since 1986
Domestic Industries in Chipping Sodbury, 1755–1757

12.2 Revision Techniques

It is up to you to work out the revision technique which suits you best. Your plan could look like this:

Revision Programme

- *End of February* Look through your 'mock' examination answer papers. Which questions did you do well on? Where did you make mistakes? How can you improve your mark in May/June?

  Try to learn from your mistakes. The main reason for setting you a 'mock' examination was to give you *practice* at answering questions under examination conditions. You may find writing answers under examination conditions a difficult thing to do. If so, you need as much practice at *examination technique* between February and May as possible.

  Work out a *timetable* using the chapters in this book, your exercise book and your school textbooks. The timetable should cover March and April. You should aim to do plenty of revision during the Easter holidays. The timetable should run from the end of February to the end of April. This will give you two weeks at the end of your revision programme to concentrate on your weaker points. It will also give you a chance to revise the main points in each topic again.

- *March and April* Spend between 45 minutes and an hour and a half on your revision each day. If you have planned your revision programme carefully, you will start to *enjoy* the revision at this point. It will be satisfying to feel that you are on course for a good GCSE examination result!

- *May* Revise the main points, using the work out sections at the end of each chapter and any headings you have written on cards or slips of paper. Check that you know *when and where* the examination is taking place.

- *The Day of the Examination* Have an early night before the examination. Get along to the examination room early. Make sure that you have pens, pencils, a ruler and a rubber with you. Read the examination paper very carefully. Tick off the questions you think you can answer. Choose the questions you intend to do. If you are answering an essay-type question, do plan your paragraphs in advance.

How to Revise

Below there are *ten* tried and tested methods of revising? Which method(s) appeal to you most? Try each method out. Then rank each method in your own order of importance.

Method 1

(i) Get hold of an ordinary exercise book. Leave the first page blank. You can write your *index* here.

(ii) Using the GCSE *WORK OUT* book, decide which topics you are going to revise. *Always* revise more topics than you think will come up on the exam paper. You need a few reserve topics to fall back on in an emergency!

(iii) Write the title of the topic in BLOCK CAPITALS at the top of the left-hand page in your exercise book. Make notes from your exercise book and/or your school textbook. Your notes for each topic should not fill up more than *two sides* (i.e. a double page of your exercise book).

(iv) Revise each topic from the double page. Try to learn or relearn *a topic a day* in the four weeks prior to the examination.

Method 2: Index Cards

(i) You need to buy a packet of *blank postcards* from a stationer. If you are revising 12 topics, you need at least 12 cards.

(ii) Use method 1 to summarise the main points in your notes and school textbook.

(iii) Write down the *main headings* of each topic on your postcards. Below the headings write names, dates, places, figures, definitions.

(iv) Whenever you have a spare moment, read through the *headings* on your cards. Then try to remember the most important facts you have written down below each heading. Look at the cards when you are waiting for a bus to arrive or before breakfast or while you're waiting for a lesson to start.

Method 3

Imagine you are a GCSE History examiner. Look at last year's paper. Set yourself a GCSE History paper which covers most of the main topics on the syllabus. If you like, work out a *mark scheme*. Then try to answer the questions you have set on your paper. Time yourself carefully. How much time do you have to answer each question?

Method 4: Test Yourself

Go through your notes and the textbook. Set yourself *100* short-answer questions on each topic. Your revision sheets on each topic could look like this:

Population	(Fold back along dotted line)
Questions	Answers
1. What was the population of England and Wales in 1700?	1. $5\frac{1}{2}$ million
2. Who drew up an estimate of the size of England and Wales in 1695?	2. Gregory King
3. Name the Anglican vicar who wrote a book in 1798 claiming there would be a population explosion.	3. Thomas Malthus
4. Define the term 'death-rate' . . . etc.	4. ....

Method 5: Talking

Choose a History topic with a friend. Revise the topic. Then meet to discuss the topic. Talk about any points you don't understand. Then test each other on the topic until you both know it thoroughly.

Warning   This method of revising requires great self-discipline on the part of both the students involved. Don't work with a friend unless you are sure that he/she wants to revise as well. Otherwise you might end up wasting precious time.

Method 6: Audio Tapes

Record the notes you have made in method 1 on a cassette. Play back your recorded notes at every opportunity. If you have a Walkman-type cassette player, you can listen to your revision topics while walking to school, sitting on the bus or going to the park.

Method 7: Mnemonics

You can sometimes remember facts by the use of a device called a *mnemonic*. You invent a sentence or rhyme which helps you to remember things better. For example, some people remember the colours of the rainbow by using the initial letter of each colour to form a sentence.

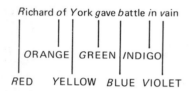

Richard of York gave battle in vain

RED · ORANGE · YELLOW · GREEN · BLUE · INDIGO · VIOLET

Ask your teachers whether they know any mnemonics. Here are two useful examples:

Textile Inventors (in correct chronological order)

King Henry ate cream cakes

KAY   HARGREAVES   ARKWRIGHT   CROMPTON   CARTWRIGHT

Textile Machines (in correct chronological order)

Few short women marry policemen

FLYING SHUTTLE   SPINNING-JENNY   WATER-FRAME   MULE   POWER LOOM

Method 8: Revision Games

Try inventing some revision games. The board could look like the example below:

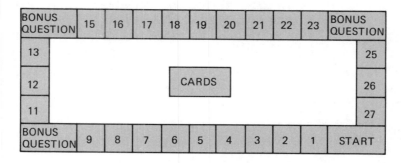

Write 500 History questions on pieces of card and place them in the centre of the board. Take it in turns to answer questions. You move forward *two* places for each correct answer. You move back *one* place for each incorrect answer. The winner is the first person to get back to '*Start*'.

Method 9: Practice Makes Perfect

Your teacher will probably give you a number of *key revision topics*. Find an old question paper which sets questions on one or more of these topics. Pick a question. Write out the answer in full or in note form. Get someone to check your answer. How many marks would you have scored on a question like this in the examination?

Method 10: Puzzles and Quizzes

This is an entertaining way of revising. You can make up wordsearches or quiz-type games quite easily.

Trackdate   Use the grid below to track the dates of the FIVE most important textile machines of the eighteenth century. You can track horizontally, vertically or diagonally from the figure 1 on the left-hand side.

5		
8	6	7
1	7	9
3	3	

Wordsearch   Find the names of:

    (i) The man who modified the Newcomen steam pump
   (ii) An agricultural improver
  (iii) An early eighteenth-century roadbuilder
  (iv) The Queen of England, 1702–1714
   (v) The ironmaster who developed 'puddling and rolling'

```
T  T  A  W
U  R  N  A
L  O  N  D
L  C  E  E
```

GOOD LUCK WITH YOUR REVISION!

Further Reading

The best books on GCSE History are:

The Blackwell History Project (Ed. Jon Nichol)

    Agrarian Britain 1700–1980
    The Industrial Revolution
    Transport 1750–1980
    Social Problems 1760–1914
    Trade Unions and Social Change 1750–1980
    Using Evidence
    Medicine

(Basil Blackwell, Oxford)

History For You (Britain Since 1700), Robert Unwin, Hutchinson, 1986
Making Modern Britain, Christopher Culpin, Collins, 1987
A Social and Economic History of Industrial Britain, John Robottom, Longmans, 1986
Rapid Revision Notes — British Economic History, D. C. Perkins, Celtic Revision Aids

Two old 'O' level textbooks would be extremely useful for further reference:

The Age of Industrial Expansion, A. J. Holland, Nelson, 1975
British Economic and Social History 1700–1975, C. P. Hill, Arnold, 1977

Answers to Short-answer Questions

Chapter 2: Population

1. $5\frac{1}{2}$ million
2. Birth-rate — number of births per thousand per year
   Death-rate — number of deaths per thousand per year
3. A person who studies population figures
4. The death-rate among babies
5. Gin
6. *An Essay on the Principles of Population*
7. Wars, famines
8. Wars with France
9. A government official who carried out a census in 1801
10. Nine million
11. Every ten years
12. East Anglia, Somerset, the Cotswolds
13. Lancashire
14. Liverpool, Manchester
15. Railways
16. Money collected for the poor
17. Poor Law Amendment Act
18. Ireland
19. 80 per cent
20. Coal, iron, steel, textiles

Chapter 3: Agriculture

1. 2.6 per cent
2. The Midlands and the South
3. Three
4. One acre ($\frac{1}{2}$ hectare)
5. It was the amount of land a man could plough in one day
6. Wheat, barley, oats
7. A field left unploughed so that the soil could regain its goodness
8. The squire
9. Land belonging to the Church
10. Even the poorest farmers had *some* land; co-operative farming was possible; villagers had grazing rights; it provided enough food for the population
11. Balks, fallows, grassy tracks
12. Mating your best animals to produce strong, healthy stock

13. Arthur Young, Nathaniel Kent, William Cobbett
14. They argued that the changes we call 'The Agricultural Revolution' took place very slowly and varied from area to area
15. Increase in population; new farming techniques were not suited to open-field farming; landowners were keen to try out new methods and make money
16. Grassland which has been fenced off and turned into 'patchwork' fields
17. Villagers swapping parcels of land so that their holdings were all in one place
18. So that farmers could produce more food and make greater profits
19. They surveyed each village and tried to sort out who the land belonged to
20. 1801
21. 1810–1819
22. High prices, unemployment, wars with France
23. Farmers could try out new machines, crops, fertilisers; there was more farm land in England; huge new estates were formed
24. Marquis of Rockingham, Lord Braybrook
25. Seed-drill, horse-drawn hoe
26. He grew root crops on his estates in Norfolk
27. Sheep-shearing festivals
28. They saw well-fed animals in clean stalls and sheds
29. Windsor Park
30. 1793–1815
31. To prevent the price of home-produced wheat, barley and oats falling
32. He introduced a sliding-scale
33. They were organised by a mythical 'Captain Swing'
34. Manchester
35. 1846–1870
36. He developed a new system of drainage
37. Justus von Liebig
38. McCormick
39. Seagull-droppings from Peru
40. Linseed, oilseed, maize
41. Foreign competition
42. U.S.A., France, Germany
43. A cottage which a farm worker was allowed to live in as part of his conditions of work
44. National Agricultural Labourers Union
45. Agricultural Development Act, County War Agricultural Committees, Agricultural Improvement Council
46. To feed cattle, check production figures, work out farm accounts
47. Rearing animals intensively in 'belsens' and 'batteries'
48. 1973
49. The CAP keeps food prices at a fixed amount by imposing tariffs on food grown outside the EEC
50. EEC surpluses in butter and wine.

Chapter 4: Industry

1. The change from an economy based on agriculture to an economy based on industry
2. The process of workers making goods in their own homes
3. Wool
4. East Anglia, the South-west, the West Riding of Yorkshire

5. Cottage workers received 'payment in kind' (payment in goods rather than money)
6. Combing out the wool to separate and straighten the individual strands
7. Spinning — twisting woollen fibres together to make *threads*
   Weaving — passing weft thread under and over warp thread to make *cloth*
8. Some wool-producing areas were a long way from the coalfields
9. Liverpool
10. The Pennines
11. 1771
12. The flying shuttle
13. Lewis Paul
14. It could produce more than one thread at a time
15. Crompton's machine was a combination of the spinning-jenny and the water-frame; a mule is a cross between a horse and an ass
16. The American Civil War resulted in a shortage of raw cotton
17. Lancashire
18. Man-made fibres
19. There is a world-wide demand for British tweeds and worsteds
20. A mine with a horizontal entrance with a drainage channel below the entrance
21. The increase in population; a shortage of timber; the development of steam power
22. Northumberland
23. Keels — river boats
    Colliers — sea-going coalships
24. Methane
25. Canaries are affected by poisonous gas more quickly than people
26. Men who worked in coal-mines during the Second World War
27. There was a shortage of charcoal for smelting
28. Across the River Severn, south of Coalbrookdale
29. The reverberatory furnace
30 (i) Neilson (ii) Nasmyth
31. The converter
32. The temperature of the furnace could be controlled easily
33. Taxes on imported goods
34. Water
35. He realised that the Newcomen engine wasted a lot of fuel
36. The separate condenser (1765); rotary motion (1781); the valve box (1782)
37. Queensware
38. Claude Berthollet
39. Imperial Chemical Industries
40. Henry Maudslay
41. Belfast; the River Clyde; Barrow-in-Furness; the River Tyne
42. To enable Britain to show off her technical and industrial achievements
43. 1870–1900
44. Textiles, coal, iron and steel, shipbuilding
45. William Murdoch
46. Charles Parsons
47. A national network of power lines
48. Petrochemicals; atomic energy; computers
49. Transport, communications, information technology
50. Government non-intervention

1. To make it easier to prosecute workers who combined together for higher rates of pay
2. Francis Place and Joseph Hume
3. For trying to form a branch of the G.N.C.T.U.
4. It stated that an employee was not a member of a trade union
5. William Lovett, Francis Place, Thomas Attwood, Feargus O'Connor
6. 1848
7. Lancashire Chartists removed the plugs from the boilers of steam engines
8. Five
9. Co-operative Wholesale Society
10. The A.S.J.C. was a union for skilled workers paying high subscriptions
11. William Allen
12. The leaders of New Model Unions living in London
13. Cutlers dropped a can of gunpowder down the chimney of a 'blackleg'
14. Peaceful picketing was made illegal
15. Joseph Arch
16. Girls working for Bryant and May in 1888
17. The dockers' wage of 6d. ($2\frac{1}{2}$p) an hour
18. Unions which called a strike could be held responsible for employers' losses
19. He was a member of the Liberal Party who objected to paying part of his union subscription to the Labour party
20. Unions negotiating with employers over pay and conditions
21. Black Friday — 15 April 1921. The railwaymen and transport workers failed to support the miners
    Red Friday — 31 July 1925. The government offered a subsidy of £24 million to the Miners Federation
22. Railwaymen, transport workers, miners
23. A. J. Cooke
24. Nine days
25. The government
26. General strikes and sympathetic strikes were declared illegal
27. Steel, coal, textiles
28. State ownership
29. Ernest Bevin
30. Coal, railways, civil aviation
31. There was a quarrel over pay restraint
32. Money losing its value
33. The National Incomes Council Act
34. Strikes which do not have the backing of a union
35. Harold Wilson
36. 1970
37. In 1974 shortages of fuel led to a shorter working week in industry
38. Miners demanded a large pay increase
39. Hospital workers, local government workers, ambulancemen, teachers
40. Employment Acts (1980/1982)
    Trade Union Act (1984)

Chapter 6: Social Change

1. A prison warder
2. Typhus fever

3. The High Sheriff of Bedfordshire
4. Newgate
5. Robert Peel
6. Convicts started sentences in prison, then did hard labour and were finally released on probation
7. Henry Fielding
8. 3000 men
9. Towns and boroughs were controlled by corporations
10. 1910
11. Policemen carrying out foot patrols and getting to know members of the community well
12. Society for the Promotion of Christian Knowledge
13. The Church of England; bequests and wills
14. They were set up because Raikes was shocked by the behaviour of local children on Sundays
15. Children whose parents were out working
16. Joseph Lancaster and Andrew Bell
17. The teacher taught the monitors; the monitors taught the children
18. 1820
19. Lord Shaftesbury and Charles Dickens
20. Public schools
21. They taught Latin and Greek grammar
22. Book-keeping, science and natural history
23. £20 000
24. Less than half of Britain's children went to school; only one-half of these learned to read and write
25. 1870
26. 5–11 years
27. 15
28. £50
29. Dr Southwood Smith and Dr Kay Shuttleworth
30. He used the medical officers of the Poor Law Unions
31. The Poor Law Commissioners thought it would annoy too many people
32. Bread
33. Lack of vitamins in the diet
34. Some families got more milk, eggs and meat than before the war
35. People are concerned about additives in food
36. When trade was good and employees worked long hours to satisfy the demand for textile goods
37. Robert Owen, Benjamin Gott
38. The men who worked at the coal-face
39. There were no factory inspectors
40. 58 hours
41. Boys under the age of 15 were not allowed to work machinery
42. Quakers, Baptists, Unitarians
43. She believed that people would be more sober, respectful, obedient members of society
44. Money losing its value
45. 20 000
46. There was a terrible potato famine
47. There was a shortage of skilled jobs
48. 1965, 1968, 1976
49. London, Bristol, Liverpool
50. Poor social conditions, low wages, unemployment

1. In monasteries
2. St. Bartholomew's, St. Thomas's, St. Mary's
3. 1725
4. Blood poisoning
5. People employed to look after patients at night
6. They were poorly paid and unqualified
7. At home
8. Poor sanitation, water supply and hygiene
9. Tuberculosis
10. 1831–1832, 1838, 1848–1849, 1854
11. 29 per 1000
12. 40 000 per year
13. Giving a person a mild form of a disease to prevent a serious outbreak of the same disease
14. Lady Mary Wortley Montague
15. He noticed that country people who had caught cowpox never caught smallpox
16. Sunderland (the North-east)
17. 1848
18. Lord Morpeth, Lord Shaftesbury, Edwin Chadwick
19. 23 per 1000
20. A doctor trained by a medical school
21. Opium or hemp
22. Windmill Street, London
23. Cutting up the dead bodies of humans or animals
24. 1778
25. Barbiturates make you feel sleepy
26. Louis Pasteur
27. He applied carbolic acid directly to wounds
28. 1865
29. Antiseptic surgery — acid is applied directly to wounds
    Aseptic surgery — keeping clothes, hands, surgical instruments free from germs
30. Queen Anne
31. He improved midwifery techniques
32. £5 a year
33. 1855
34. They were given a uniform, regular meals, accommodation
35. Sobriety, veracity, trustworthiness, punctuality, cleanliness
36. Chadwick, one member of the Board, had made many enemies
37. Dr John Simon
38. New laws to deal with sanitation and water supply had to be passed by Parliament
39. In universities or medical schools
40. Orthopaedics — children's diseases
    Pathology — the study of disease
    Radiology — the study of X-rays
41. 1946
42. Koch identified the germs that cause sepsis, tuberculosis and cholera
43. In the stomachs of certain kinds of mosquito
44. Germs which resist a disease
45. A doctor in the Indian Medical Service who researched the causes of malaria

46. It will magnify up to 200 000 times
47. Acquired Immune Deficiency Syndrome
48. While growing bacteria on a dish
49. Substances which kill other disease-causing organisms
50. It was discovered in 1947 and used to treat TB patients

Chapter 8: The Welfare State

1. A state which looks after the welfare of all its citizens 'from the cradle to the grave.'
2. (a) Money collected from each household to be handed out to those in need
   (b) A place where the poor and sick could live
   (c) Looking after paupers in the workhouse
   (d) Money, food, clothing for poor people living *outside* the workhouse
3. The Act empowered parishes to form poorhouse unions
4. Poor harvests and high prices in the 1790s meant that farm workers were not earning enough to feed themselves
5. It was calculated according to the cost of bread and the size of a farm worker's family
6. It encouraged workers to be idle; the cost of the poor-rate shot up
7. There had been food riots in 1830; the cost of poor relief had reached record levels
8. 1834
9. Conditions in the workhouse were to be made as harsh as possible
10. The sick, the infirm and those over 60 years of age
11. Edwin Chadwick
12. (a) He/she was examined by a doctor
    (b) He/she was sent to a small cell and expected to live on bread and water
13. In the industrial North there were so many paupers that the new system of poor relief broke down
14. Oakum picking, breaking bones and stones, household jobs
15. Their diet had to be more unpleasant than the food eaten by the poorest farm-workers outside the workhouse
16. Charles Booth was a wealthy ship-owner. He published *The Life and Labour of the London Poor* in 1889
17. York
18. They were given school meals, medical services and Infant Welfare Centres
19. 70
20. Back-to-back houses
21. Winston Churchill
22. 4d. (2p)
23. Building, engineering, shipbuilding
24. 'Dole' payments
25. Sums of money were paid out by the Unemployment Assistance Board according to a Means Test
26. Want, disease, ignorance, squalor, idleness
27. Ten shillings (50p)
28. The Ministry of Social Insurance
29. The blind, the old, vagrants, T.B. patients
30. £7898 million

1. 4–6 days
2. Groups of businessmen and landowners who took over and repaired stretches of road
3. Many people objected to paying for what had once been free
4. Telford
5. Jobs for coach-builders, inn-keepers, drivers and grooms
6. 1835
7. The M1
8. The report recommended that main roads should not run through the centres of busy towns
9. Coal
10. John Gilbert
11. 1761
12. The Leeds–Liverpool Canal
13. A craze for canal-building
14. Shardlow
15. Sailing ships with long, sharp bows
16. Clipper ships could not use the canal because of cross-winds
17. The *Sirius*
18. The load-line
19. Northumberland
20. The Surrey Iron Railway
21. Trevithick
22. 1821–1825
23. Chat Moss, the Sankey River, Olive Mount
24. To see which design of locomotive would be best for the Liverpool and Manchester Railway
25. Seven feet
26. A train which had to run once a day along the whole length of line, stopping at all stations
27. George Hudson
28. Canals and turnpike trusts went out of business
29. Brighton, Torquay, Southend
30. London, Midland and Scottish; London and North-East Railway; Great Western Railway; Southern Railway
31. 1947
32. The Beeching Report
33. John Palmer
34. Parliament had placed taxes on letters
35. William Cooke and Charles Wheatstone
36. An early form of bicycle
37. 1906
38. To celebrate the repeal of the Red Flag Act
39. Morris Cowley
40. Louis Bleriot
41. It proved the transatlantic commercial flights were a possibility
42. British Overseas Airways Corporation; British and European Airways
43. The *Daily Mail*
44. John Delane
45. Alfred Harmsworth
46. Jarrow
47. A giant oil-tanker

48. Guglielmo Marconi
49. Radio detection and ranging
50. 1964

Chapter 10: Trade and the Economy

1. To ensure that only British ships traded between Britain and her colonies
2. A tax on foreign goods
3. A system of restricted trade
4. The Isle of Man, Romney Marsh, Devon and Cornwall
5. A Scottish economist
6. A policy of government non-intervention
7. Pitt, Huskisson
8. Britain and France reduced taxes on each other's goods
9. Lancashire merchants
10. 1860
11. A pattern of trade between Britain, Africa and the West Indies
12. William Wilberforce
13. 26
14. Goldsmiths
15. Britain was fighting a war against France
16. 1946
17. Many banks had gone out of business
18. Customs duties on tea, wine, spirits, tobacco
19. Beer, candles, soap, leather
20. William Pitt
21. An increase in indirect taxation
22. Robert Peel
23. 1p
24. Lloyd George's budget to pay for old age pensions
25. 15 per cent
26. The difference between what the nation spends and what the nation earns
27. Joseph Chamberlain
28. The collapse of the American stock market
29. Because of the 1931 economic depression
30. 1973

Chapter 11: The Role of Women

1. 1928
2. Women became wage-earners
3. Domestic service
4. 'Hurriers' and 'putters' were women who carried coal from the coal-face to the mine shaft
5. 1842
6. The work was cleaner, more respectable; there were regular meals
7. One of the first women doctors
8. William Rathbone
9. The headmistresses of the North London Collegiate School and the Cheltenham Ladies College
10. The campaign for a fairer deal for women
11. They could keep their earnings while living with their husbands

12. Suffragists — men and women who supported the campaign to give more people the vote

Suffragettes — women campaigning for the vote

13. The government released starving suffragettes from prison and rearrested them as soon as they were fit
14. The country went to war against Germany
15. Clerical work, nursing, catering, cleaning, making weapons, porters, bus-conductors, postwomen, farm-workers
16. Women's Auxiliary Air Force; Women's Royal Naval Service; Women's Auxiliary Army Corps; Auxiliary Territorial Service
17. Women teachers
18. The Equal Opportunities Commission
19. She opened the first birth-control clinic in London
20. Germaine Greer